CW01640380

I ONE

Y

Introduction

There are various hypotheses with regard to the earliest civilisations. The analysis in this book is from existing historical, archaeological and forensic evidence, to expose a picture of an original pioneering British Nation, who possibly colonized the Americas BC. Evidently the British surveyed the astral system for eons, to found a basic formula they used for measurement, time and surveying, which is prevalent in most of the ancient constructions, particularly Stonehenge. This narrative is intended to demonstrate their superiority in exploration and innovative early technologies, with an independent founding organisation and refined education system, which infrastructure sprang into agriculture, trade and export. It is also identified that the British defended against all invaders for their land and "freedom"; and the evidence will dispel the supposition that they were ignorant savage barbarians. Many Britons have bloodlines that extend into the past that lay claim to being true British. Also explored are the names Irish, Scottish, Cornish, Manx and Welsh, are Saxon names; and according to some historians the English region and name was invented by a Saxon monk called Bede, to be a misconception of the true lineages of the British Nation. The evidence submitted is for you to decide who the British really are and where they originate from. This evidence may induce some Cornish, Irish, Manx, Scots and Welsh and, perhaps some Britons from the English regions, as well as some Scandinavians, Americans, Australians and New Zealanders, to identify they are the true descendants of the British Nation.

Chapter 1

Distant Footprints

To put British development into perspective, consider the finds of Boxgrove Man in Sussex, dated at 500,000 BC and the cave burial of the Red Man of Paviland in South Wales, dated up to and after 30,000 BC. These are the earliest of intelligent British people residing at this most "front line" northwest location, independent of any races of lower latitudes. The evidences will prove that the ancestors and descendants of Boxgrove and Red Man are the first settlers of the British lands.

However, many historians say that Neanderthal was "front line", who are evidenced from about 230,000 BC to 30,000 BC and settled in France (is not the British area is it)? Other fossils of early modern humans types to be identified are *Cro-Magnon* from about 23,000 to 27,000 years old; they were discovered in a rock shelter at Les Eyzies in the Dordogne, who may have came up from the south and perhaps coexisted with and are accredited to Neanderthal's extinction. They may owe their name to the "French" dialects of Cro "cavity" and Magnon "large" i.e. large-cave. *Homo sapiens*, labelled modern human, are believed to have evolved from East Africa; some historians' say took over Neanderthal.
Apparently this evidence does not refute that Boxgrove and the Red Man were of a front line Nation settled in the British Lands; and the amount of other British archaeology that supports this is considerable, of which we can examine and compare following.

Some historians believe that Homo-Sapiens/Cro magnon migrated out of Africa, and exterminated or bred out Neanderthal in areas of France at about 30,000 BC; however there is no evidence of this. Some historians have wrongly named these people "modern-humans" to have had superior minds and abilities to that of Neanderthal. Some even suggest that the emergence of Homo-Sapiens was the start of a "human revolution" at 30,000 BC, a sudden God given, freak, genetic mutation of speech at this time, allowing these so called "modern-humans" to exist "exclusively".

However British evidence exists to the contrary. It is also evidenced that Neanderthals shared the same significant human traits, and in fact had superior voice organ amplification, so could possibly communicate much better than any "modern-humans", so again these historian are incorrect. It is also evidenced that both had the same brain capacity, which allowed the same types of thought and speech processes.

I suggest that it is reasonable for us to assume that Neanderthals were absorbed into a larger populous coming out from the British areas and from lower latitudes, whereby the physical features of Neanderthal were bread out, or they had died from disease, rather than the extermination theory, by a specific people arriving in France out of Africa.

There is clear evidence that Boxgrove and the Red Man had modern human features and resided in the British lands in front of Neanderthal.

Historians who insist that the British came out of Africa, to overtake Neanderthal in France, to reside in the British lands, cannot be correct?

Archaeologists Cline and Hensleswood (of the George Washington University and the African Heritage centre) made discoveries of prehistoric artefacts in a cave in Africa. The finds dated to about 75,000 BC, were of shaped bone points that could have been used for weapons. They also found 8,000 pieces of ochre; two pieces were marked with cross-hatching designs, clearly showing that the people who produced them exhibited creative talents. Brooks (of the George Washington University) said the latter was a product of human thought; saying to get to this stage in evolution took thousands of years, which is correct. But the clear evidence is that Boxgrove predates Neanderthal and the Red Man evidence predates the modern humans, which came up from Africa to take over Neanderthal.

So what did Boxgrove and the Red Man's people leave behind for us to evaluate? From fossil records we know more about the animals that roamed the world in the mists of time than by the archaeological finds of our ancestors. We speak of fossilised footprints, which sometimes show the lifestyle of Boxgrove and the Red Man who left many footprints on the landscape. They utilised what nature provided to make their tools, build their habitat and find their food. They learned to control fire, and once early man managed to capture flame and bring it back to his often dark, damp, cold cave; he progressed to something that would, in time, revolutionise his life. For all the evidence clearly stems from Boxgrove to the Red Man flourishing in a fruitful British land supported by the Gulf Stream running into a landfall to ice-shelf catchment area.

Boxgrove man no longer ate raw flesh and sat in darkness after sunset, fearing attack from wild beasts; he had heat and light and this brought security and comfort. It must have seemed like a gift from a benevolent God, something to be cherished and utilised.
To elaborate on this progression from Boxgrove to Red Man. Archaeologist Christopher Stringer investigated a shin bone of Boxgrove man, a few of whose remains were found in the gravel pit in Sussex, along with flint tools and animal bones that were dated to about 500,000 BC, although controversy still rages about the accuracy of the dating measures used. A scan revealed that Boxgrove man was taller and more heavily built than a Neanderthal. The finds include evidence of a rhinoceros killing with scratch marks of butchering on its bones, evidencing the kill was made by humans and not by any predatory animal. In a horse's shoulder blade find there was evidence of a spear wound and also evidence of the smashing of animal bones to extract the marrow.
In this Boxgrove site, a tool made from deer antler was also found, which had been carried and used over a long period of time, showing a degree of thought and inventiveness. The team also found a bone of another individual and a human tooth. All the latter is good evidence of human planning, of social organisation, and of big game hunting strategies.
Historians will have to rethink their "modern-human" theory which claim that human evolution started at 30,000 BC, when modern humans came up from Africa to take over Neanderthal in France; I say this because Boxgrove and Red Man were an intelligent race residing in Britain at least 470 and 30,000 years earlier.

I elaborate here to evidence that the early British existed with natural fire and progressed to creating it by rubbing dry sticks, and later striking two flints; thereafter by carrying a horse hoof skin-ember that would be carried from site to site. This control of fire was advanced and capitalised into other amazing British achievements, progressing into the Tin, Lead, Copper, Bronze and Iron Age; and the British innovative sciences of metallurgy, of mixing certain combinations of metals to forge for the making of implements, tools and weapons in later years. British existence progressed over many thousands of years up to the clear evidences of the Red Man's location and existence after 30,000 BC.

Britain was the farthest habitable land to the north-west which became Islands apart from Europe; it had a superior coastline, with the warm waters of the Gulf-Stream creating the perfect environment for good fishing and good hunting, so this was a prime location for any human evolution to spring from, for the British to have evolved as a frontline pioneering nation.

Boxgrove and Red Man provisionally dated from around 500.000 and 30,000 BC and thereafter, had actually evolved in the area of Britain in front of Neanderthal or the said "modern-humans" coming out of Africa at 30,000 BC. The early British resided northwest below the ice-shelf and quite apparently would have moved west and east and also back into the south from this latitude and this very location. It is the Boxgrove and Red Man's people who are the only candidates to be the very early British.

Academics also argue that every human came out of Africa. If that is so then the British were the first to come out of Africa to arrive in Britain. Britain was the furthest place northwest from Africa under the ice-shelf and up against the Atlantic Ocean, in front of any other race out of Africa. Whoever moved into the east on a lower latitude out of Africa are those peoples that are there now, who are not British. If the British evolved or were first to arrive in Britain, then they can only be the same true British Nation.
In recent evidence such as the TV documentary called "Stone Age Apocalypse" it was suggested we evolved from apes; and the human revolution started at about 75,000 years BC (not 30,000 BC, as some historians insist) and a vast area around Indonesia was wiped out by a super volcano eruption at about 75,000 BC, after which, it was stated, that most of the origins of man came out of East Africa, from a small leftover DNA pool of people who survived.
Other academics say we evolved from apes, then why from 4 million years are the apes still aping; and if evolution predicts that brain capacity gets larger, then why do humans have a head 30% smaller than the first apes? All dogs came from the wolf, which apparently dogs are still the same old dogs; so is this evidence of a weakest link barking up the wrong tree of human life?
Boxgrove and the Red Man were residing in Britain up to and after 500,000 and 30,000 BC and this must evidence a front line original people who were not affected by the Indonesian super volcano eruption; or the subsequent leftover DNA pool out of East Africa at 75,000 BC. The British are race apart from this source.

Lets look back to analyse this:- In the 1830s, Sir Roderick Murchison excavated 405 million years old sedimentary rocks in South Wales; he named the Silurian layer after an early British Clan who later inhabited this area, which fossil records since, he say's places this area as the cradle of life.
(I note here, there is further reference to the Silurian British in a book called "Searching for the Silures" by Ray Howell, which identifies a remarkable innovative people who defended ceaselessly and won many battles against the Romans, are some of the same British).
Britain has been on the Gulf Stream since before 500,000 BC, evidenced by the skeleton finds of many animals including mammoth, horse, bison, small mammals, fish and, particularly eels which return from their migrations on the Gulf Stream, found in a gravel pit in Stanton Harcourt in Oxfordshire. Up to and after 30,000 BC the Red Man's people were residing on the Gower Peninsula in South Wales, who must be the direct descendents of Boxgrove man.
These British people were in the farthest land North West, at least 16,000 years ahead of any other race in technological terms regarding astronomy and following sciences of these British people, which technologies followed on from the refined artefacts and implements found in the Red Man's cave burial, in a chamber called "Goat's Cave". The skeleton is now called the Paviland "Red Man" which finds in this area have been dated up to and after 30,000 BC. Many other artefacts have been found in other caves on this location. A roundhouse air conditioning features, shape and format can be detected in this cave structure, depicted following.

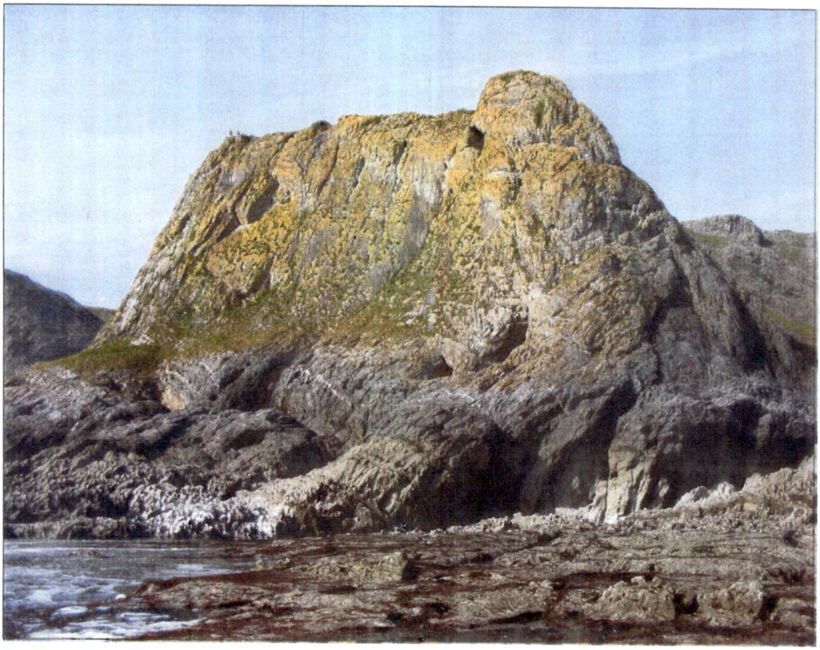

Paviland Caves

In the above photograph, you can see an impressive stronghold of caves, and you can detect a roundhouse shape in the cave area. The caves would have been looking out over a vast delta-plain at 30,000 BC, with many wild animals foraging there, and with the Gulf Stream flowing into low lying beach areas and possibly salt marshes. Some of the higher caves are now at the current high-tide-mark and lichen-line. Archaeologist Paul Pettit investigated the cave burial, possibly the earliest and most important to be recorded, which was initially named the Paviland "Red Lady". Recent forensic evidence establishes that it was the remains of a man, which I refer to as the "Red Man".

The chamber of one cave is about 30 ft high by 20 ft wide, with a natural flue-shaft, opening 60 ft above, where daylight enters and smoke from a fire could filter through. This cave would have been organised to possibly have a wattle and daub door-frontage, with reed thatch to the upper shaft area; this may have been a precursor to the basic (round) house format.

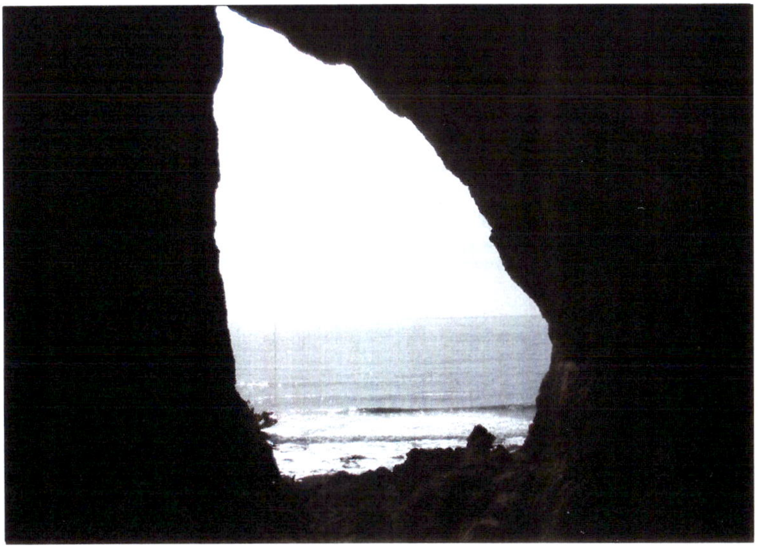

View from one of the caves.

Red Man's bones were dyed with red ochre before they were laid to rest in Goat's Cave. With him were a mammoth's skull and what was probably a neck adornment consisting of drilled periwinkle shells and fox canines. Animal bones such as antler were laid on and around the body, with bone needles, flints (4,000 found in this area) and sculptures made from mammoth teeth, and tusk-ivory bracelets.

We can only guess at whether there was some sort of religious ceremony attached to the burial; most academics would say the artefacts were intended for the use of the dead person in the afterlife. I would say they were placed as a matter of remembrance and respect. Birth, marriage and death are still the events surrounded by ceremony, and it is not surprising to think that the Red Man found these important stages in life to be worth celebrating, as we still do today. He must have belonged to one of the earliest orders residing in Britain, long before Neanderthal reached the lower latitudes near France. Evidence shows that he was a fit young man, who varied his diet and could endure the hardships of these times, and by the evidence of the fine workmanship in the artefacts, these people would certainly have been able to make very good clothing and probably sealskin covered boats. It is believed, from the considerable artefacts and animal bones found in Goat's Cave and adjoining caves, that the Red Man was a very significant person, visited from all over Britain. Similar artefacts are found throughout the British Isles, which evidence that the British people flourished and moved northwards, west and east on this latitude, behind the receding ice-shelf, and the British of today must be the descendant of these very same people.

Near Goat's Cave at Cefn-Bryn, is a ridge that overlooks the same plains area, is a structure called Arthur's Stone, depicted following. The capstone weighs about 20 tons; surely this refutes the supposition, these people were hunter-gatherers on the move, why would they have undertaken such a huge task? Surely these structures' were used functionally by the living, who had settled.

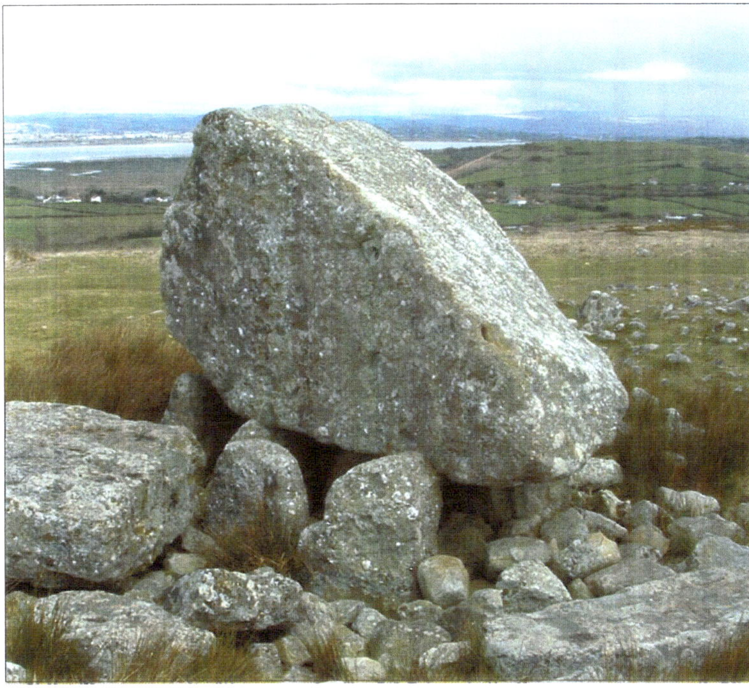

Arthur's Stone

The well that springs up inside the chamber of Arthur's Stone is said by historians to be a healing well.

About 50 yards away from Arthur's Stone is a Neolithic burial cairn (pictured following). There are at least 60 cairns on this ridge, three of which were excavated to prove an ancient history. Should it follow that Arthur's Stone was used for a function besides burial when all these other burial cairns exist? It seems inappropriate that all these structures were all built for burial? There must be another function for these huge structures.

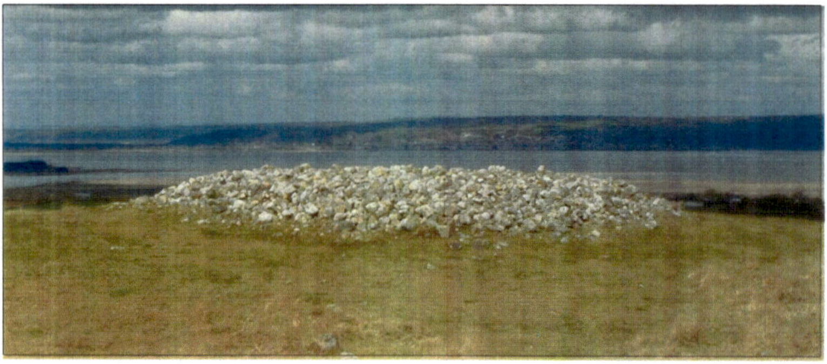

Burial Cairn

The illustration following is an idea of an area under the Preseli bluestone outcrop in West Wales, with mammoth roaming the plains.

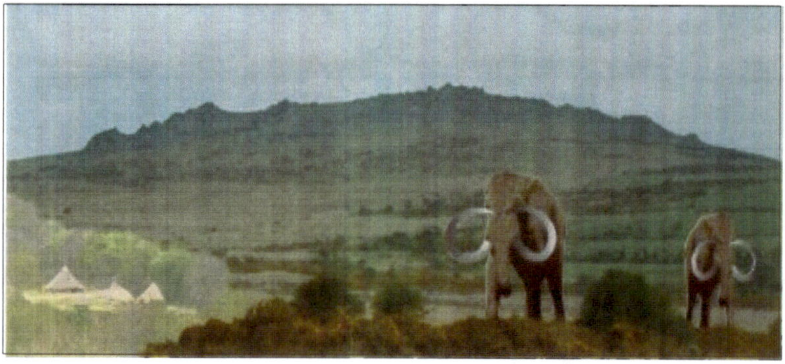

Were our ancestors venturing back into the south? Unlike Neanderthal man, the British, up to and after 30,000 BC left some considerable footprints on the landscape; easily identified many years later. Current investigations give us an opportunity to follow and interpret the evidence that exists, as follows.

Footprints have been examined by Professor Martin Bell, which date between 30,000 BC up to 7,000 BC and some of them were found along the delta coastal mudflats in areas of southern Britain. Others were found in the mudflats of South Wales near the Severn Estuary, the Gwent Levels and the sands of Merthyr Mawr and Kenfig. These sands, created by the last Ice Age are being washed away to reveal a type of mud-stone, containing fossilised ancient footprints.

The early cave burial of the Red Man places the British in a front-line position, following behind the receding ice shelf and, establishes evidence of a nation of innovative Britons. This must be the most important burial find to be made to date. The intention is to show that the British nation (ancient names Britan or Britanishan) is possibly a nation of nations extending into the Americas and eastward. This makes a good starting point for sound investigations about our ancestry.

Life for early man was short and his end was probably painful. We have never discovered whether herbs were made use of for medicinal purposes, or to relieve pain, but we do understand that many herbs were eaten to be discovered as good medicines and cures for certain ailments. We understand that this knowledge does not just spring into existence, it was passed down to each generation; of which has extended into the medicines of today, apparently through the later British practices of remembrances in rhyme.

Early man tackled some formidable animals in his search for food and skins, and his hunting weapons had to be adapted for certain strategies. The British progressed into family and social groups.

To evidence British development we look back to some early British, flint, single and double-edged bi-facial blades, used for tools, implements, knives and weapons. These early knives and axe heads are difficult to spot amongst the general mix of stones to be found, specialists have identified them as blades for weapons, knives or axes, usually found near remnants of communal fires, middens and also amongst and embedded in animal bones. Flint was a popular type of stone; it breaks with sharp edges and might well have been firstly used as it was found and later, specifically knapped.

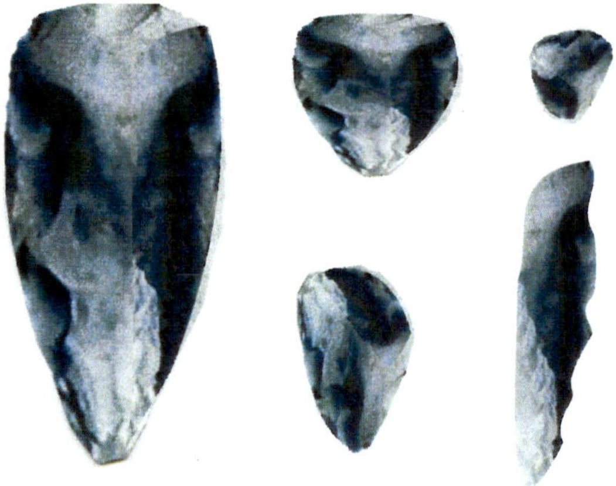

From dated evidence it is reasonable to confirm that up to and after 30,000 BC the ice-shelf extended down over the Mid Wales regions and also over southern Ireland. The evidence is taken from the ice-flow gorges and the Red Man's dated burial. The ice shelf was slowly receding northward after this time and so it was not possible to enter America via the north and through the Bering Straits. I elaborate further as follows.

It is presumed by scientists that eastern people called Clovis entered the Americas via the Bering Straits at about 13,000 BC. However there is new evidence that another race of people entered into America at about 20,000 BC, which I say are possibly the British.
To support my opinion that the British entered into America at about 20,000 BC I cite the evidences following: It is known from scientific and geographical data that there was a series of glaciations, when the ice cap advanced and covered most of Britain, which resulted in these northern ice-desert areas being too hostile to support humans, making it impossible for any race to have travelled northward.
Interglacial periods also occurred when the ice retreated and the climate grew warmer, and according to records, at 20,000 BC it was a few degrees colder than today, with the ice cover just above the Red Man's location and receding. Geophysicists relate major climate changes to the behaviour of the earth, which is subject to 'wobbles'; these fluctuations are pendulum-like and the ice-ages are followed by warm periods, however this period was the beginning of the last ice age and so the ice was receding.
However, archaeologists suggest that another race of people called "Solutrians" of Southern France and Spain entered into the Americas at 20,000 BC along the "ice shelf". I say this claim is impossible because the Solutrians were living near to the equator, centrally adjacent to the vast, open and violent 5,000 kilometre expanse of the Atlantic Ocean at this time, which lay between them and America and it would have been impossible for numbers of these Solutrians in loaded down flimsy sealskin boats to have crossed.

Solutrians did not have any knowledge of navigation to have crossed this vast expanse of extremely violent seas in small flimsy boats.

I also evidence that the ice was gradually receding from above Goat's Cave after 30/20,000 BC and the ice-shelf never returned back to France and Southern Spain after this time; and so Solutrians could not have crossed on any "ice shelf" after 30,000 or about 20,000 BC.

I say the British were the only people, given their location are the best candidates for migrating to the Americas. They could have identified giant turtles, beans, and exotic tree remnants, washing up along their shoreline-to-ice-shelf Gulf Stream catchment area, to notice it was from another land. At about 20,000 BC I deduce that the British, to satisfy their pioneering curiosity could have crossed the Atlantic to follow this straightforward navigational trail. They could have boat-hop-trekked across the ice shelf, and flow, that would have been moving towards the west at about 4 MPH on the returning Gulf Stream currents, with following mega-winds. This journey would have taken about a month or so to travel across this 3,000-mile stretch of sea, to reach landfall on the Grande Banks, which would have been islands at this date. It would have been a hazardous adventure, but with good provisions of dried fruit and certain grasses to combat scurvy and living off sea flotsam, kale, kelp, cabbage and molluscs; along with seal, walrus, and good drift fishing, the journey was more than possible. British migration eastward was also a straightforward course, to travel across the bottom of this same ice shelf latitude, up to and after 30/20,000 BC.

Chapter 2

Other nations which are possibly blood relatives of the Britons

The British were pioneering forward as they had always done, looking for good hunting and fishing. There were no maps to follow, no knowledge of what awaited them at the next landfall and neither did they have any foreknowledge of any enemies they might encounter, until they were first in their land north-west just under the ice shelf in Britain, for there was nothing above this location but pack-ice, with no human enemy above there. The trend was to pioneer forward in the hope of finding a better land to where the sun was setting and that was the way forward to the west. Perhaps the British were monitoring the Sun, Moon and Stars travelling towards the west and may have assumed that the earth was flat, as did people in recent times. They may have imagined the Sun, Moon and Stars were entering into the water or earth in the best land to the west and to rise again in the east in a re-birth, so possibly this was the sign to follow into the west. This may also relate to a reason for British lake offerings and burials, was to follow the planets into the earth. Nevertheless they would have viewed the same procession of planets and stars moving into the west. This location was the farthest land north-west and apparently the ice-shelf was the only following course they could follow into the west, and I assume that is just what they actually did; for it was impossible to go northward up to an after 20,000 BC; of which I cite AD pioneers following, to evidence so.

To evidence the impossibilities of trekking north after 20,000 BC, it was not until AD, the Greeks in the 4th century were aware of the Arctic regions, which by this time were settled by Inuit Eskimo. Vikings reached the Arctic regions in 982 AD when Eric the Red sighted Greenland. However, a very long time had elapsed since the British explorers set out from home at about 20,000 BC. It is perhaps pertinent to firstly pose the question here: Were the Vikings descended from the British who travelled to the east on this latitude? There is some evidence to support this possibility.

Viking long ships were made from Irish oak and carried straps of Welsh bronze. This is indicative of trading and communication between these peoples, evidencing that Vikings may truly be blood relatives of the British. The evidence also suggests that Viking worship was akin to that of the British. Stone circles, burial mounds, grave goods and burials are similar in both nations. One burial of a warrior queen, with a four-wheeled cart, a chair and other grave goods, show that Viking women were of equal status to men and were occasionally elevated to superior positions, which is a similar status for women in the British culture.

Other examples are found in the dragon carvings on Viking boats, and the sundial used for navigation; similarities reinforce the view that here is a race of people akin to the British. Further evidence comes with finds of 14,000 various coins ranging from Britain to the Arabian Empire; pure silver bracelets and iron swords are evidence of the Vikings trading from Gotland into the Baltic, the Black Sea and Byzantium; are similar to British trading areas of these times.

I identify relevant British connections here for it will become more apparent later. I now continue to identify the impossibilities of trekking north, up to and after 20,000 BC, by the facts of the impossibilities AD.
The Search for the North West Passage began in AD 1490, by Navigator John Cabot. In 1553 Navigator Sir Hugh Willoughby was seeking to find the North East Passage. Danish navigator Vitus Jonassen Bering discovered the Straits in 1728 that bear his name; the Straits separate Siberia and Alaska. American Explorer Robert Peary reached the Northern most point of land in 1900 and named it Cape Morris Jesup. He proved that Greenland was an island and also led an expedition in 1909 to reach the North Pole location; so apparently there were considerable problems navigating these vast Polar ice desert regions in AD.
The first question is 'how in heaven' did the French/Spanish Solutrians cross the Atlantic at 20,000 BC as aforementioned? Or how did the eastern Clovis people navigate to trek northwards through this very hostile region at about 13,000 BC?
Surely any reasonable person would conclude that it was not at all possible for groups of people to have trekked through these Polar deserts without modern technology, BC. It is also known that the first voyage by ship through the North West Passage was accomplished by Norwegian explorer Roald Amundsen 1903-1906. So how could these eastern Clovis people have trekked through this area or navigated it in flimsy sealskin boats at 13,000 BC? Let's analyse this further, because it seem that there is no possibility that Clovis travelled the inner arctic regions at 13,000 BC.

Apparently the ice shelf would have receded north as far as the Siberia - Alaska latitude by about 13,000 BC. The supposition that anyone crossed the "inner" vast Polar ice-desert regions, following herds of wild animals cannot possibly be correct, for there would have been no lichen or other vegetation for herbivores to feed on, in 20,000 or 13,000 BC and for some time after. The ice shelf must have receded to a northern position but given all the latter evidence of AD, how could Clovis have crossed these regions at 13,000 BC?

The Clovis evidence in the Americas is possibly British, let's analyse this following:-

Bi-facial flint blades said to be used by Clovis people have been discovered in Cactus Hill, Virginia, and in the Great Lakes region; they date to about 12,000 BC.

Evidentially, given that the Britons' location was up against the ice-shelf from at least 30,000 BC, there was nowhere else to go other than across the ice-shelf west; and so the British would have entered into the America has the evidence predicts at 20,000 BC. Then of course the bifacial flint implements could possibly be that of the British, which has been dated at 20 and 13,000 BC.

I also evidence here while we are on this subject, the British did pioneer east into Scandinavia and beyond and, understandably they would also have been returning to the south at certain times, in order to hunt and perhaps trade their pioneering implements with the people in the east and south, and to further evidence following.

Geneticists Brown and Wallace (of Smithsonian Institute and Emory University USA) working with female mitochondrial DNA, gave evidence of migrations into America at about 20,000 BC of people with an X marker chromosome, is ABC X D, and also indicated that there were several waves of migrations of earlier people than Clovis. Clovis people did not have the X marker within their ABCD chromosome; as did the earlier settlers of 20,000 BC, evidencing another race crossed over.
In the book "*Atlantis in America*" a Mayan culture comprised of early settlers, evidenced by skeletons found in caves 2,000 feet under the sea. The existing natives tell of an ancient civilisation arriving in boats along the seashore and not via the Bering Straits. Also other tests for female mitochondria DNA to find the X chromosome to ABC X D, showed that it is absent from 42 other types of eastern DNA, including Clovis.
Archaeologists Stanford of the Smithsonian Institute and Bradley of Exeter University, produced evidence to suggest that Solutrians existed in Southern France and Spain, who had crossed to America from that location at 20,000 BC. But as aforementioned, Solutrians could not have crossed the open Atlantic to America at anytime up to 20,000 BC, or afterwards.
You will see on the map following a geophysicist's prediction of the last ice shelf position at 30 and 20,000 BC. You will see that Southern France and Spain are adjacent to the vast open violent seas of the Atlantic Ocean, of which it was not possible for anyone to have crossed this great expanse of violent sea in flimsy sealskin boats from that area at 20,000 BC?

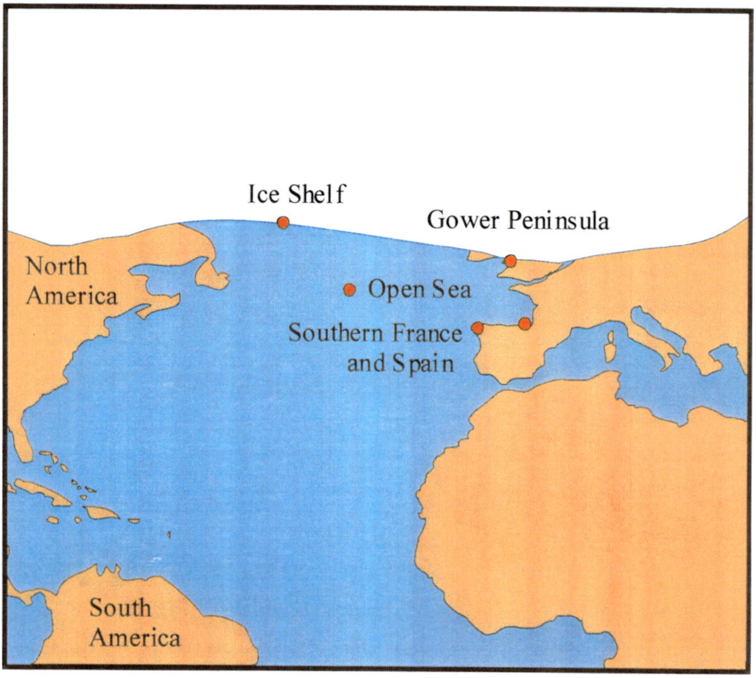

The latter is further evidenced by engineers who were digging tunnels for the London Underground who found evidence of the edge of the ice shelf which was estimated to have been 100 metres thick, spanning across South Wales, through London and across to Amsterdam and Hamburg at about 28,000 BC; so logically the ice-shelf would have been receding from this time.

Also, Geologist Anthony Long estimates that there was about a kilometre thickness of ice over Scotland, tapering down to about 20 metres in the mid Wales area at about 22,000 BC, which again supports an ice-shelf position, and a British front line pioneering people's location in this area at this date.

Further evidence in a TV documentary called *'Wild Europe'*, revealed that the area from mid Wales and across to Scandinavia was covered in ice at about 24,000 BC. It was stated: - The ice retreat from the valleys revealed marine shingle dumps and sand beaches where human evolution flourished, following behind the ice-shelf. The Ice crust extended over much of the Earth's northern hemisphere and apparently, it ended at the close of the Pleistocene era, in about 8,000 BC.
These dates concur to evidence that the ice shelf was still receding at about the time of the Red Man's evidence, in around and after 30,000 BC. It was also stated that in this warmer period, the rise in temperature allowed plants and animals to flourish, thus allowing the descendants of Paviland Red Man to flourish.
If you calculate back from the Red Mans evidences after 30 and 24,000 BC and the Scandinavian date of 24,000 BC, allowing for the ice shelf to be receding at a fairly regular slow rate at this point in time, then the Ice shelf could not have been in Spain at 20,000 BC. Again at these dates the only possible way to cross to America was on this ice shelf from the Red Man's area of Britain, by the British.
It would seem that the footprints of the Red Man are well travelled indeed and the fact that the British people set out from their original locations. I will now follow the Red Man's people from the Gower Peninsula in South Wales from about 30,000 BC, to evidence that after this time the British had discovered the first paint mixtures and preservatives, body painting, eyed bone needles, sculptured jewellery, flint weapons and tools, placed as grave goods, with the Red Man of Paviland.

It is also evidenced that these people cared for one another. They were capable of producing sealskin 'coastal' going boats, tools, farming implements and weapons for hunting and who also at this time had developed a religious culture so it seems by the artefacts laid in the Red Man's burial.
The British were an innovative people as shown by their bi-facial flint blades, spears, knives and arrow heads, manufactured at least 12,000 years before the eastern Clovis and it is these implements that may have been found in America, some of which have been found in mammoth fossils, likewise were amongst the grave goods of the Paviland Red Man and his people.
The British followed the great herds and developed new fishing and hunting skills, on which they depended for food and clothing. The Red Man's existence on this ice-shelf-gulf-stream location, allowed for the very best coastal fishing and inland hunting, which included woolly mammoth, rhinoceros, horses, deer and many smaller mammals to be had, which had become land-locked to the south, but could travel the delta-plains and ice-shelf to the west and east. The Red-Man's people progressed to erect permanent structures in order to hunt these wild animals near their track-ways and migratory corridors onto the ice-shelf and delta-plains, as the ice-shelf slowly receded to expose more land, for they were certainly staying in these locations longer than necessary, erecting huge constructions; as apposed to a hunter gatherers habitual relentless trail.

Chapter 3

The Britons' Legacy of the British Isles

Britons' survival depended on several factors; this was water to sustain plants and animals, sunlight, and fertile soil to maintain the balance of flora and fauna. Sudden or major changes in the supply of any of these would alter the balance, and at the same time influence the British to move forward or back, to more favourable locations at these times. Man requires a diet that contains sufficient nourishment and a balance of vitamins and minerals to sustain health. Good health was essential to hunters who had to be able to chase fast moving animals, and carry the carcasses back to the women and children, and fight off attacking lions and wolves. When game animals were scarce, they depended on the fruits, nuts, roots and cereals of the countryside. A harsh winter may have meant death to the weakest in the clans and would have encouraged them to stock up for better times. On this Gulf-Stream location the British were at a good productive place to settle, and could explore towards the west and east on the ice shelf, up to and after 30,000 BC. Many animals survived even the harshest of winters. Some large game animals were hunted to extinction, which is recorded in reliable archaeological data. The early Britons had to compete with scavengers and predators, including hyenas, bears, tigers and lions. Their use of implements for culinary purposes and to make clothing from animal skins, deployment of weapons, and use of fire for warmth were very important defences in this hostile environment.

There are many features in the landscape that give clues to how hunters defended against and trapped their prey, such as Mammoth and other animals, some of the early animals are depicted following are the Paraceratherium, Titanotheriam, Sabre-Tooth-Tiger and Uintatherium.

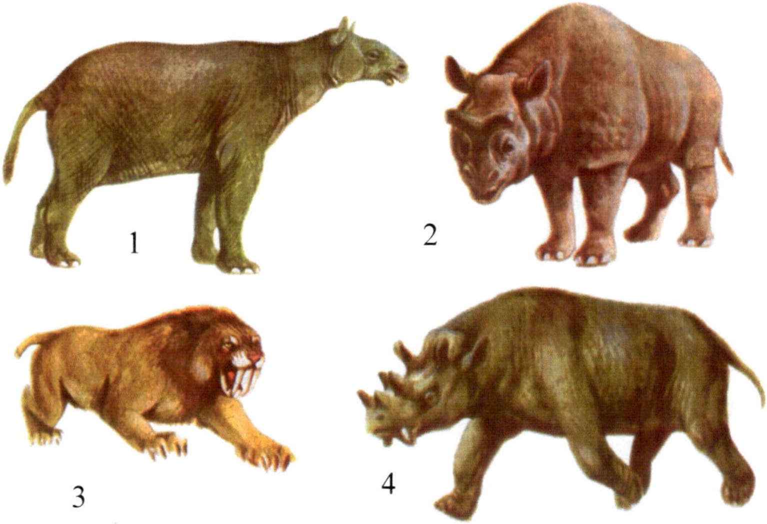

There are many stone structures found in the British Isles; one is on the south side coastal path at Manorbier in Pembrokeshire named "King's Quoit" depicted following. From a settler hunter's perspective, this was used as a lookout over a vast delta plain, which had been left behind by the receding ice. The side stones are estimated to weigh 10 tons each, and the supports and capstone about 15 tons. Animals leaving the plains would have used this cliff trail and this would have been a very advantageous place to lay an ambush for them.

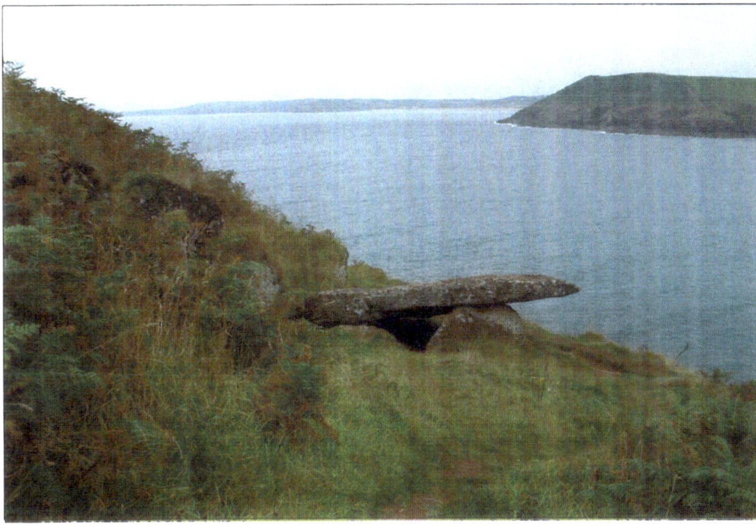

King's Quoit

This hide was possibly covered with wattle-laced brush, to conceal the hunters, who could spear any passing animal to send it over the cliff. Some archaeologists have suggested that these were ritual burial places, but this single explanation for the building of such elaborate strongholds is barely sufficient. Hunters attacking passing animals might well have been killed at these sites and they are likely to have been cremated or buried here in honour of the hunter and animal alike. It may also have been a waste of manpower to carry corpses away for burial, and likewise near Arthur's Stone on the Gower ridge depicted earlier, there are adjacent cairns that were used specifically for burials, so why label all the structures as burial places? So possibly each enormous stone-capped Carreg was built as a hide attack post.

Further north along the Pembrokeshire coast at White Sands Bay near St David's, is a structure called Carn Llidi, shown in the following photograph. You can see, like Arthur's Stone and King's Quoit, this is a strategic lookout area, and from a hunter's point of view, this location is an excellent hunting and encampment site, looking over a trail leading onto and from what was once a delta plain.

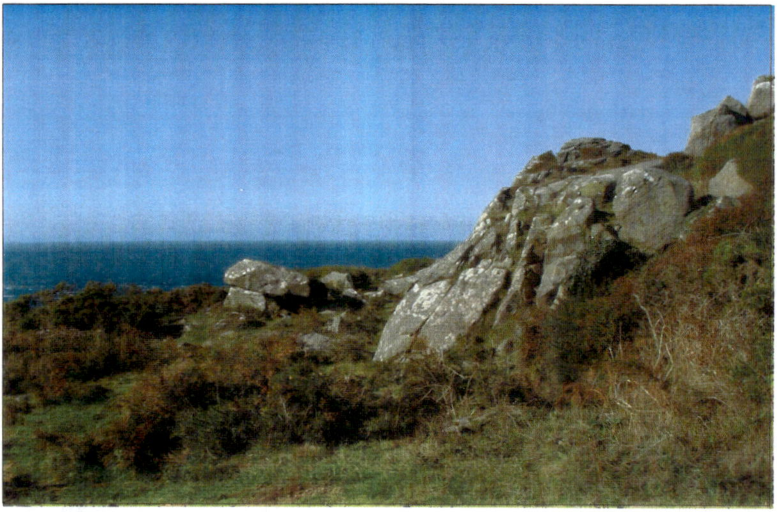

Carn Llidi

Further north is another strategically built structure "Coetan Arthur" depicted following, perhaps another stone hide. Again, this whole area looks to be a good settlement or hunting encampment area, which overlooks onto Carn Llidi (is the hilltop on the horizon) with a plains track between; any animals moving through this trail could easily be ambushed from both sides.

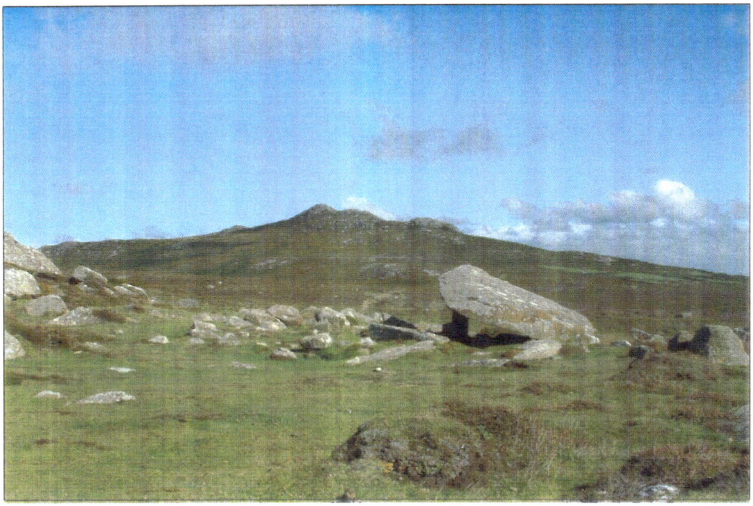

Coetan Arthur (Carn Llidi is in the distance)

There are at least 70 standing stones, 35 cairns, 30 cromlechs, and 27 ancient hill-fortresses to be found in Pembrokeshire, and many more not yet listed. Following is a standing stone, looking over a plains corridor trail.

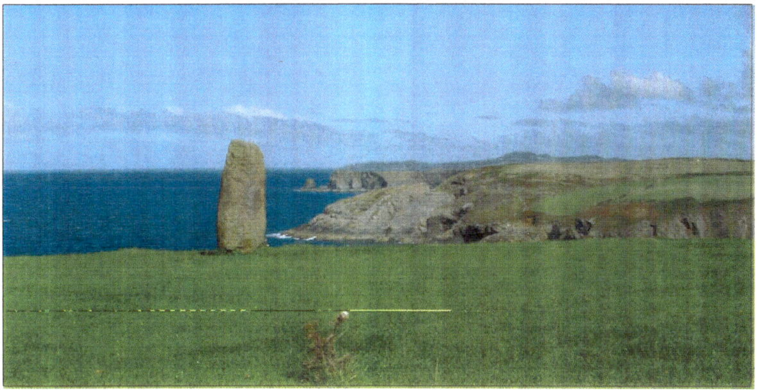

Standing Stone

North is a structure (unlisted)

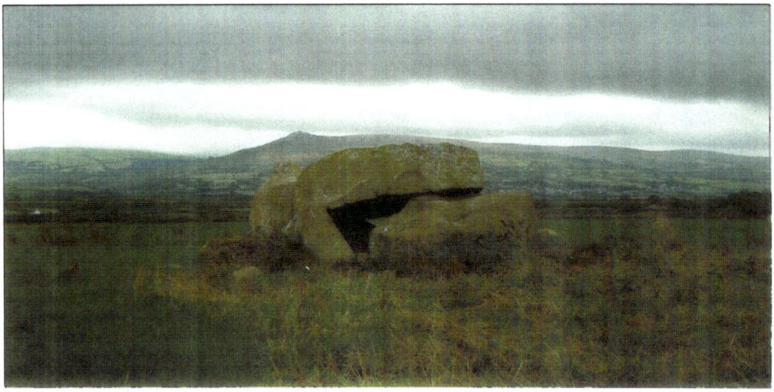

Following is a Carreg listed as a burial tomb.

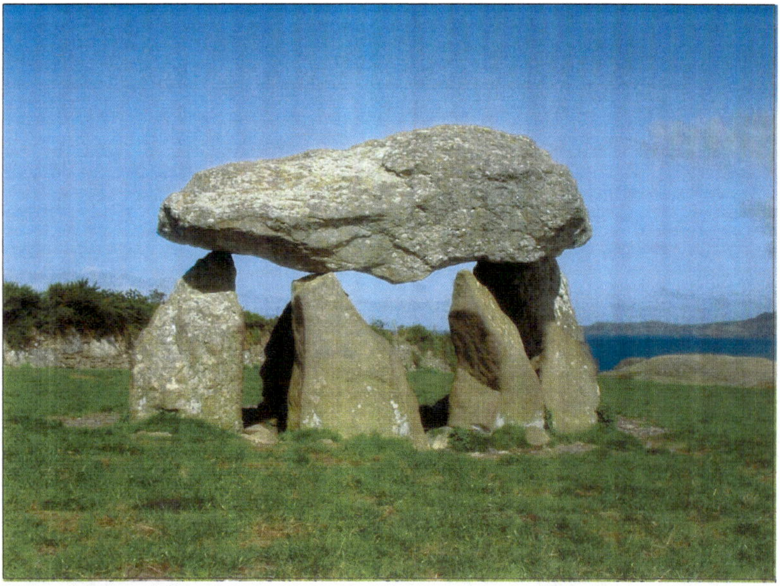

Carreg Samson

The capstone of Carreg Samson weighs about 19 tons and its support stones are at least 4 tons each. The description 'burial tomb' offers an unsatisfactory explanation for this heavyweight monument and does scant justice to the technological advancements and new engineering skills that went into its construction. This monument is also strategically placed overlooking a plains area and I can imagine panels of brush covering the sides and blending in with the many stone outcrops of this area. Little is known of the exact way in which British hunting strategy operated. It is visualised that huntsmen lay in wait inside a Carreg, with a bank of spears bows and arrows, and would attack say a passing Oryx. If they failed to kill but wounded an animal, it would attack the huntsmen, who could retreat to the safety of the hide. Tusked animals could stab into the hide but the huntsmen could emerge from any other opening, and finish the job; for tusked animal at this point could not defend itself other than walk backwards, not an easy task for many of the largest beasts. The huntsmen could then make a relatively safe kill. If any animal chose not to attack the stone-hide, a huntsman could mount the capstone, to goad it. The animal would try to mount the hide from the lower side of the capstone, whereby any huntsmen inside the hide could spear the animal in its underbelly and, these strategies appear to be the most logical uses for these structures. Huntsmen would have been killed at these sites and may have been laid on the capstone for their bones to dry in the sun, before they were painted with red ochre and buried. Or cremated and then their ashes scattered. (The tomb theory could be a much later use).

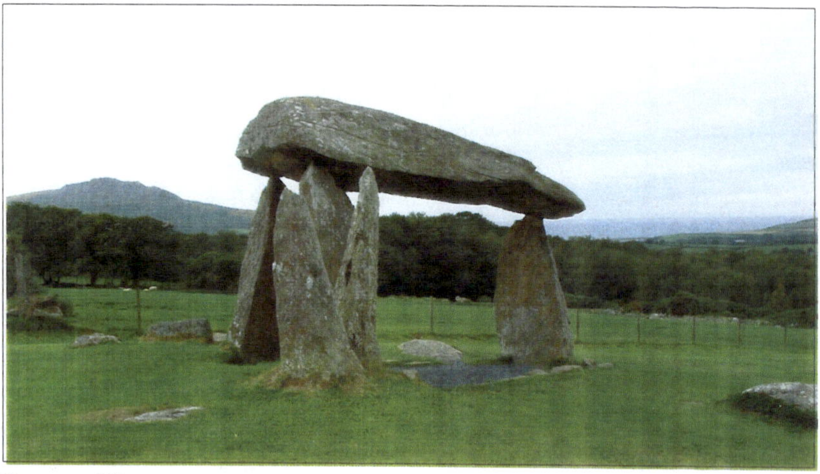

Pentre Ifan

"Pentre Ifan" is also listed as a burial chamber. This structure also overlooks what would have been a plains area, with the Preseli mountain range in the background. The capstone is impressive, weighing at least 16 tons, with support stones of around 5 tons. In this structure some of the supports have fallen or have been removed.

At "Carreg Coetan" following, some of the supporting stones have fallen but the original architecture and strategy of the builders can readily be visualised and the further north you go, these structures are becoming more elaborate. The capstone weighs about 20 tons and support stones each weighing about 4 tons. To identify anyone who built Stonehenge these Britons are a good bet, for the planning and engineering skills that went into the construction of these monuments must progress to relate to the similar enormous task of the construction of Stonehenge.

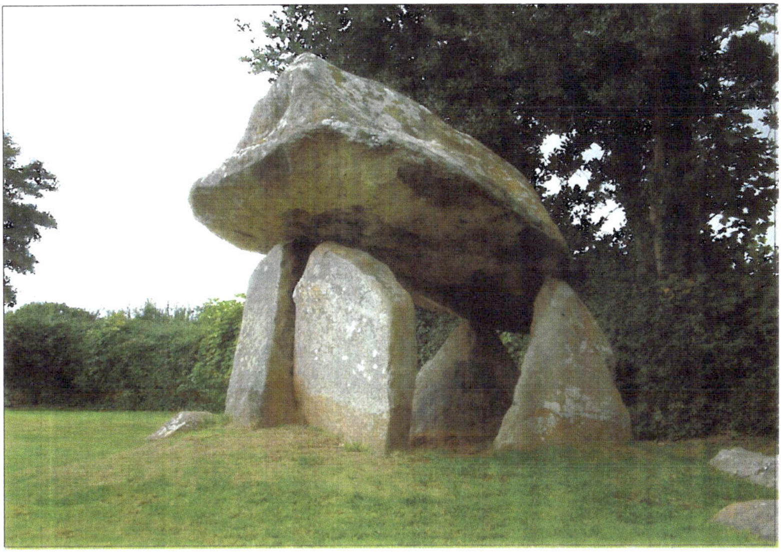

Carreg Coetan

From a construction engineer's perception, the supports were erected and embedded into ground pits and then the spoil was cast into and around the support stones to cover them completely, with a ramp to the lower side. The capstone was then levered, or drawn over log-rollers onto the mound by manpower, or combined animal team. The earth was then removed to reveal the structure, more or less as you see it today.

Near these constructions we usually find the yew tree. Ancient Britons worshiped the yew which represents long life existing in perpetuity, in their land. The British used the natural two ply structure of the yew, when centrally split to leave heartwood and outer-wood, to make the longbow. When this ply-strength longbow is drawn it will produce 150lbs of stored power.

The British longbow would have evolved from their earlier type of bow made from witch-hazel. One bow kept in the British Museum is made from a solid block of the heartwood of a yew tree dated to about 2,700 BC. The string and bindings were made from the leg sinews of a red deer. These evolving innovations show the British expertise in weapon manufacture that was very advanced in technological terms at this time.

It is astonishing how some technological advances were made afterwards, on opposite sides of the world. The ancient Chinese had developed a crude type of bow which was made from a single tapering branch, which was drawn with the arrow about one third up from the bottom, to balance for the tapering thickness. The later bows in the east may have been copied from the British yew longbow, substituting glued animal horns and other composites to try to simulate the ply-strengths of the yew bow. The British yew longbow was the most innovative forerunner of all bows and the most effective weapon of its time; it is still in use today, pretty much unchanged.

I example here one later use of the longbow in battle, is that of Henry V in 1415, enlisting a British strategy of the (Welsh) Longbow-men at Agincourt. The Britons gave their enemies the two finger-salute, (which salute exists today) which meant these archers' fingers would draw the string of the longbow to release the arrow that ends your life. Incidentally a Welshman named Davey Gamm, Henry's personal bodyguard, defended in front of Henry to cut down a number of knights to save Henrys life, to Gamm's demise. Henry Knighted Gamm, posthumously of course.

To further evidence British technological migration to the east, Victor Mair, and Spencer Wells of the National Geographic Society have excavated and researched burials in the Tarin Basin of the Chin-Jung Province in China, of ancient mummies with heights of about six feet tall with fair hair, having similar features of the early British; that were buried with the dignity of a Royal. The mummies are carbon dated to about 2,000 BC. Their faces were painted with intricate perhaps British Celtic patterns. Textile Expert Good (of Harvard University) examined their colourful tartan and plaid woollen clothing with an electron microscope to evidence the wool was from sheep that came from the far west; possibly relating to the British plaid clothing styles. Particularly the trousers as described by Greek geographer Poseidonius, who wrote about the Britons of the second century BC saying: '... were startling in appearance, wearing colourful tartan cloaks, and trousers they call *braceae*. Also Greek explorer and geographer, Strabo (63 BC to AD 24), wrote of the visit to Athens of a Briton, who was as he put it, an *astronomer of his day* '...he came not clad in skins like a Scythian, but with a bow in his hand, a quiver hanging over his shoulder, a plaid wrapped around his body, a gilded belt encircling his loins and, trousers reaching down from the waist to the soles of his feet'. Is it possible that British influence reached China in 2,000 BC? Felix Jin (Fudan University) evidenced that these people had migrated from the west (with bronze artefacts) to settle on the Pontic Steppe. We know that the British were smelting tin with copper to make Bronze probably before 3,500 BC; would this link British connections with the east at 2,000 BC.

Other evidence shows that obsidian bifacial tools and implements that came from the volcanoes in Turkey were similar to early British flint artefacts. Later artefacts that were traded throughout the regions of the Silk-Route could also have been influenced by the British who migrated east into these regions.
There is also evidence that British Celtic influences had advanced as far as the Aegean by 279 BC, for British Celtic items have been discovered there.
Evidences in the west are coming from American scientists and archaeologists who have recently been excavating a Florida peat bog, which was once a lake; the burials are comparable to British lake burials, with what seemed like wattle type weave and tweed fabrics, dated up to 8,000 BC.
To recap and place the latter into chronological perspective, the descendants of Red Man from about 30,000 BC and to the end of the Pleistocene period at around 8,000 BC were manufacturing bifacial tools and flint points for spears; suggesting that good hunting remained their most important life sustaining activity in these settled areas. The latter demonstrates many major technological steps forward, including the wattle and tweed designs in construction and fabrics.
Physicists estimate that temperatures were one degree warmer than today and so life would have flourished. A wide range of wild fruits and other vegetable foods would have been available. It is possible to tell a good deal about the vegetation of that early time, from pollens found in gravesites, as well as from fossilised leaves and tree remnants. The land evolved into mixed woodland, occupied by herds of wild animals.

This fruitful, temperate environment encouraged the continuing development of new technologies and new lifestyles among the British clans who depended on it. The hunt for food was eased by improving climatic conditions and the acquisition of better implements, weapons and hunting techniques, as well as burgeoning husbandry practices were becoming prevalent.

Following are some of the copper to bronze to iron tools of which the British were progressing towards. You can see the distinctive technological progression from one to the other, for certain types of weapons or implements for specific uses. These new metallurgical innovations were designed for specific uses and must have evolved over hundreds if not thousands of years.

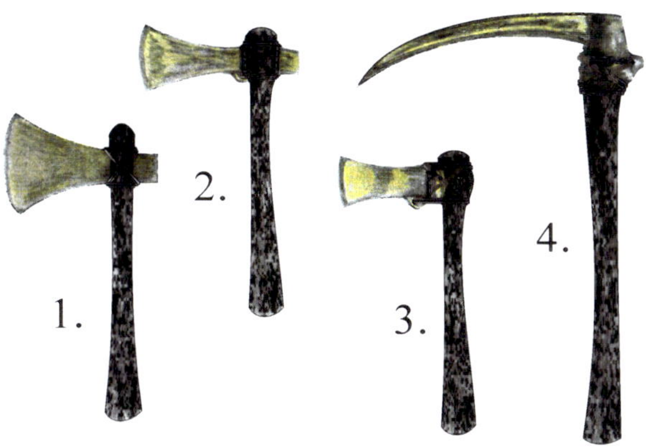

Copper to Bronze to Iron implements

1. Hand-to-shaft-axe, 2. Niche, 3. Fluted, 4. Scythe.

Chapter 4

New horizons

Let's look at the Red Man's progression after 30,000 BC, while the ice edge was in his vicinity and receding. The environment over most of northern Britain was clearly too hostile to support human life. The seas along this western British coastline would have been very good fishing grounds, providing an abundant source of protein and vitamins. Healthy bodies encourage brain activity and we shall see how this was true of the British.

As alleged, an "eastern" people called Clovis entered North America at 12,000 BC, by which their bi-facial flint blades are unique. However, British-like bi-facial blades found there, have been dated from an earlier date; so how can Clovis blades be unique?

Supporting the latter is the Red Man's bifacial flints from about 24,000 BC; and recent finds in Montverde, Chile, Virginia and Pennsylvania indicate that a pre-Clovis migration, *in all probability*, were the Ancient British; whereby the oldest stone tools excavated in America were found in sites on the eastern seaboard, in Pennsylvania, Virginia and Carolina dated at 20,000 BC.

Also, British folklore and religion is akin to that of the Ojibwa, Chippewa and Palaeo Native American Indian tribes; also the Mayan, Aztec, Olmec, Inca and Nazca civilisations. Ojibwa mythology is elaborate and centred on the Medewiwin, or grand medicine society, which religious deities are of the Sun (Life), Moon (Mother), Earth (Seed), Wind (Breath) and Water (Blood). They relate to nature, and are common to ancient British rites.

More recent comparable finds by Jim Alan, Author of "Atlantis in the Andes", who is exploring a vast open elevated plain in Bolivia, with canal systems and a dock site, with artefacts he excavated relating to the Mayan culture of the super city of Teotihuacan. Some metal and clay artefacts found have similarities to the religious and astronomical definitions of the ancient sites of the British.

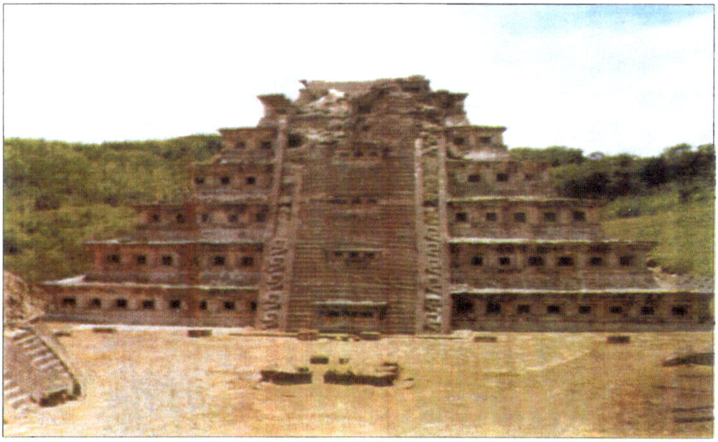

Mayan temple

Archaeologists working on an Aztec site found a bronze disc calendar dated to about 2,000 BC, depicting the 365 days and 12 months of the year, the phases of the moon, indicative of Stonehenge and other British sites, for the best times for crop seeding and harvesting. They also predict the five ages of human progression; the last of which the Aztecs have dated ends in the year 2,012 AD. According to archaeologists the Aztec were making clay bricks and had invented rubber by about 1,600 BC.

The Aztecs also had piped mineral water into their homes and they had refuse collections each week. Archaeological finds also evidence they had dental treatment and they cleaned their teeth with charcoal; it is known they also invented chocolate which perhaps included sugar, may be the reason they cleaned their teeth in order to prevent decay. The level of civilisation reached at this early date is astonishing and comparable to the Ancient British.

Likewise the British on the Great Orme BC; the Inca were pioneering metallurgists, ingeniously mixing 50% copper and gold, which they heat-treated to a cherry red heat-colour, then quenched it in water. The burnt copper on the surface turned to black copper oxide. This was then placed into a boiling combination of perhaps water and alum, whereby the copper oxide was eaten off to reveal a pure gold surface. This is probably the first instance of (reverse) metal plating. The Spanish, after 1519 AD, must have been right "brassed off" when they realised they only had 50% gold, perhaps this is where that expression came from. The Inca were also proficient astronomers, surveyors, engineers, and master masons; this is clearly shown by all the innovations used in the construction of their citadel, Machu Picchu. The latter is familiar to British innovation and progression.

The tribes of the Americas had a similar form of worship to the ancient British whose many deities encompass all the natural life giving phenomena of one god and so it is quite possible that this form of religion was taken west by the British, who were possibly the first to colonise the Americas; and apparently there is no evidence that such religion existed there previously.

Care is needed here not to confuse any issues, for people who lived close to nature depended on the seasons for their food, they faced life and death, sickness and disease, accident and attack from all quarters. There was a human need to find excuses for the bad things in life and have someone to turn to in time of trouble. What gods they devised for their worship and propitiation we cannot say with certainty. The world over at an early stage of development, as well as today, mankind faced identical problems: - years of famine and plenty, seasons of heat and cold, loss by bereavement, accident and war. There was always a need of someone to pray to and to give hope.
So if the ancient British were the first to cross to the Americas up to an after 20,000 BC then it must follow they took their early religion with them, and it is possible it is that which may have evolved to be found there.
To identify the Britons pioneering course to the west at 20,000 BC, the ice would still have been over most of the northern hemisphere of Britain. The mid country was habitable and there would have been a vast, flat, delta plain that stretched across to what is now called Ireland. It has been established by eminent geologists that Britain once formed part of the landmass of America, from which it parted company alone, due to continental drift, separated by the Atlantic Ocean. I note here that there is no evidence of Pre-historic evolution in America, so it is likely that the earliest of humans arrived in America at about 20,000 BC; were possibly the British.
Are there similarities between the Native American Indian and the British in their behavioural patterns; are there further aspects alike in both races?

Most of the Native American Clans adorned paint and often placed 3 feathers in their headbands. The weapons and tools and implements were certainly similar. It is not in dispute that Native American Indians' wigwams, and wikiup wattle and daub roundhouses bear certain strong similarities, as depicted following.

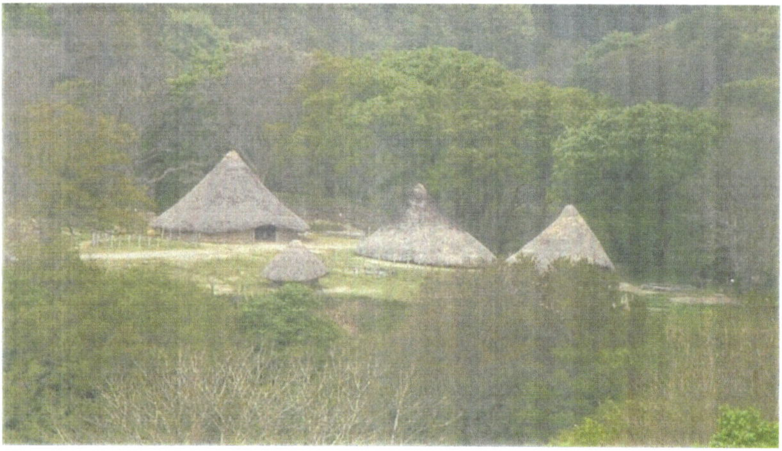

Archaeologists have also evidenced recently, super prehistoric cities standing in the thousands of square kilometres in the Amazon Basin and on the plains and Savannas of Brazil in South America, there are long and round houses raised on man made islands, with causeways between and tracts of land and canals, which are similar to the ancient islands and causeways, particularly found in the Thames Valley and throughout the British Isles and Ireland. Both are dated at about the same time; is this coincidence or instinctive knowledge?

In line with nature, the South Americans had invented a way of sustaining the soil with charcoal, which is called Terrafraiter, sometimes as much as two metres thick, which is now a highly prized source of compost, which actually grows each year by micro organism bio-reproduction. Scientists suggest this could bring a halt to slash and burn, if these nature friendly ancient practices are taken on board today. The latter can be identified with British progression, which had migrated to the Americas at 20,000 BC from the prime British location on the Gower peninsular.

Let's analyse the above statement: - Post 30,000 BC, Ireland was once part of Britain, attached to what is now called Wales by a vast flat delta plain, stretching across what is now called the Irish Sea. The ice sheets eventually melted, and with the tremendous weight removed from the land surface, the northern parts of the country were able to rise up and the southern parts dipped down; this is a phenomenon known as 'glacial rebound'. Similarly, Europe also became separated from Britain as the ice melted and the seas rolled in.

This separation is confirmed by the findings in the Solent made by Frank Battsford, who discovered artefacts of microliths and ancient forests dated to about 8,500 BC. A log-boat was also found inland, dated to about 1,500 BC. In several places along the western edge of Wales, other ancient forest are revealed at very low tides dated at 4,000 BC, and a legend of *Cantre Gwaelod* relates to these early times, when the sea swallowed the low-lying land and at least sixteen townships sank into Cardigan Bay. One wonders what archaeology as been lost to the seas, particularly to the west of Ireland.

Supporting evidence is that glacial rebound caused the seas to roll into Cardigan Bay to form what is now called Ireland and, flooded the low-lying delta areas including the British Channel; which is now called the English Channel. Up to about 10,000 BC in the retreat of this last ice age, parts of the southern coastal areas of Britain sank by up to about 50 metres, when vast areas of land around Britain were lost to the sea.
Professor David Smith and geologist Donald Jameson, found sperm whale vertebrae inland at a site near Stirling in what is now called Scotland. This seems to be convincing evidence that this area was once covered to a considerable depth by the sea, and Scotland was rising up, while the south of Britain was sinking. Up to 10,000 BC, the North Sea and Atlantic land bridges had been flooded by melt water and Britain became a cluster of independent islands.
At a site at Star Carr in Yorkshire, dated to about 10,000 BC, is a camp built on an artificial timber platform, at the edge of a lake. Here is evidence of a burial of the first trained hunting dog of thc British. Animal bone finds suggest the butchering of deer with small flint blades called microliths; some of these flints formed the tips and barbs of arrows used for hunting, similar to those found in the Paviland Red Man's burial site.

The latter proves that the ice shelf was receding and Britain was attached to Ireland with the Gulf Stream running into a catchment area up against the ice shelf and land, by which an easily following course was established by sea current, wind and ice shelf edge, which followed to the Americas.

From 30,000 to 10,000 BC the ice had retreated to expose more northern areas, which is good evidence of the last ice retreat and glacial rebound.

Following is a reconstruction of a scaled down version of a Crannog roundhouse, on a raised platform or island, on Llangorse Lake in the Brecon Beacons, which lake is a left over from the last ice age.

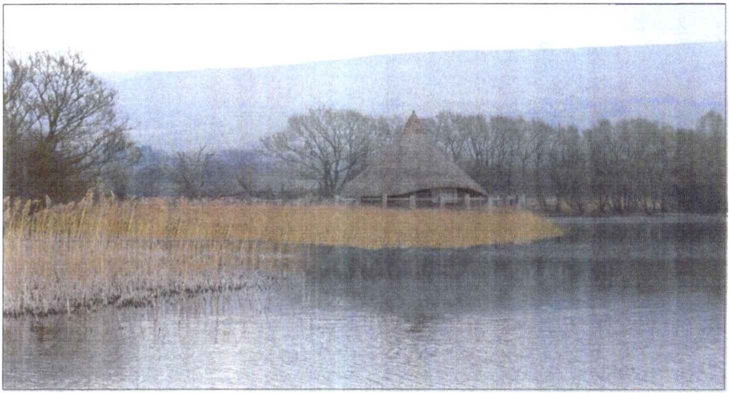

Crannog

I mention here while referencing this location in other respect; recent excavations reveals an ancient connection to Llangorse Lake and the surrounding lands, which there are many hillfort locations in this area, wherein the British resided to settle.
Imagine this area would also have been vastly wooded BC, and deer and other animals would have been a plentiful source,
Ogham stones and other artefacts have also been found at this location, which identifies early writings of the British, of the land that became the British Isles.

Chapter 5

The development of a new society with technological advancements

Evidenced from the vast amount of archaeological finds the British pioneered forward. Big game would have been hunted to the edge of extinction and out of necessity settled agricultural communities were formed. As they expanded and thrived they encouraged the development of new technologies and cultural and social organisation, with religious and ceremonial activities coming in their wake. The British had to progress to new implements and ways of life, and a considerable communal effort was required to prepare ground for planting, to scatter seed, control weeds and to harvest and store crops. It was no longer the domain of hunters to feed the community and so agricultural expertise became a benefit. This in turn gave associated work for women and the old folk, winnowing and grinding cereal to make flour, baking the bread, tending the animals and storing and preparing other plant foodstuff, which indicates that agriculture and stock control was developing alongside hunting. This led to new types of tools to break up and prepare the soil for seeding (these were precursors of the modern plough and harrow) which gave rise for quern stones to grind the grain and various pots in which to bake and stew.

Depicted following are some rotary grinders of which the British progressed to. The corn was ground between the stones that filtered out from the sides as baking flour, likewise our commercial flourmills of recent days.

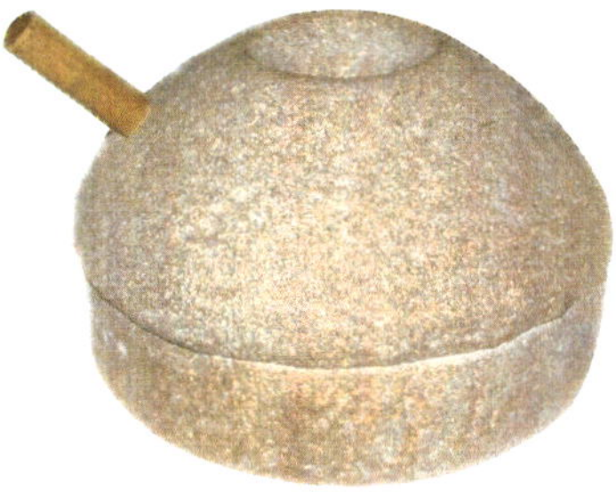 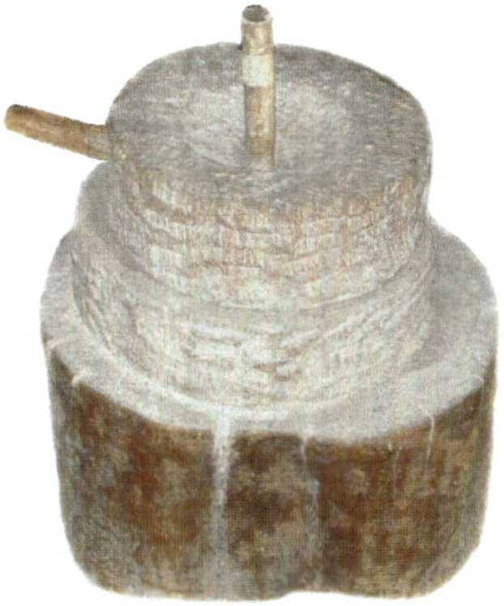

This was the start of a new type of socialisation in Britain. Communal stores had to be constructed to preserve food over the winter months. Feed for domesticated grazing animals had to be gathered and stored to keep alive the best animals as breeding stock for future times. There was strength and safety in the new communal style of living, which led to the exchange of ideas on how to improve tools and the invention of new ones. New types of buildings were needed. Greater manpower could now be deployed to create and maintain defences around settlements. This was a pioneering civilisation that produced innovators, explorers, sailors, new technologies, and men capable of settling new lands.

Like the American tribes the British left no written records of their existence. Only the archaeological, architectural and technological evidence remains, and yet this evidence is substantial, for their footprints in the stone were substantial indeed.

As is the case with all advances in any society, changes came gradually to the British, driven by their need for sustenance and self-protection.
The Red Man's burial is possibly the most significant British cave burial find which establishes who were the best candidates for our ancient British ancestors. It is a reasonable supposition that his descendants would have established their ownership of this land as the population increased and the supply of big game reduced.
The landscape of Britain had changed irrevocably since the days of the mammoth and as the ice sheet departed, the great valleys and riverbeds were formed and fertile silt was deposited. Vegetation took hold, vast forests spread across the land and small mammals became plentiful, with wild boar, deer and other creatures. Once man evolved and as he slowly exchanged his hunting and gathering habits for agriculture and herding, he had to clear areas of the forest to allow grass and cereals to grow, to feed his family and his grazing animals. The felled trees were used for building his home, fuel for cooking, and keeping them warm. All these activities progressed to people creating open spaces in the forest into tracts of workable land. Expansion in all types of mining was emerging from as early as polished stone axes and other implements, to using mined flint to replace the stone and, this quarrying led to techniques for building homes, with slate for floor and roofing material. The digging of flints from the chalk gave rise to lime mortar to fertilise crop fields, and lime-paint-wash for clay-plastered wattle walls, which clay was also used to make kilns for metal and pottery. This natural progression evolved from necessity and inventiveness.

To emphasise here, there is evidence showing that there were many British communities living in many regions, which made up the whole pedigree of the British Nation. To evidence the latter, it was the Romans who identified and named (interpreted) these many regions, which are depicted on the following map. These regions establish that an independent Britain progressed through all the ages, to these resident regional areas throughout the whole of the British Islands.

On the following map you will also see the edge of the ice-shelf is near the line of the British regions of the Silures and Atribates. The ice edge is shown as a dotted line where it would have been after about 30,000 BC, near the Gower Peninsula in South Wales.

I must also reference by this map: - With such a massive sea-barrier to overcome, how did the Romans launch an attack on Britain from the open seas after 56 BC. I would also like to point out that during the Roman invasion and up to 410 AD there was no division into the Saxon named regions such as Wales, Ireland, Scotland, or England, as the map depicts. All of Britain was inhabited by the kin related British in the whole of the "British Isles". Another misrepresentation is by the fact that no British achievements have been allowed to be taught in British schools since any invasion, for the syllabus has been set to what the Romans, Saxons and Normans allegedly achieved in Britain. It is apparent however that the Britons are an established Nation in their own British lands before and after any invasion and evidence exists to show that the whole of the British Isles are inhabited by the British; so is this another continued Roman deception?

Map of the British Isles

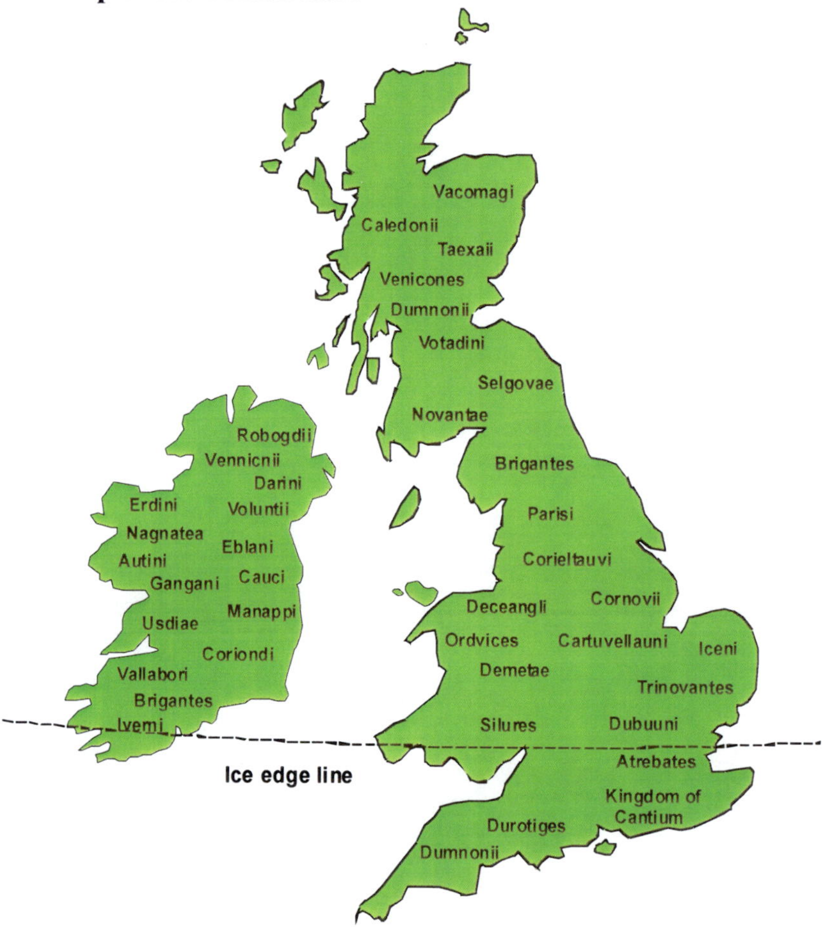

It is said that some Irishmen say - the Scots are actually Irish migrants, I agree of course, but therefore are the Irish Welsh migrants? It is also suggested that St Patrick was born in Onllwyn, in the Swansea Valley; but all are descendants of the Ancient British of course.

This is the very misconception brought about by each invader of the British Isles, because all Britons are in fact related British. Ireland, Scotland, England and Wales are Saxon-invented names, an invader's division of the British Isles. And it only takes at least three generations to (meme) brainwash any nation into whatever any controllers want them to be. The reality is though, unequivocally, that the British Nation exists.

In further evidence of the British Nation: - Products were bartered or exchanged over long distances. Evidences of some axes came from a documented site in Langdale (Cumbria) and are widespread in the East Riding of Yorkshire. Evidently, at the latter end of the mining of Flint at Grime's Graves and Langdale, the Great Orme was already in production and being mined for copper. Progression from mining was emerging from flint to tin to copper and the making of Bronze, to Iron, showing the entire process of mining through to each individual end product. Surely these ages must be from earlier dates if you factor in the embryonic start of any project to the actual made products found, e.g. from the first stone axe to the bronze axe, must have taken thousands of years of evolution for the British to have evolved in scientific and technological terms.

Understandably any development would involve a great exchange of ideas and ideals taking place through communal communications with the whole of the British Isles.

The appearances of the many regional areas are testament to this need for more cooperation and a good reason for the British to barter and trade throughout the islands and apparently with Europe at these times.

The British knew how to construct the wheel, as they firstly used in farming and then in their war chariots, to defend their technology against would-be invaders. The wheel gives mobility and allows for a motive force to be applied to a conveyance, expressed even today, in terms of horsepower, manpower and engine power. There became a need for implements for everyday use and weapons of war for defending Britain and possibly for trading abroad; mining for metals became more significant to the early British. The uses to which metal was engineered, demonstrated their inventiveness with a refined representation in their artistry, by using gems alongside the decorations made from silver and gold and, in their intricate designs inscribed thereon, was an expression of who they were and where they came from.

The British progressed intellectually until they were able to calculate time and measurement, judging by what they left behind for us to study. It would for instance take some considerable degree of intellect, cooperation and management in order to design and construct Wood or Stonehenge. Stone circles are found throughout the British Isles particularly in Wales, where there are many stone circles, cairns and burial mounds, some of which were associated with the measurement of time, day and night, the progression of sun and moon, the seasons, and lunar months.

Britons depending on agriculture for their food and a calendar was a good indicator of times to plant seed. Once they started to extend their territories, they would wish to avoid the seasons of heavy rain, snow and gales; their knowledge of all these attributes are abundantly clear from the evidences they have left us to read.

The possession of a calendar assists in the formulation of ceremonies to celebrate harvest, mid winter and mid summer, to predict the equinoctial gales and high tides, and the arrival of shoals of fish and so on. It is a significant development as we know.
The British were leaders in many technological advances and it was well within their capability to design major projects, and they had the expertise to transport the sacred blue stones used at Stonehenge, from Preseli in South Wales, to Salisbury. There is a suggestion by some archaeologists that the 90 Preseli blue stones, all of near equal size, were transported to Salisbury by the ice flow. If that is the case, it must have happened at about 100,000 BC, or earlier, to place this into any historic perspective. But how could stones travel east sideways? They would firstly have had to travel for about 80 kilometres, and then travel down a South Wales Valley for about another 100 kilometres. There is no advice offered as to which valley any stone might have followed, or how the stones then took a sharp left turn to continue for another 200 kilometres or so, moving through delta plains, bogs, rivers and the sea, before finally ending up on the Salisbury Plain near Stonehenge. This explanation seems bizarre! Perhaps these archaeologists think this was Druid magic at work! Or, was it British expertise that transported them? It is said today that the bluestones feel warm to the touch, is possibly the phenomenon for which these stones were selected to be used perhaps for ceremony, which were considered for their use in the colossal astronomical details of the mathematical calculation and the planning and construction aspects of Stonehenge.

The following photograph is of the Preseli bluestone outcrop. Looking at the skyline, it is said that true Britons will see the ancient image of the dragon sleeping. No coincidence today's Welsh Flag depicts the similar outline of this dragon image. Forefront and left are standing stones.

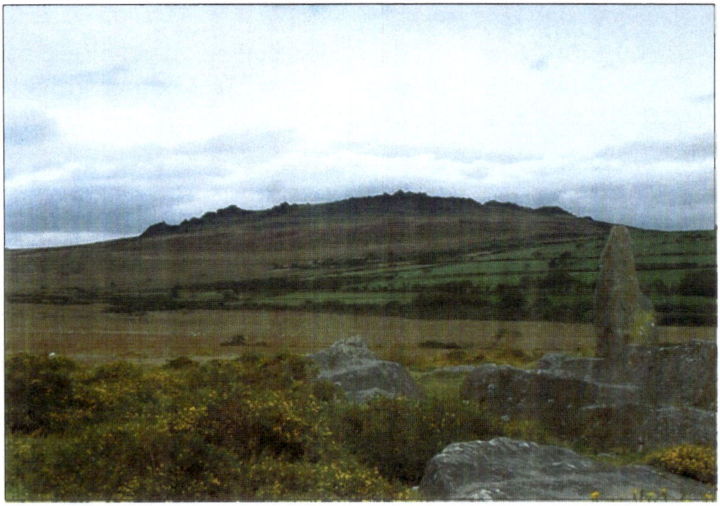

Preseli bluestone outcrop and standing stones

In the picture following, shows the same line but a few miles away, here is a stone circle (relative to Stonehenge). The Preseli outcrop is in the distance. Apparently the astronomically designed circles of Wood and Stonehenge were possibly strategically built in middle Britain, so that all the British clans could travel to one place for joint ritual festivals, games, or assembly in the management of the British Isles.

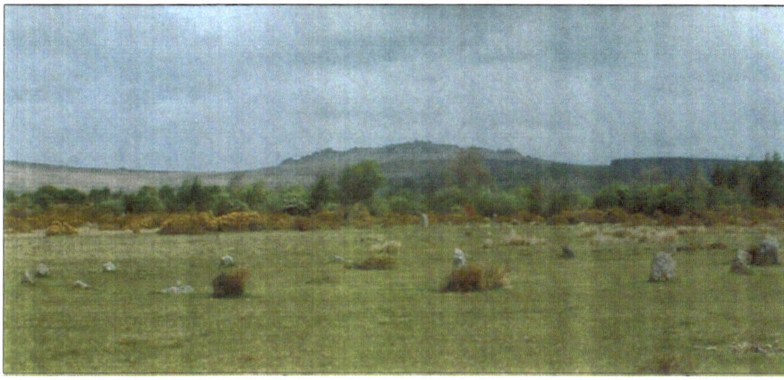

Stone Circle near the Preseli outcrop (3.500 BC)

At Stonehenge perhaps the leaders would have settled disputes, discussed defence matters to protect Britain's shorelines, and strategies involving the deployment of combined forces against any invaders. They may have considered religious rites, festivals, games, commerce, agriculture, technological advances, and astronomy. This was still an age when most people were closely related to one another and these meetings must have been seen as important enough to justify travelling a considerable distance to attend, twice a year at least, on each solstice. Recently, hundreds of human bones have been excavated on Boscombe Down near Stonehenge, along with their grave goods, including bows and arrows. Historians have named these people the "Boscombe Bowmen". Genetic markers in their tooth enamel indicate that these people originated in the west of Britain, perhaps from Preseli in Wales, wherefrom it was these people who transported the bluestones to Stonehenge. These bowmen also lend weight to the real possibility that it was the British who progressed to make the yew (natural ply) longbow.

Further confirmation has come from fragments of antler bone and other artefacts found at Stonehenge, in the last phase of the monument dated to about 2,500 BC. The latter date also coincides with the Britons' huge scale mining of copper and the technological developments and advances in metallurgy and smelting and forging on the Great Orme, which shows incredible innovative abilities' and the vision of a Great British Nation.

Ancient British astronomy and technology must have evolved into the ancient lunar calculator called the Coligny Calendar of the Celtic Sequani Clan, which was found near Coligny in France; which used the same principles as the stone engravings found at the Knowth site in Ireland. Other instruments that followed were such as the astrolabe. Julius Caesar also described this in his writings about the Gaelic Wars, saying: - "this tradition (of lunar forecast) has been handed down by the Druids". Logically he means the British; because it is the British who are the real innovators, (Druid is a later faction of the British). These instruments can forecast with astonishing accuracy, the planets' positions at future dates, which is a step forward from the basic Luna formula of Stonehenge. Evidently, advanced instruments do not suddenly come about in isolation. Clearly, the British were using geometrical calculations in their constructions thousands of years earlier than Pythagoras. As aforementioned, the British would have monitored the course of the stars to arrive at the farthest place northwest, a position under the ice-shelf where the Red Man was buried. After residing in the British Isles for thousands of years, it would make sense that this nation would have evolved to present day.

British innovation was in line with what they learnt from the stars; and the clans met together at Stonehenge, in a complex of which mathematical and astral related methods and basic formula still work today.
At this juncture I would like to put forward my interpretation of Stonehenge in consideration of what the British would have evaluated over thousands of years, as follows: - Stonehenge is not aligned to compass east-west, it is located on a latitude north of the equator, aligned with the midsummer solstice sunrise on June 21st, the longest day, which is seen to the northeast (through the main portals); and the midwinter solstice sunset on Dec 21st, the shortest day, to the southwest. The full-moon alignments will be opposite to the sun at the winter and summer solstice and both will be seen as spectacular full gleaming orbs, in the main portals of the monument at rise and set, sequentially. The equinoxes are an equal day and night and are aligned east-west, but are not aligned through the main portals of the monument. True compass can be found by the equinox, or by dissecting the pass-through line to the solstice. References to this can be found in Newman 1972 "The Astronomical Significance of Stonehenge" and HMSO "What is Stonehenge".
Understandably, the Ancient British would have logged each astronomical event to the relevant stone positions of Stonehenge and therefore could have calculated any position of any event in any sector.
In the 1st phase of Stonehenge, it is discovered what are called the (56) outer Aubrey holes (and outer ditches with internal post-holes) named after the founder John Aubrey (depicted on the following Stonehenge Layout).

There are however 60 holes to be found (by including the inner ditch post-holes) because it is evident that by the 2nd and 3rd a, b and c, phases of construction, the British had scaled down in each from the 60 outer holes to a smaller circle of 30 outer stones (of which 30 stones and spaces are consistently 60 (for all purposes and intent). It is apparent the British were not placing stones at random, for the design from phase 1 to 2, as from 2 to 3a/b/c, is consistent. Equally convincing there are 60 and 30 inner bluestones remnants to be found, which would be relative to the 60 outer holes in ratio, in order to make mathematical scaled down sense. The British had an amazing grasp of mathematics, surveying and astronomy at this time, to have refined these calculations of alignments from surveying astronomical events over thousands of years.

On the avenue leading into the monument and on the causeway, you will see a number of postholes that have been discovered, which must be the means for sighting and surveying. The British would have learned how to find the solstice days, from thousands of years of observations and a good guess is, that all the post places on and about the monument are the remnants of their surveying techniques.

Near the Heel Stone you will see 4 postholes in line, and I deduce there was a sighting pole behind this line, further back towards the east, whereby sighting through the pole to a post, would align it with the solstice sunset peak. The further back the sighting pole, the more accurate the line of sight, (just like a long rifle barrel sight is more accurate than a short pistol barrel sight) will give a more precise alignment to the sunset.

Over the years, the British would have observed a small shift in the front post (the foresight) in relation to the sunset and, would have placed a second post in line with the solstice in subsequent years, and over four years they would have noticed the return to a previously placed post, which is each a quarter of a degree shift, pertaining to a leap year. This brings the sightings back to a start post, by which Stonehenge was aligned.

It is seen that the four post holes on the causeway are of a regular specific distance apart, and the sighting pole (which may be found today if the remnants exist) would be the back sight to and through any one of the four posts of each year's solstice (as shown in the solstice pictures following).

Understandably the British were capable of scaling down the four post holes actual width to a hand usable smaller width measurement scale (as in the imperial yard which is depicted following).

As we now know, the earth is 93 million miles away from the sun and any degree of angle on the earth is a minute subdivision of the distance angle, relative to any datum point, foresight, and the solstice Sun peak.

On the following solstice depictions, by aligning (like an engineer's datum point of today) one of the post-holes with any solstice sunset, the British would have placed a fixed aperture, pole or stone back-sight, as shown (white), and a foresight post (yellow) at the peak of the solstice Sun peak, and this would have given them a year start and an alignment with Sun peak, as you will be able to establish on the pictures of the 1st, 2nd, 3rd and 4th year solstice sunsets, which many monuments throughout Britain are aligned with.

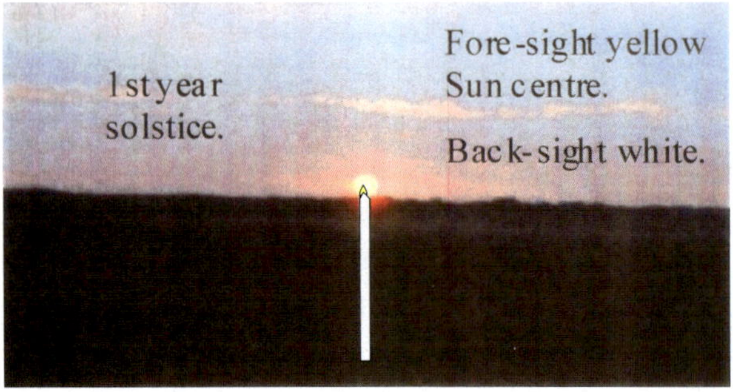

In following years, the solstice is not exactly in line; this must be a fraction of a whole degree. So, at this point another (yellow) post foresight is positioned (as in the following depictions).

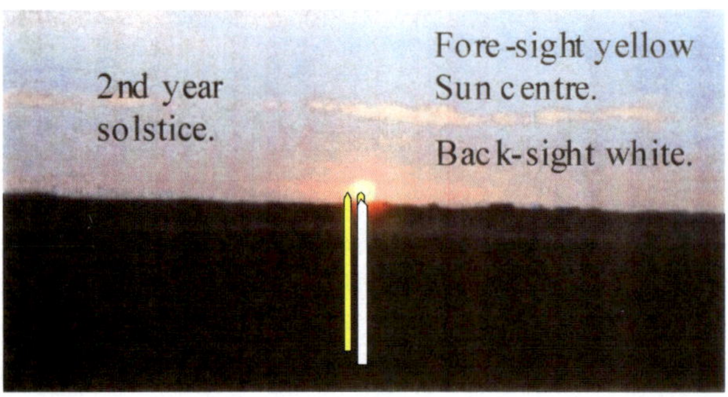

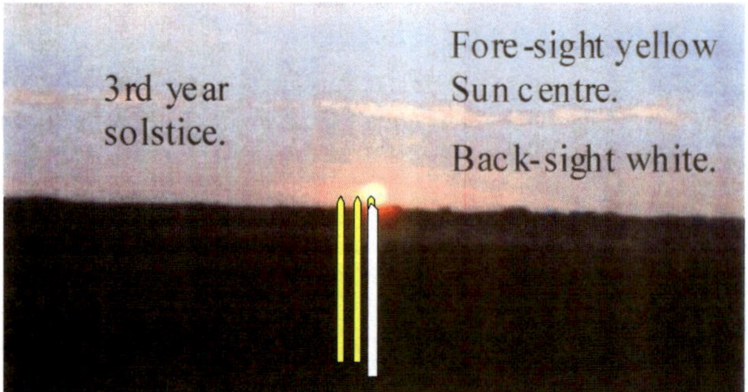

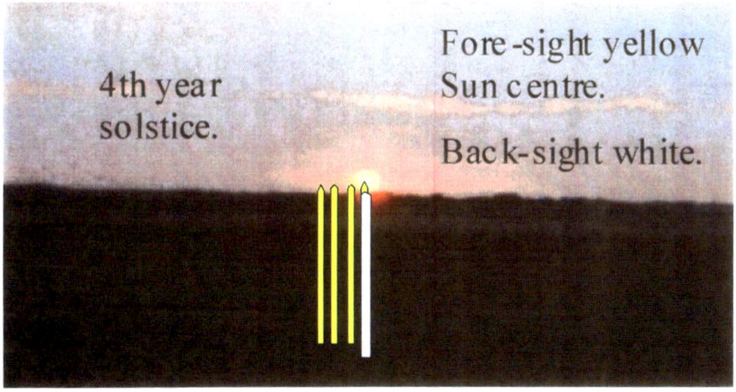

The British would have come to this annual sequence by simply monitoring the heavens over very long periods of time, establishing a quarter of a degree shift each year to establish one extra (degree) day in every four years, to what we now call a leap year. This is all relevant to the rotations of distance and angle of the sun, to and by the earth. This method of placing the 4 post points will give 3 divisions, when viewed through to the great circle (shown as the imperial yard, following).

The next logical step would be to place a circle to represent the Sun (and nights Moon) cycles through the days, months and year, to follow the cast shadows, similar to a sundial or (associated) Viking sun compass. The length of cast shadows will give direction and the exact year start and progress to the year end, marking the degrees of time between; likewise represented by the alignment of the circle of Stonehenge. These motions are completely relative to the laws of the universe and of its structure. The British, whilst monitoring these events were able to lay out their celestial maps on their sacred site at Stonehenge.

Having made a study of the Layout of Stonehenge I offer following, my interpretation of its formula, which is relative to time and the motions of the earth, sun, moon and stars. The best possible way to start is to look at the details of Stonehenge and then place them into an uncomplicated perspective of a sound basic formula. Apparently the Ancient British evolved to use this basic but sound formula, which has extended into what we actually use today.

The Stonehenge Layout depicted following has 30 outer stones; these are shown with superimposed black lines, representing the average of thirty days of each month. The months are shown as red lines. The stones' formula reveals random days to each full moon and moon crescent in each month, and the circle can also predict the sun (as a sundial) moving through each day.

The next steps to which the British may have evolved are as follows: - There are averages of 30 days in each month, as shown by the 30 outer stones of Stonehenge. There is an average 12 full moons in a year equivalent to twelve months, divided into 4 quarters (seasons) equivalent to 3 full moons in each quarter, as can be seen by the stones' Layout. It is clear from this how far the British had progressed at Stonehenge, which is basically used in our calendars today. It has been modified to some extent to our modern day divisions, by scaling it into smaller units for the use in a clocks hour minutes and seconds; and further subdivided into a 360 degree circle, which is all from the very same Stonehenge basic formula.

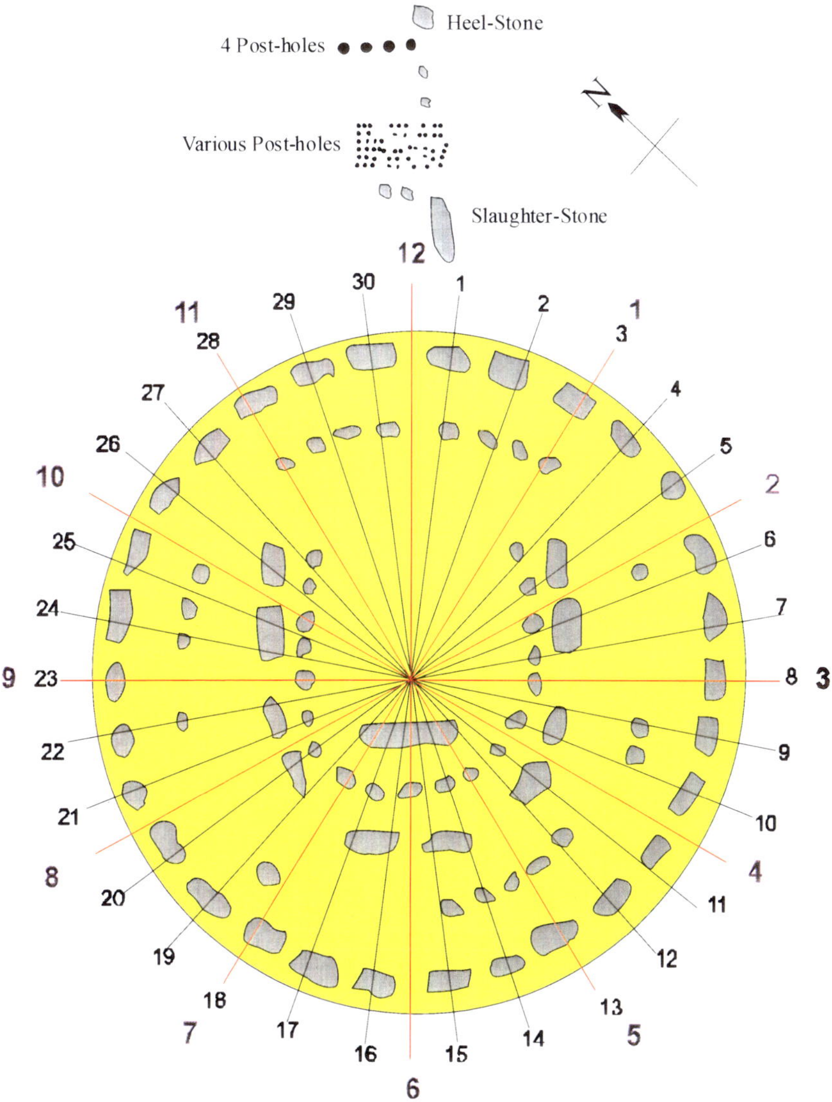

Stonehenge Layout *(Not to scale)*

Each of the 4 quarters have been divided into three parts of 5 minutes, equal to 15 minutes per quarter, whereby 2 quarters are equal to 30 minutes, or half of one hour and 4 quarters of 15 minutes into 60 minutes in each hour (as depicted in the arrangement of stones and spaces). The latter is equal to 12 hours in half a day, 24 hours in a whole day, 365 ¼ days in the year, relative to the moon's phase rotations to the earth, and the earth's rotations around the sun, consisting of a complete cycle of one year. This is the typical basis of the basic formula seen at Stonehenge.

Another step forward could have been the devising of units of measurement. Firstly, as described previously; the 4 posts, denoting solstice peaks over four years, establish the degree of a year. Each post is displaced one ¼ of a degree each year, which may represent the imperial yard (as depicted following). The 4 posts are divided by 3 spaces; each is a 3-part (yard) division, which gives the formula of the British imperial yard unit of measurement.

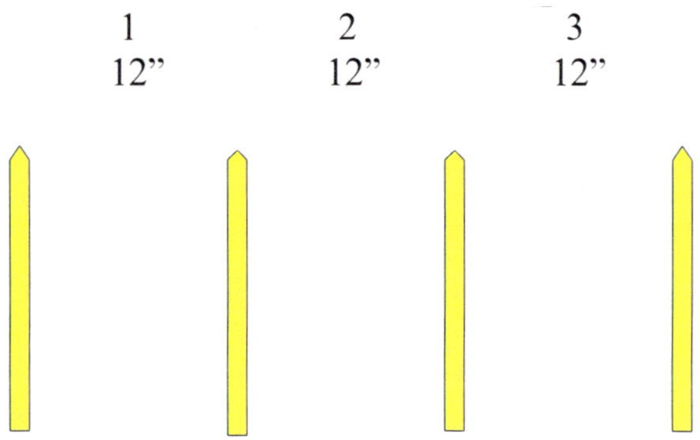

"Imperial Yard"

It has been suggested that the imperial yard came from the Egyptians or Romans, but if Britons were using this measurement BC then again this must be a British invention of an understanding which came from observing the universe, as shown at Stonehenge.
Understandably, for ease of calculating, a year became 360 (days), when divided by 3 is 120 parts of each space, which is too fine a calculation to place into a rule and, so would have been subdivided by 10 equal 12 divisions, this will become a 3 part (12 inch), is the 36 (inch) British Imperial Yard. This yard in our time has been subdivided into tenths, to furnish us with 360 divisions.
We also know that the metre is approximately 39 inches and provides a modern-day modification for finer measurement, nearer to the original 365 ¼ days of the year; nevertheless, this is a sound modification; as can be deduced by the construction stages of Stonehenge. Evidently, it was the British who were first to refine these measurements.
Using the same Stonehenge basic formula, it is another easy step to establish the 360 degree circle, based on a one tenth scale, where 12 (months) times the 30 stones, is close to the 360 days of one year. And so the circle made up of 360 divisions, with 3 parts of a degree in each quarter, is 3 times 30 which equals 90, and 90 x 4, equals 360, again comes from the typical British Stonehenge basic formula, which is established by the Stonehenge Layout. Possibly, the Stonehenge 90 bluestone's is the quarter division for defining the 360 degree circle? Also, evidentially, by using a surveying device this 360 degree circle evolved to provide today's means to calculate by triangulation.

The 360 degree circle became the step forward to establish latitude and to measure the time and motion of the universe, which evolved from this basic formula.
This formula is actually taken from the movement and dimensions of the universe and so it must be relatively precise. The importance of this original formula is to establish the correct length of a yard (degree) that must be determined by the heavenly bodies in the visible universe, relative to the earth. And the best subdivision of that yard or metre (degree) is determined by how you proceed to subdivide it. We know by experts' advice there has been a half a degree shift up to today's evaluations of the setting Sun, and the universe is expanding, so fine tuning will always be the norm.
A reference by Christopher Knight and Alan Butler in their book called "Civilisation One" their evidence suggests that Britain may have been one of the first civilisations, particularly in Chapter 12 titled "Sun, Moon and Megalithic Measurement", of the data cited therein of professor Alexander Thom who gathered mathematical information from his many analyses of Megalithic sites in Britain, to notice parallels in each monument's dimensions relative to what they named a "megalithic yard". Knight and Butler have done some extremely good research and have cited very sound complex calculations, which indeed are all relevant to the astronomy of our solar system and our measurements of time and space. The Ancient Britons would have used a less complicated, down-to-earth explanation of basic formula, from some of the fundamental essential elements associated with Stonehenge.

Again, this is an instance of sound support research, to show that Ancient Britons were indeed an extremely advanced civilisation. You will also see at Stonehenge that the sun's beam would shine through each solstice aperture to meet possibly a King, Queen or priest at the centre of the monument. The inner stones may represent eclipses and other astronomical events.
In every certain 19th year, the moon's position appears to horseshoe-arc over the winter's sun-setting position over this direct sun-beam-line through the portals, this was a magnificent sight for the Ancient Britons to see. Is it no coincidence there are nineteen bluestones in the inner stone horseshoe-arc design of the Stonehenge layout; one wonders how this was used. These events in every 19th year also depict the sun and moon standstill settings, when they seem to join below the horizon, perhaps to be seen as a metaphor by the ancients as a marriage and to rise in the east as re-birth. These moon events will happen in every month of the year, which can only be described as monumental. All these sophisticated details show a precision and accuracy of observation, learning, surveying, astronomy and mathematics at Stonehenge, indicative of an innovative people that have surveyed the solar system for aeons, well before 3,500 BC.
Burial chambers on Anglesey and Newgrange in Ireland are provisionally dated to about 3,500 BC, where you will find similar British designs and incredibly accurate, sophisticated, architectural features as found at Stonehenge, which must have resulted from intelligent, joint, long term, astral observations, apparently observed by the British, in their own British Isles.

The British stone carved artwork designs, ritual, innovation, technology and learning were cutting edge up to and after 3,500 BC, found throughout the British Isles, particularly Ireland where no foreigners entered BC. Clearly, this pre-dates anything in Europe and beyond, so the British culture was unique.
Finds of bronze discs with moon phases on them have recently been found, and also cone-shaped bronze hats inscribed with incredible details of the solar system, found near Alicia in Europe and dated to sometime AD. It is evident that British astronomy was developed far earlier than this. Possibly, there was somehow an allied corridor of learning from Britain into Europe. These coned hats seem familiar to Welsh hats (although the name Welsh is a later Saxon invented name); perhaps of these hats is an echo from the past?
We may also wonder whether our pre-decimal coinage are also echoes of which came from the ancient British source which is relative to British astronomy that has reflected into our coinages, for there were the farthing, halfpenny, penny, three-penny piece, sixpence, and shilling, half-crown (crescent) and crown; divisions of 4, 2, 1, 3, 6, 12, 24, 60 and so on. I have made some calculations of these divisions relative to seasons, crescents and moons, but more information to cross reference them is needed before any remote relationship to the typical formula of Stonehenge can possibly be assessed.
It would seem that the Stonehenge basic formula, which is relative to the universe, has evolved into all aspects of our measurement and time, which is a true evaluation of British existence.

I further evidence here that our ancestors were possibly first to be aware of there being 365¼ days to every year, adjustable to include an extra day in a leap year, as found in our ancient British calendar and to the west BC - particularly in the Inca, Aztec, Maya Olmec, and Nazca civilisations of the Americas – for the calendar number of days in a year is found in the architecture of their great temples and sun-worship altars, with flights of 365 steps and other subtle details. Likewise, it is by the Britons' tracking of the cycles of the earth, sun and moon over thousands of years, they established that earth's movement must be relative to and in harmony with the visible bodies in the whole universe.

In Richard Danbury's book "The Inca Trail" you will see the American clans progressing in parallel with the British clans and a large part of his book is relative to the ancient British culture, particularly the development of engineering skills, such as their canal systems and masonry etc. Other similarities are seen in social structure: is the Inca nobleman called the Orejones and their Druidic counterparts; there was also the Britons' early worship of lakes, earth, wind, sun and moon etc.

At the super city of Teotihuacan, in Mexico, which was larger than imperial Rome, there is evidence that these early peoples aligned monuments to the sun by the means of a sighting pole and post, indicative of what was achieved at Stonehenge, so it is possible the British colonised America at 20,000 BC as mentioned earlier. The Teotihuacan people have never been properly identified, nor have they left any written records of their lives. All we have are their monuments of stone, architectures and artefacts.

We have seen how like the Teotihuacan people, the early Britons came to an understanding of the cycles of the heavenly bodies and taught themselves about time and measurement, and we deduce they had a form of religion, one that encouraged harmony in relationships and community activity for mutual benefit, evidencing that like the British, these rulers were working for the benefit of their nation, not ruling to live off it.

We cannot know exactly what beliefs Britons held, but from archaeological finds and their sophisticated art, we see that it was based on a love of the natural world, on which they depended for their livelihood, and possibly was monotheistic in the sense that all the natural phenomenon of nature of which they respected, were of one God. It would perhaps be overrating their moral code to suggest that these nations always lived in harmony with one another, and were never at odds with neighbouring kin-clans. Based on what we know of human nature it is safe to assume that all was not sweetness and light, but may have been regulated by the high priests, similar to the later British Druids.

Richard Danbury shows that early South Americans, dated to 10,000 BC were farming domestic animals by 8,500 BC and were living in close communities by 4,000 BC. They were planting crops at about 3,000 BC, about the same time as the British, and like the British were later invaded, plagued and enslaved.

As invasion crops up here, I mention that Rome had an inferior ten-month calendar; and when they realised their mistake AD they placed two extra months, July and August, named after Julius and Augustus of the Roman Empire, so evidently were not skilled in this area.

We also know that the Romans stole other nations' technologies and destroyed evidence of its origins, to make it seem as if it were their own. If there had been evidence of a 365 ¼ - day calendar, in the east or south, BC, surely the Romans would have seized upon it. The point is that predators will come in to take what they want if they realise its worth, and will disease or annihilate a nation, or absorb it to assimilate and enslave. This knowledge of astronomy at Stonehenge was brought about by the innovation of learning and understanding in order to have plotted the astral system over thousands of years BC, which enabled the British architects to incorporate astronomical alignments and events that would have been important to the British. Briton's evolved to use a twelve month calendar from their year start to end and the times for planting and harvesting, religious festivals and rites. It is these astronomical features as well as the enormous engineering factors of the construction of the Stonehenge monument, which makes it so momentous BC.

This was the beginning of a technological revolution brought about by successive advances in metalworking on the Great Orme. Copper needed an iron mix in it, so from this smelting the British naturally progressed to Bronze and into the Iron Age and so on.

From the footprints of the Red Man and to Stonehenge, the laws of nature and the universe had become relatively understood and respected; what else is there to learn from Stonehenge's design? British intellect and innovation bred refinement, which led to novel implements and instruments such as in the intricate details of the British Cross (Called the Celtic-Cross).

I put forward here my interpretation of the British Cross of BC which has a similar mortise and tenon joint to the lintel joints of Stonehenge, as could be used in a basic surveying device, I will explain following: -
Britons did not practise the Roman crucifixion, which was to draw out the suffering and deaths of their victims, nor did the British mark their graves with crucifix markers BC, and so it is possible the British Cross was used for surveying BC (thereafter became a carved standing stone grave-marker). The Romans in AD had a surveying instrument which incorporated a range-pole and cross bar, with plumb lines hanging, which gave the means of plumbing, lining and levelling, but had to be further aided with a square or triangle. The Ancient British Cross could be an uncomplicated hand or ground retainer held surveying instrument, which will give a ranging means, a levelling and plumbing means, degrees of a circle and angle of degrees and, rotation means. This is speculation, just as any historian may speculate; however the basic Stonehenge formula is sound, so a surveying means is possible. The British could have progressed from the simple means of lining posts to a more sophisticated means for surveying precise circles, arcs and squares and so on. To plan Stonehenge to place massive stones into precise ground holes, with matching dressed mortise, tenon and dowel joints, in order to connect with a massive raised circular lintel platform, in line with the inner circles and the actual surveyed universe, then a surveying instrument is quite feasible. This means is exampled following in more detail.

The British Celtic-Cross

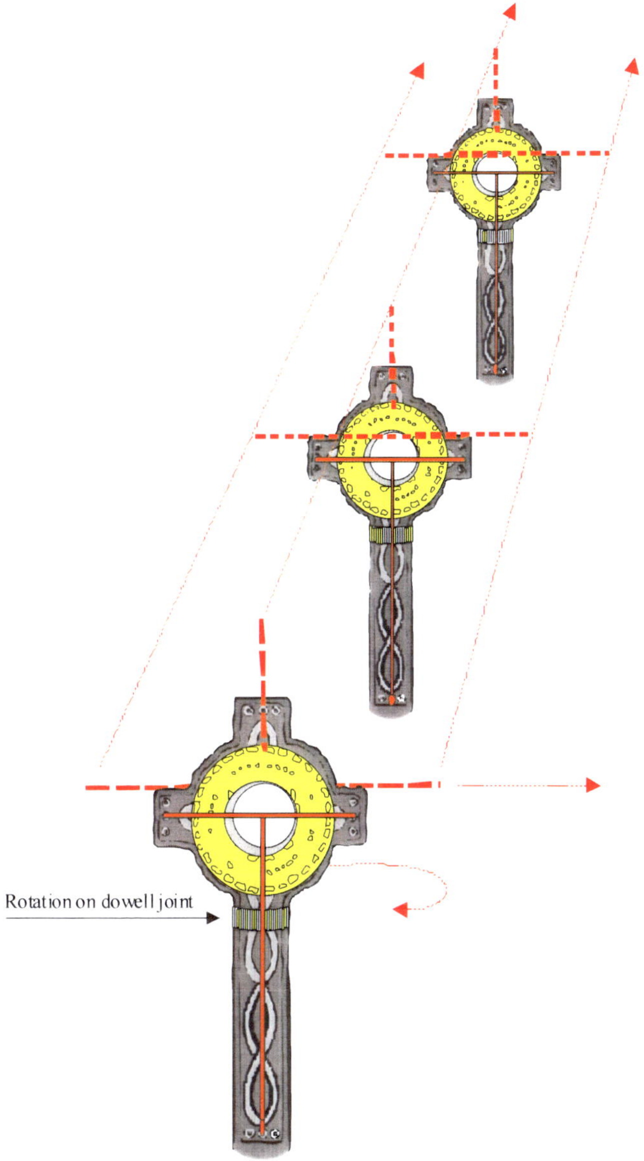

The British Cross incorporates a dowel joint, which in the cross' sighting means can be rotated, whereby you sight through the apertures or cross-arms.
Understandably, the ancient Britons may not have used a finite scale, but you will see the uncomplicated basic Stonehenge formula shown. The (yellow highlighted) Stonehenge Layout of 30 stones and 12 (months), which is 30 x 12 = 360 degrees scaled centre on the cross, which would have been represented by 36, giving the means to project angles off the plumb (vertical).
The middle rotation dowel joint may also have had 36 degrees of scales marked just below the wheel head; this will give a rotation of 36 (finite 360) degrees of any rotational angles. The horizontal and vertical full red plumb-bob line at the middle of the cross will give true plumb and levelling. This is achieved by sighting across the ranging members with cross at vertical (plumb).
The broken straight red lines show the sighting points for lining and levelling.
The hole through in the centre of each cross will give you an aperture sight for aligning through; also by sighting through a hole to any second cross' hole, for the second holes' outer-line to be effectively within the sighting means inner circle hole, it appears that this will give a regular distance from one cross to the other.
The radius, a broken red line, indicates that the cross can be rotated to degrees on the dowel joint, and the degrees read off the yellow line marks of the upright, possibly in 4 quarter marks of 9 (90 degrees) giving 36 x 10th of a 360 degree circle. Logically, the Ancient Britons would be using the scales of which they could easily manage at any time.

This cross will also give angled lines off the plumb line, for building buttresses, slopes of roads and irrigation channels and so on.
The ancient Britons were far advanced in astronomy and so were capable of meeting with the vast complexities of constructing Stonehenge, which included a precision of mathematics. The latter surveying basics are really only a basis for what we call today is a "ranging" or "boning rod" procedure. It is more than possible the British had a surveying means, and these basics did progress to what we have today, more or less. It seems to be likely that the cross is an uncomplicated easy to use surveying instrument, one that the ancient British would have developed quite easily, given their superior knowledge of the universe to firstly identify a basic formula and the ability to plan, organise, and manage to construct such an astronomical Stonehenge monument.
Britons we know - progressed to use the imperial yard measurement to calculate the speed of a vessel. Also ropes with knots tied in every yard of their length could also be used to judge depth of water, in much the same way as the sailing ship's captains measured depth in quite recent times, perhaps another echo of the past, all relative to a Stonehenge basic formula.
This formula allows us to triangulate, to measure most anything; to navigate the oceans by latitude and measure the universe by volume and time. This technology would have been necessary for surveying roads, aqueducts, terraces, buildings, buttresses, canals and temples etc; has found in the Americas. We know the Romans never got to the Americas, so they cannot lay claim to such technology or device.

If it was the British who crossed to America at about 20,000 BC, then this basic ranging-rod cross, could have progressed to measure something as intricate as the Nazca geometrical angles and irrigation lines; these are geoglyphs and geometric line clearings in the Peruvian desert, made by the Nazca people, who flourished between 200 BC and 600 AD, along rivers and streams that flow from the Andes. The desert itself runs for over 1,400 miles along the Pacific Ocean. Dark red surface stones and soil have been cleared away, exposing the lighter-coloured subsoil, creating the 'lines'. There is no sand in this desert. From the air it is seen that the 'lines' include not only geometric shapes, but also depictions of animals and plants in stylized forms; including images of humans, which grace the steep hillsides at the edge of the desert. The Nazca lines took hundreds of years to create and required certain educated people working on this planned project.

We also have small but similar land-art, in the chalk clay in Britain, such as the White Horse of Uffington on the north-facing slope of the Berkshire Downs close to a hillfort. This is dated similarly to about early Iron Age and is of a similar date as the Nazca lines; this art form is similar.

Coincidentally, if you lay the ancient Celtic cross on the ground with the degrees upon it, with the head pointing at the solstice, you will see the Layout shape of our ancient Britons' avenue and the circle of Stonehenge.

Britons were the pioneering inventive people of the time, who would most certainly have progressed to these understandably uncomplicated and yet comprehensive technologies.

No hard evidence of the ancient British cross remains because, as seen by the decayed surveying post-hole remnants at Stonehenge, it would have been made from wood and wood deteriorates. There may be more technological innovations and physical and astrological uses of the Stonehenge monument than meet the eye, which remain to be discovered. Possibly, the inner stones would reveal more if the exact numbers originally placed there could be established. It would be interesting to find out more about Stonehenge.
There are hosts of books offering various complex explanations for the original purpose of Stonehenge. One is by American Gerald Hawkins, called *Stonehenge Decoded*; Hawkins used his computer in a genuine attempt to try to prove that Stonehenge could have been used to observe the sun and moons rise and sets. However R. J. C. Atkinson, one expert on Stonehenge, wrote an article in 'Antiquity' 40 (1966) 212-16, said to be the world leading journal on archaeology, by which Atkinson debunks Hawkins' theories in his book entitled 'Moonshine over Stonehenge'. But perhaps a "Blue-Moon over Stonehenge" will illuminate a down to earth British basic formula!

Quote: "The aristocracy are not British; then who are"?

Question: I am a person the Greeks named Celt, from a place the Romans identified as the Silures, in the region the Saxons named Wales and the people Welsh, and other inhabitants Irish, Scottish, Cornish, Manx and English. Is it apparent we are all of a bloodline from the same Ancient British Nation?

Chapter 6

The spread of knowledge and the Dragon awakens

I will now mostly identify with Welsh British and I am sure the British in other Saxon named areas can identify locally: There is unequivocal archaeological evidence of British technologies found throughout the British Isles. Knowledge, especially industrial cutting edge is any nation's prized asset, which derives from intelligent source. The British Druids knew how to keep secret their knowledge in their libraries of remembrance to the benefit of their nation, and kin-clan allies.

The British moved from the Gower across to Ireland and up onto the Dyfi estuary, the Great Orme, and Anglesey North Wales. Nick Jowett, explorer and pothole expert, excavated some of the oldest copper mines, dated pre 2,500 BC, in the Great Orme (Orme means dragon, which was an island in BC). These copper mines have more than five miles of hand-excavated tunnels, which yielded 37,000 fragments of bone and stone tools, producing an estimated 1,700 tons of copper mined there, enough to make ten million axe heads. Jowett also excavated here, the first industrial smelting plant in the world, dated pre 1,580 BC.

If the British had mined 1,700 tons of copper from more than five miles of tunnels before 2,500 BC, and had set up an industrial smelting plant before 1,580 BC, then the Copper and the Bronze Age must be pushed back to the middle, or the early part of the Flint Age; for understandably it takes many years to perfect a technology to reach a certain standard in time.

Copper and bronze may have evolved from pre 3,000 BC, for these technological advancements must have coexisted at an earlier stage, to have progressed to this industrial enterprise scale on the Great Orme. The British were producing copper on a scale that is evidence of a surplus for trade and possibly export.

I will mention here: - In 1991 an Ice mummy, called Oetzi, was found in the Alps, dated at 3.500 BC. Scientists who investigated Oetzi found evidences of copper particles and arsenic in his hair, which inferred he had been engaged in copper production (not bronze). However it was then stated: at the time of his demise he was shepherding a flock. In his possessions were a copper axe, a bow and quiver of arrows, also leather straps and sinews, suggesting he was on the move. It was also alleged that very small opencast pits in this region were producing copper at this time. This is evidence that copper was later used in Europe post 3,500 BC.

The Great Orme mine may be the start of the industrial revolution in Britain and possibly the world. I point out here that the Romans made Britain the slave shop of the world and how this happened will be revealed in due course.

DNA from human bones found at the Great Orme mine proves a (Welsh) British ancestry. Understandable this technological advancement would have been a sacred, secret asset, which was slowly brought into existence over hundreds, perhaps thousands of years prior to 3,500 BC, as indeed, any technological advancement would have been slowly learned and protected at this time. It would take many footprints in the stone to have progressed from flint to copper to bronze and so on.

Copper would have been seen as a wondrous, sacred metal and a great trading asset in Britain and abroad, as the Britons traded back into the south and east.

Let's identify here how the British had progressed up to and after 3,500 BC: There were innovators, hunters, teachers, astronomers, strategists, chieftains, warriors, kings, queens, clergy, politicians, designers, architects, surveyors, masons, carpenters, farmers, stockmen, mariners, fishermen, potters, weavers, artists, scientists, metallurgists, engineers, smelters and so on. They had forges and foundries producing copper and bronze goods far exceeding their requirements. Their surplus was traded at home, enabling the acquisition of local produce; and for the export and import of goods made elsewhere; an early form of entrepreneurship can be detected here.

The Great Orme has also been called the 'Sleeping Dragon', and when mining and smelting took place here it must have looked as if there was a great fire-breathing dragon on this island, with the glowing furnaces below and smoke from the fires curling overhead. In the blackness of night it must have been an awesome site for the locals to see.

British in the South (Cornwall) mined tin ore, which was transported to the Great Orme to be forged with copper to make bronze. Later, tin was used with lead from the Cardigan mines to make pewter. Also lead gold and silver were mined in Wales in these early days BC. We know the Romans, in AD, exploited this British mining industry to enslave Britons into providing them with every item of engineering, including lead water pipes, and roofing materials for their villas and bath houses.

The British at 3,500 BC were at the forefront of innovation in most technologies, evidenced by their expertise in mining to extract tin, copper, iron and lead from ore and then to forge the correct combinations to cast bronze and pewter in pre-formed stone and clay and, using the process of finely carving beeswax models, to be placed inside a clay casting mould. This mould was then fired to burn off the wax, whereby molten metal was then poured into the mould to leave a finely crafted object. This procedure is still used today and is called the "Lost Wax Process". This type of clay moulding would have progressed from ordinary clay pots, to have fired the maker's imagination into making clay metal castings. With this knowledge and expertise, the British entered the Iron Age. Metallurgy must have been a weird and wonderful science at this time and it is no wonder the British kept it a secret for so long, from any predator invaders. Very likely this smelting plant when viewed from the opposite shoreline to the Great Orme may be the origin of our Welsh emblem, the "fire-breathing" red dragon. It would have been a good deterrent, to keep prying eyes off the Great Orme Island, to preserve the details of the mining and what was actually taking place. It must have taken many footprints to advance to this great technological importance - of knowing how to use charcoal in kiln smelting plants to get to the correct temperatures, and all the trials and errors of finding the correct combinations of copper with tin and some iron, to make bronze. To remember these sciences of many combinations must have been a greater fete than writing it down, apparently these Britons were very advanced indeed.

Following are depictions which relate to the Welsh hornpipe, that may have progressed into the Dragon passant. Also a Celtic shield design, and sword.

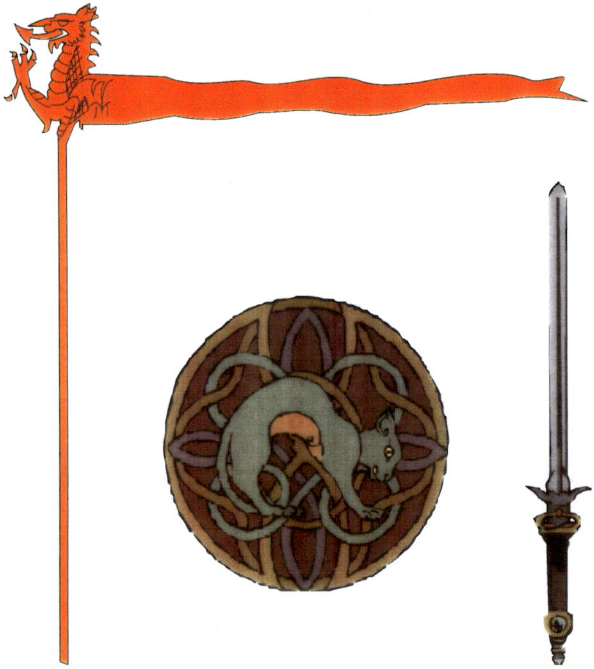

In order to highlight the Britons' progression, listed following are some Ancient British sites, dated from the Flint to the Bronze and Iron Age which will serve to show that the British progressed independently up to the Roman invasions, and also, after they left. You must appreciate that this is a small selection, because to list most would involve the writing of volumes (Listed in the back of this book are more places of interest to visit, with various comments of support).

On the Gower Peninsula, in South Wales, are many Ancient British sites from BC. They date from Stone to Flint, through Tin to Copper to Bronze to Lead and to the Iron Age. Many were communal sites, which became hill forts.

Caldy Island, in Pembrokeshire, has been inhabited since the Stone Age, and has been linked to British trading into Byzantium (pre Roman).

At Brodgar Ring, Orkney is a henge circle of approximately 100 yards diameter, inside an excavated ditch. Nearby are the comet stones and a henge circle of 60 stones and a ditch of Stenness, which are relative to the basic formula of Stonehenge, and shows that the British had extended their regions into the far north.

The Trippet Stones in Cornwall is a circle of about 30 stones of about 30 yards diameter, again associated with the formula of Stonehenge.

Long Meg and Her Daughters in Cumbria, is a stone circle of approximately 100 yards diameter, with an entrance of double portals; beyond stands Long Meg in-line with the midwinter sunset, all are relative to Stonehenge.

At Tregeseal Cornwall is a pair of circles. Originally, 19 tall stones stood on the border. It is known that the moon is at its southernmost lowest position in line with the winter solstice every 19 years, which may relate to this same cycle associated with Stonehenge.

At Merry Maidens Cornwall is a stone circle, and nearby a chambered tomb with cup-marked entrance. One wonders if these cup marks, which turn up on many ancient monuments, have some significance to toasting, perhaps to offer the wine to nature - or casting metal.

Toasting is evident by the British Horn of Plenty, the Cauldron, the Quaich (existing in Scotland) and the Wooden Chalice healing cup, which is kept in Nanteouse house in Aberystwyth, Wales.
Geographically you will see that these great monuments are predominantly in Britain, however, some are on areas of the shorelines of Brittany and the Isles of Scilly, which were once part of Britain. None are significantly found in deep Europe (Note: I use imperial measurement which is relative to the monuments period and the Stonehenge basic formula of measurement to relate).
On the Island of Er-Lannic, southern Brittany, there is a site of approximately 60 by 60 yards with a second semicircle of 60 yards across. Excavations give evidence of occupation from the Middle Neolithic to the Iron Age. Cattle footprints have been found in the mud flats near the Severn Estuary in South Wales are dated to 4,000 BC; here is confirmation that Britons were driving their cattle great distances and clearing the lowlands of trees, to grow grass for winter grazing, all evidence that the British were well established and here to stay.
On the Orkneys, where wood was scarce, there are standing stone circles and burial chambers aligned to correspond with the solar system. There is also the stone-built village of Skara Brae, with roofing slates and ornate stone dressed internal utility formations, with air conditioning and indoor toilets. There are also the circular stone corbelled air conditioned broch's with cavity walls and a spiral staircase leading to at least three upper floors, of which principals of BC are still used in constructions of today; (which are more sophisticated than any stone pyramid chamber in Egypt).

The great Cairn of Maeshowe is carefully built of crafted stones; one weighing up to 30 tons, the chamber is illuminated on the winter solstice. In the near Minehowe chamber there are 30 well preserved stone steps leading to a rock floored subterranean cavern 20 feet below, with a hidden chamber in behind the main cavern, this monument is dated to around 3,000 BC.
The British were using wattle and daub, and then stone to build tombs, housing and astronomical monuments, pre 3.500 BC, before most of the eastern stone built structures and were freely using natural resources of wood and other materials to build enormous residences. At this time the Egyptians were building mud pyramids for their Pharaohs, with no functional design other than a tomb for a self styled ruler, who presided as a living God. Later in 2,667 BC, the first "stone" pyramid was built, for the Pharaoh Djoser.
In the *Time-Team* documentary, featuring archaeologists Gibson, Richards, and Professor Richardson, they excavated a natural arena-type enclosure at Minehowe: the dig revealed a 60-yard diameter - stone-bridged mound site protected by a ditch enclosure and, in the middle of this mound was a 20-yard deep subterranean chamber. Also found was a bone needle, Bronze-Age arrowhead, and a mould for casting a bronze mace type spear-base. Iron-Age pottery was also discovered on this site, showing a continuation of British use. It is speculated that these chambers could have been used as a contact point with the underworld, similar to the Greek Oracle's consultations, but earlier at 3,000 BC, another export to the east perhaps?

In a nearby excavation of about the same date is another similar construction, where perhaps an Oracle could have conveyed instruction from the hidden chamber. Anyone visiting here would easily believe that the voice they heard was emerging from the underworld. Alexander the Great was known to consult an Oracle; is it possible that this ritual migrated to the east from Britain?

In the living landscape of Wales there are at least 600 regional hill forts that have been identified so far. (And there is an enormous amount throughout the British Isles). These hill forts took a significant amount of co-operation in their planning, building and design. We know that Britons had all these abilities in abundance. One of the greatest strengths of these early people was their ability to combine their resources, information and manpower, for mutual benefit. They built defences around their inhabited sites for their flocks and herds. They set markers to separate the land into units and agreed the boundaries. This pattern of defence and demarcation is still recognised today.

There were also large amounts of natural resources to exploit, such as hazel, oak and water reed, used to construct and roof round houses, each of which needed about 34 oak beams, 2,000 bundles of water reed, and 125 bundles of hazel wattle, and mud daub. Martin Bell used dendrochronology to date the oak planks on these sites to about 2,743 BC. It has also been established that the yew tree existed here at this time, as earlier evidenced was essential for making the natural-ply strength long bow.

Following is a photograph of some of the round houses of BC, reconstructed on their original foundations, at Castle Henllys near Nevern in Pembrokeshire. This site is within a vast hill-top location with a circular fenced rampart and a lower defensive ditch surround, with pointed stone pitched obstructions and walls and fences at the bottom. Initially, these were defences against wild animals and perhaps poachers. It is seen that Britons were using natural resources, and if you look into the structure, you will realise its unique central fire air-conditioning design, which rising smoke-tar seeped through to preserve its timbers, roof and wall structure, in a healthy, louse free environment.

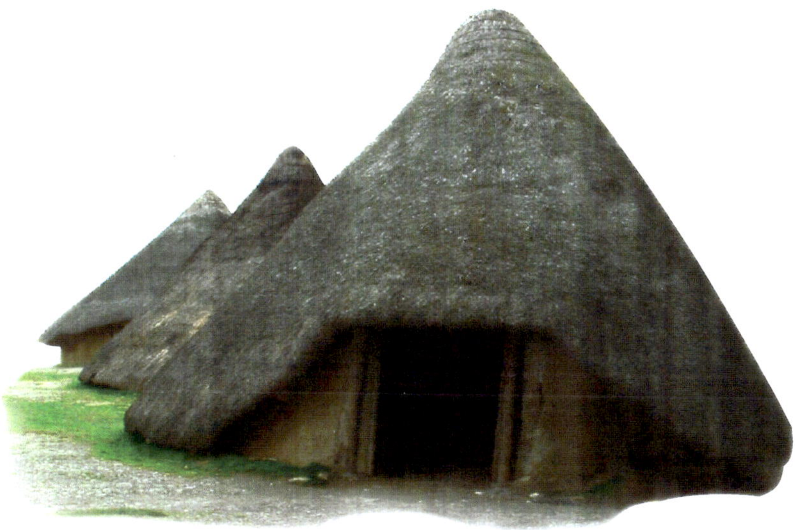

Castle Henllys Roundhouses

Castle Henllys was strategically built by a British chieftain, who would have presided over this communal stronghold and region, and would have been one of the many warriors that made up the pedigree of a whole British Nation. The exchange of knowledge and ideas between regional communes led to an integration of industry, which included mining, engineering metalwork, pottery, domesticated animals, agriculture, woodcraft, reed-thatching, weaving and commerce etc; with schooling, training, and religious practices. This infrastructure, once set up, led to communication with other regional communities. It proves that there was an established British Nation in place, well before any invaders arrived.

Following is the massive Bronze to Iron Age hill-fortress of Foel Drygarn in the Preseli hills, which shows that the British were a well organised nation.

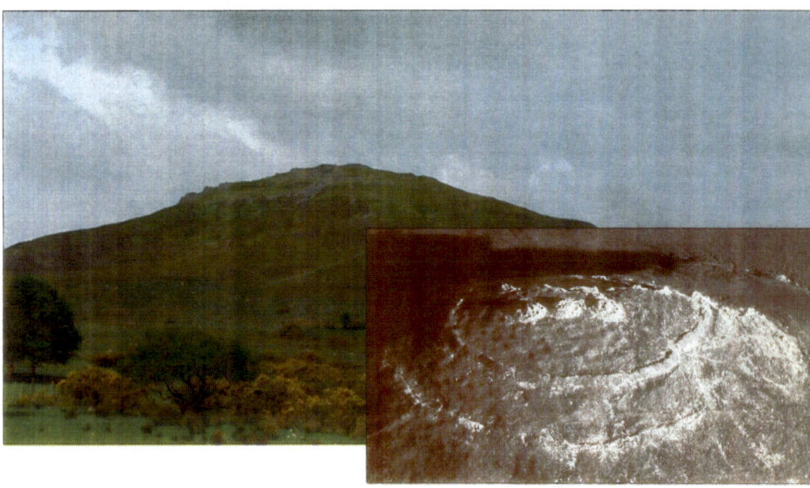

Foel Drygarn. **Fortress layout.**

Within the Foel Drygarn outlaying enclosure there are at least 220 stone hut foundations. It is suggested that three chieftain kings who presided here in succession, are buried in the three cairns (shown on the inset photo). The British clearly evolved to building these great regional strongholds and, it follows that they would certainly have had a good strategy for defence against invaders. There are hundreds of such hillforts throughout the British Isles which sites have been used by Britons through the Flint, Copper, Bronze and Iron Ages.
Wide tracts of forests were cleared for farming and agriculture, confirming a nation that was well organised, undertaking communal work, with ritual ceremony at its forefront. Also found are round mound barrows, and rectangular long barrows of earth burial places, such as the 50 burials, found at Fussell's Lodge (Wiltshire) suggesting a communal grave-yard.
Earlier burials suggest the bodies were perhaps left in the sun to dry and bleach, before being dyed with red ochre, this suggests that the preparation of the bodies before burial were part of a religious rite. Cremation was also a factor especially in eastern Yorkshire at Willerby Wold and East Heslerton.
From about 3,500 BC there appeared at burials sites new distinctive rites of placing jewellery, and dagger-blades of copper, then bronze, then to iron, then to other metal objects that have been found in Britain.
An excavated site at Oddendale (Cumbria) produced radiocarbon dates of around 2,800 BC, which is relative in time to the industrial revolution of tin, copper and bronze smelting on the Great Orme and followed by the Iron Age.

Near Migdale lock, Inverness, Scotland, a bronze hoard was found in a rock crevice, dated at 2,000 BC. An axe head was tinned (a new plating process) with anklets and armbands of Bavarian influence, likely for export.
Highly decorated grooved clay-ware has been found at henge sites is evidence of communal life, particularly as mentioned, in the village of Skara Brae (Orkney) is a group of finely built stone houses linked by stone passageways. The houses are laid out with beds, seats and storage places of stone and shows the British were building permanent structures to settle.
A new form of beaker shaped decorated pottery vessel appeared in Britain, from which is derived the name applied to this new type, the "Beaker" folk. But surely these routine pots were made by Britons in Britain and were not that complicated to make, considering Britons were actually making "clay-cast" and "lost-wax" clay moulds, are processes of refined metalwork smelting, thousands of years before any simply made "Beaker" clay pot.
After this time many structures throughout Britain, such as Windmill Hill (Wiltshire) appeared showing regular use of the slaughter of cattle and the trade of goods, as well as large industry, commerce, agriculture, farming and regional communal life.
The Britons founded all the major British towns and the roads to and from them before any Roman or Saxon invasion. We know less about the Iron Age than others because Iron Age burials are rarely found, perhaps because the offerings to lakes or rivers left few traces, but it is a fact that the Britons are the true residents, who established Britain, is the British nation.

A burial in Welwyn, Hertfordshire, contained items of imported luxury goods, domestic implements and vessels associated with wine, indicative of a continual trading of goods and ideas with countries abroad.
Burials were usually under round barrows of stone or earth, such as the example at Bush Barrow Wiltshire; but in northern Britain they were in flat graves, some of which were lined with stone. Clay objects identified with Beaker Culture are found all over Europe, and the closest parallels for the British material are found in the Netherlands and Rhineland, so it is likely these commonplace clay items were widely copied or traded.
In Berkshire, Wiltshire and Dorset, dated around 1,600 BC, excavations turned up gold, jewellery and items of personal adornment together with new types of bronze daggers and axes.
At Sutton-Hoo, Suffolk, is a later, isolated, alleged Angle or Saxon boat-burial, containing artefacts of bronze axes, a stone-cast mace-head and refineries etc; to bury expensive or luxury items in a grave suggests that some individuals had accrued considerable wealth; but surely this was British material and workmanship in Britain.
The term "Wessex Culture" may in reality be British Culture, of trading its agriculture with metals of the west on the Great Orme, and also regions in Ireland, Scotland, Europe the Mediterranean and to Byzantium.
This high degree of technical innovation showed the progression of a distinct British Nation. Regional innovation evolved into a broad framework of common culture and social organisations and ceremonial sites, the most important site being that of Stonehenge.

The Bronze Age flourished into a society in line with communal life, commerce, agriculture, farming, high technological advances in fortress design and defensive strategies, mining, metallurgy, moulding, engineering and design. It seems the control of the sources of mining and manufacturing of metal objects, especially of weapons, increasingly emerged as the foundation for trading and became a source of British wealth and power.

Huge tracts of land in middle Britain came under intensive agricultural and farming use, where cattle and sheep were grazed and cereal crops were grown. Extensive farming has long been known in the south of England, the Yorkshire Dales and Lake District, whilst the industrial mines and metal smelting plants were situated in Cornwall and Wales etc, where tin, coal and copper were plentiful, is evidence of the emergence of a powerful British Nation. Evidence of pottery continues to crop up in sites dated up to 1,400 BC, including new kinds of clayware used to preserve cremation ashes.

Metalwork continued to cvolvc rcsulting in new types of implements being produced by the British industrial plant on the Great Orme, to meet British needs, which progressed from socket axes to weapons of flared spearheads. Swords and round shields could also have been influenced and commissioned for the requirements of continental traders, for new types of weapons for their local wars. Unfortunately this technology was later turned against the Britons, as you will read later.

British metalwork has been found in what one would consider places of religious importance such as in rivers and lakes.

The British Clans were by now a major force of British society who must have fought over certain regional rights; but understandably would have joined to defend Britain from foreign invasion.
Chariots were of great importance to the British, and sometimes formed part of the grave goods of warriors. These chariots sprang from the production of carts in which to bring the harvest home, to carry heavy loads and to save manpower for more important tasks. Early strongholds were built of timber and comprised box ramparts and single ditches and then new techniques came along; and the designs were much improved, resulting in huge fortifications with multiple ditches and sloping ramparts. Maiden Castle (Dorset) is a good example of the progress made in building.
Before 700 BC in what would have been a remote dense untracked forest in the wilderness of western Britain, is the Llyn Fawr Lake near Hirwaun in what is now called South Wales. In this lake was found a bronze cauldron that displayed the intricate work of early British metalworkers. Also found in this lake were an iron sword, sickle and shaving blades, all dated up to around 700 BC. The significance of this find, it shows a continual British use of the lake through the Copper, Bronze, and Iron Ages who were producing British products for their own use. This remote lake evidences that these artefacts can only be associated with the Britons because this location at the time these items were deposited into this lake, would have been in a wilderness in the depths of a forested mountain region; that would have been inaccessible and of no concern for any foreigners.

At Llanmelin Wood, near Newport, is a hill fort which was strengthened in 50 BC. It is one of the British King Caradoc's tribal fortresses of the Silures Clan. The Silures also occupied Caerwent.
At Caerau, near Cardiff, is a plateau hill fort with three ramparts; this was one of the strongest Silurian hill forts in South Wales.
Merlin's Hill situated in Bryn Myrddin Carmarthenshire is legendary that Merlin lays there, is relative to the King Arthur legend (or a King called Arthur at least).
St David's Peninsula has many prehistoric remains such as Clawdd y Milwyr and Clegyr Boia, with the remains of Iron Age dwellings and traces of earlier Neolithic farms of early British origins that extend into the mists of time.
In the Black Mountains at Llyn y Fan Fach, Powys, there is a lake connected with the legend of the Lady of the Lake, again linked to Arthurian legend.
In the presently named county of Shropshire, near a town called Stretton, is the fortress of Caer Caradoc of the British Chicftain King Caradoc (welsh Caradog, the Romans called Caractacus). This site is an ancient Bronze to Iron Age hill fort; evidences that the area of the Silures extended eastward into this area. It is also evidenced that Caradoc defended Britain against the Romans for at least seven years.
I mention here, that British mining evolved into coal, iron ore extraction, slate, the many uses of steam, and all the everyday implements and appliances associated with communal life that had derived from these minerals. Britain was the cradle of industrial technology, thanks to the British and their inventions.

The British, like most developing societies had need of some forms of social control, and we know that Druidism had a form of law and order that was prevalent. Thus it is assumed that they also held religious festivals and formed royal dynasties. Society has need of leadership and it is seen that British leaders worked for their people, rather than use them as slaves.

It has been shown through time that each embryonic innovation will progress into other applications and refinements, for there must be a source for the water to spring from, and the well was Britain. Archaeological finds on sites of this period show remains of round houses, bronze axe heads and evidence of boat-building, across and below the Great Orme latitude. It is clear that the Britons were not only building communities, developing agriculture, engineering and commerce; but they were venturing away from hearth and home to an industry, in order to trade their surpluses at home and abroad.

It is feasible that the Britons were trading with the Romans before their invasion of Britain. However, Rome's expanding empire was built on force of arms and the Roman army was deployed to invade and to enslave whole nations. The Romans invaded Britain to satisfy Rome's greed and British technical expertise, and to enslave the British, to abuse as they wished.

Following are some British weapon blades of bronze and iron, manufactured using stone-mould castings. It can be seen they are typical of the kind of weapons used by the Romans; perhaps these were traded with the Romans and other nations of Europe, prior to any Roman invasion.

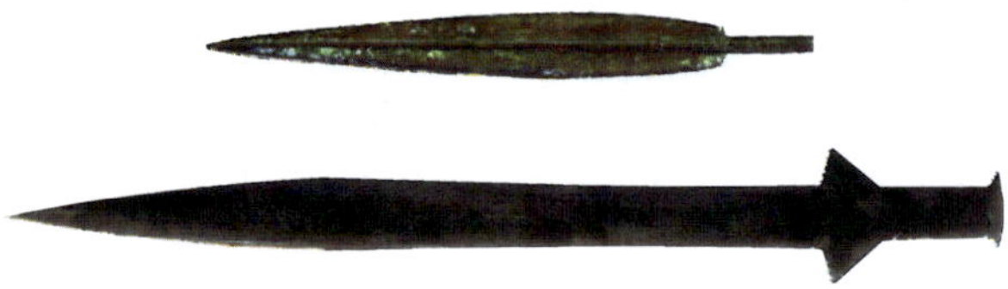

British crafted Spearhead and Short-sword

In the illustrations below are a bronze helmet, inlaid shield head, scabbard and dagger, as produced by the British.

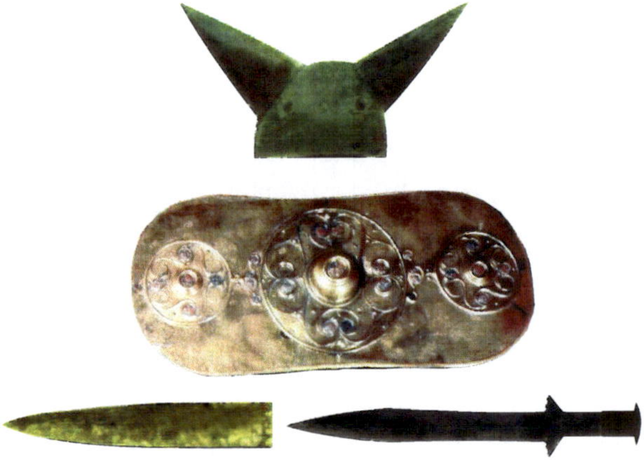

The latter is proof that the exclusive skill of early British craftsmen was unsurpassed by any of their European contemporaries and the Britons would have extended their skills to have traded abroad. These items should not be referenced as coming into Britain, as some historians insist, for apparently they were manufactured in Britain, by the Britons and also exported.

It is unfortunate that some archaeologists insist on identifying people by the artefacts unearthed from their time. They write of Beaker, Roman and Saxon people, etc. It is very misleading and it tends to make us think that the British did not exchange or make foreign commissioned products, for they certainly had the materials and skills to make ordinary items of pottery, and apparently the amazing metalwork artefacts, implements and blades. If archaeologists excavate teapots, cups, woks, and scrapped metals and Nissan cars in a thousand years' time, will they assume that the inhabitants of the British Isles were Orientals?

The British can be traced back to the earliest of times as archaeological finds clearly evidence. The British had put down their roots far and wide, after 30,000 years BC, up to and since Paviland Red Man.

The British understandably had their own language and a complete social infrastructure of schooling and caring. The clans frequently joined together to defend against foreign foes and, as history portrays, men and women were equal in courage to rise to be leaders and chieftains, and in their determination to uphold their freedom they repelled Rome on at least two occasions.

They had mines, learnt astronomy, deforested and farmed the countryside, had wheeled vehicles, surveying instruments, smelting plants, forges, moulds, chariots, chain-mail, bridles and saddles, horses bits, cavalry and infantry, and they worked in copper, tin, bronze, iron, pewter, silver and gold, to supply the known world. Small wonder then, that they made a tempting target for Rome.

It is said by some linguists and historians that the British language is a European language which spread into Cornwall, Wales, Ireland, Scotland, and the Isle of Man. Surely it would make more sense to acknowledge that the British language is their first language, which remained in the British Isles from as early as BC, as Caesar evidenced he encountered when he first landed here in 55 and 54 BC. He also said that European Druids learnt in Britain, so British Druids must have learned the European language in order to teach Europeans British Druidism. The recorder Strabo also stated that a British astronomer of his time spoke Latin as if he was brought up in the lyceum, suggesting that this Briton also had his own first language. Also Tacitus wrote that Caradoc and his sister Gwladus held the command of at least three languages, this must evidence that the early Britons learned foreign languages in order to communicate to trade and export abroad, and teach Europeans 'Druidism' in Britain. It is also documented that the aristocracy passed acts to outlaw the British from speaking their language in their own British lands. Was this the same old Roman ploy to bury any evidence of the true British?

British burial rites are also a defined product of Britain, which progressed through the ages into the Christian burials of today.

The Romans, Saxons and Normans adopted British rites. It is evidenced that Briton's such as Caradoc and his sister, according to the Roman Tacitus, were converting Romans to Christianity early AD. It is noted that the Saxons were not Christianised until about 800 AD. So it is apparent, foreigners were adopting British customs.

The Britons' first language was their ancient tongue and the British cross was not a crucifixion cross.

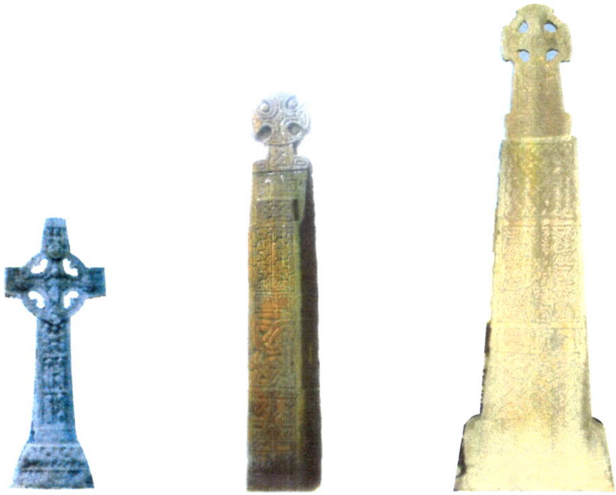

Depicted far left is a British Celtic cross standing near the Shannon River in Ireland. Centre is the Great Cross, standing 13 feet tall, in the 6th century Church of St. Brynach, at Nevern in Pembrokeshire; the angles of the arms indicate rotations against the sun; there is an ancient British inscription engraved on the Cross. Far right is the Great Cross at Carew Castle, is a gift of the Welsh King Margiteut, son of Etguin Maredudd ap Edwin, who was joint ruler of the Kingdom of Deheubarth (South West Wales), in 1033 AD.
The evidence shows, according to linguists, the Britons did not write documents, but did carve many Latin inscriptions, when duly read backwards was classical verse. The Vitalianus Stone following is inscribed in the British Ogham alphabet of which usually accompanies a Latin translation.

Caesar also recorded that the British Druids had at least 60 colleges of learning in Britain; in which each student took 20 years to acquire a high level of remembered knowledge (Jesus' missing years perhaps, you will read later) and to hold this knowledge in one's mind is a greater feat than writing it down. What the Britons kept in their minds they could more easily have put into script or art form, but they chose not to for their reasons only. Following are some carved stones, found in Wales.

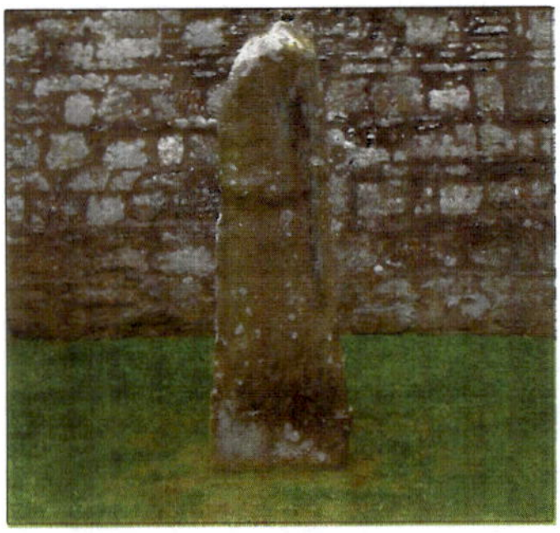

Vitalianus Stone

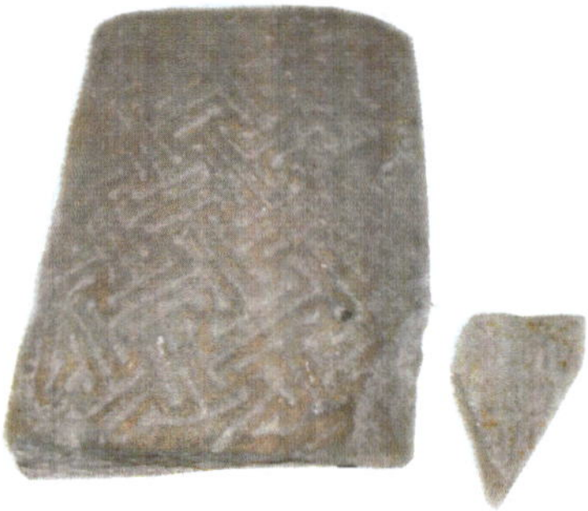

Stone fragments

There are isolated evidences of writings, often found as boundary markers or messages. About 500 inscriptions in ancient British Ogham language have been found throughout the British Isles carved on stone and wood. Some inscriptions were written in old forms of Pictish and Gaelic, others were accompanied by Latin.

Apparently, the British used their own alphabet to log or to describe by demarcation and clearly were well versed in many languages, but chose not to commit to parchment. One can only guess that the British wanted to keep their knowledge revered, from any corruptible source.

One windowsill at St Brynach Church Nevern is the Maelgwn Stone; the inscription on the surface is in Latin; on the front edge is in Ogham. The Celtic dialect connection in Irish is Magi, Scottish is Mac, the Welsh being (M)ab or ap. Ogham inscriptions are made by strokes or notches on either the side or across the edge of stone or wood. These bilingual artefacts - are the key to understanding the Ogham Alphabet. This is evidence that the British used Ogham and understood Latin.

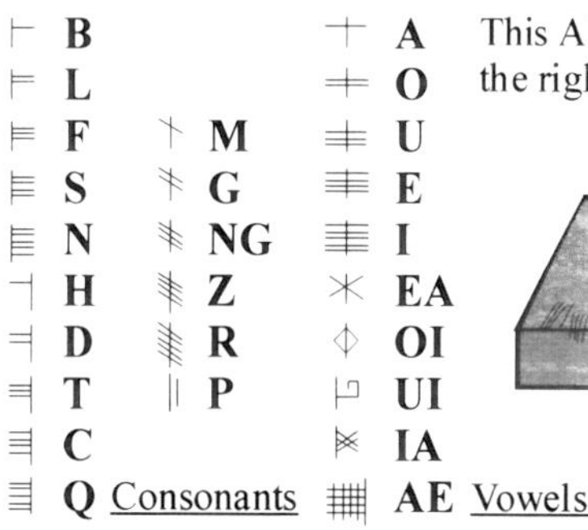

This Alphabet is in vertical writing. In the horizontal the right side would face downwards.

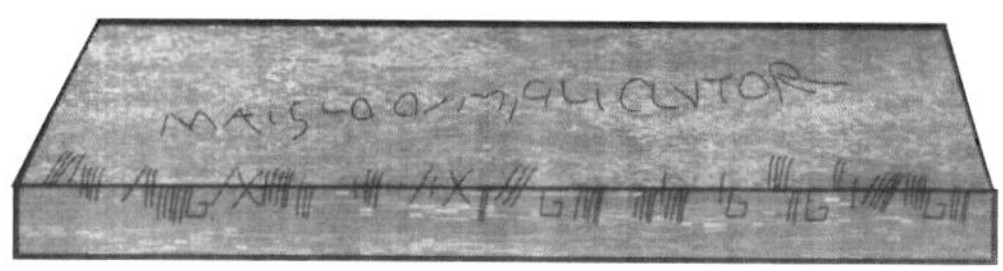

<u>Ogham Alphabet and Maelgwn Stone</u>: An exact copy of the stone is not available, so the alphabet in this instance may not relate. Precise translations are in the Church booklet.

The Cornish dialect (Kernewek) is generally assumed to be descended from the speech of the Ancient Britons. The government changed English Law in November 2002 to officially recognised Cornish as a language; so our ancient language is becoming recognised.

The Britons' language (Cymraeg) now called Welsh, is similar to (Kernewek) Cornish and today is the most flourishing of ancient languages.

When the Government passed an act establishing a universal state education in 1870, they failed to provide for the education of Cymraeg; was it to bury any evidence of our ancient language and nation for all time? This omission led to a vociferous demand for the use of the Cymraeg language in schools, and the placement of Welsh road signs throughout the Principality. For that, the Welsh had to wait for the Language Act of 1993.
The Irish dialect called "Gaeilge" is a branch of our British language. There has been no major incursion into Ireland and so the Irish language remains pure. It is the best evidence of a British language existing alone. And we know that no moles, snakes, Romans, Saxons or Normans entered into Ireland BC. We know the aristocracy took over the best of the land and built their stately homes there later; howsoever none of these foreign invaders ever spoke the British dialect called "Gaeilge". Sadly, I am told, in spite of strenuous efforts to revive the ancient Irish language through their education system, few parts of the country use this language on a day-to-day basis and, it is in danger of becoming extinct, unless the people of Ireland take more active steps to teach its younger generation.
The ancient language exists in the British Isles in the form of place-names, many of them directly attributable to the ancient Britons' tongue. One word that is to be found in Scotland and Wales is *Aber*, as in Aberdeen and Aberystwyth, meaning either estuary, or the conjunction of two rivers. Some other words from the same source have changed slightly over the years, so that *mawr* in Cymraeg becomes *mor* in Gaelic. Nevertheless it is all of the same British tongue.

The language of "Gaelic" and "Cymraeg" is comparable to the languages in Cornwall, Ireland, Scotland and Wales and, the Isle of Man, especially in poetry. Manx was spoken in the agricultural and fishing communities of the Isle of Man, is an island in the middle of the Irish Sea which again was not interfered with from incoming languages. There is now a Manx translation of the Bible, an amazing feat of translation, for the benefit of a population numbering some 200,000.

Over generations from 3,500 BC the British learned other languages, of which much later the so called Old-English language probably derives from, which syntax exists embedded within the evolved modern English of today, suggesting this was a co-operation and learning for trade. British language did not come in from Europe, it probably integrated with German vocabulary, to help Europeans to communicate and trade.

I mention the latter to show that Britain was independent and Rome would not have bothered to invade Britain if it had been a land of ignorant barbarian heathen savages, as the Romans and most historians libel the British as.

Roman interest was for Britain's mineral wealth and their technologies, so to place an elaborate foothold in Britain in order to pursue the British nation for their wealth, and enslavement. The British Druids would not give up their secrets to any invaders, so rather than trade with Britain, Rome wanted to enslave all of the British Islands by force. Perhaps it was a matter of Roman deceit not to confess to the truth of the matter, that indeed the British were a leading morally civilised cultured nation, which they wanted to denigrate or destroy any evidence of it. Let's analyse this following.

From the evidence of manufacture the Britons must have set up export and import with most of the Continent after about 2,500 BC. The Britons had the means to keep Romans out; so what happened to let them get in so easily? There are several theories to be had on the subject, one more believable than most, but firstly I must put the myth that Romans brought technology religion and moral civilisation to Britain, to the test:-

Some historians say the Romans gave us straight roads. It is not either clear which original foundations of roads are attributable to the Romans i.e. which were in existence long before they arrived in Britain. Britons had improved their surveying techniques so far as to enable them to re-build on their Stone, Bronze and Iron Age sites with interconnecting main roads. Can we, therefore, be absolutely sure that the Romans constructed all the roads and buildings attributed to them. We know Romans plundered other peoples inventions and also built over existing buildings. At Caerwent, the Romans built the town of Venta Silurum over the original foundations of the Capital of the Silures in 76 AD. This proves the Romans were not building new, but were capitalising on British foundations.

The Romans were not the first to construct the man-made arch, I say man-made for the arch was weathered out by water running through the rocks for millions of years and, all innovations come from nature, whereby Britons evolved to perceive and develop them. We know the Britons formed arches in their mining of copper and tin pre 3,500 BC, who cut into rock to form some of the first man-made arches; which is also evidenced in broch villages and corbelled tombs.

The arch is also seen in the excavations of the Hittites of about 1,000 BC, for they created cities by cutting into natural rock in mountains and beneath the sub-soil, in the region known as Cappadocia. For naturally when you cut into rock you will form an arch; when you create a rock-cavern with three tunnels running off it, you will create a triple arch; any more tunnels you will create a multiple arch; include a cavern central pillar and you will create a triple, pillar supported archway.
Did the British also influence the trading depots through the east, for there are many certain British influences being recognised there in the constructions of the supply and rest enclosures, which were constructed at about every 20 miles through the deserts, for camels could be watered to walk that distance in one day; these were created in line, to become the Silk-Route? Is the mining feature of the arch, support of another British export?
The same designs extended into castles, churches and cathedrals, which included these arches. This arch-work spread into nearly every major city along the Silk-Route, into Ankara and the great cathedral domes and architectures of the Ottoman Empire; are all pre Roman.
Strabo wrote that British envoys were travelling the known world BC, so is it possible that technologies were imparted by these envoys.
It is evidenced that a tribe similar to the British, migrated onto the Pontic Steppe, for there are burial evidences of mummies that relate to the Britons being in these areas. Is it possible these Britons merged into the populace? The copper and bronze burial artefacts found, certainly evidence a British influence in the east.

Did the Romans truly design and develop, or did they use other people's technologies for their own result? In Britain, roads are straight and others follow the natural features of mountains, for they blend in with natural contours, and in all probability the Romans utilised some ancient British routes, and improved others. Romans were certainly not the first road builders in Britain, for great roadways were constructed throughout the British Isles BC, including causeways.

At Keenagh, in Ireland, a great roadway was constructed from quarter-ton wooden blocks and, it was wide enough to take two-way traffic; it has been dated to 148 BC. I would suggest that the Romans built on existing roadways, as did the Saxons and Normans who followed them.

There is no evidence that Romans, Saxons or Normans built anything in Ireland, or the Americas; however, there are ancient straight roads in both these locations.

Why is it that some historians assume that anything of any good must have been invented by the Romans?

It is also said that Constantine destroyed British religion. Or, did he actually highjack it, to amalgamate it with his own? We still have (Sun) Sunday, (Moon) Monday, Halloween, May Day etc; and he certainly took Christianity to be a superior faith than his own.

Was it an attempt by Constantine to bring all the religions into line to conform to a Roman world order? We must wonder why he took Christianity to be a superior religion than that of his own, and we ask why did the Romans adopt British rites including burial rites? The Romans even utilised the sacred springs of Bath, converting them for their own purpose.

Rome tried to merge Pagan and Christian beliefs; however there is evidence of discarded British baptism tankards found at the bottom of wells. It is said the tankards were used in a belief of ensuring immortality, so these rites must be stemming from early British culture?

It is also said that these new Roman Christians at this time, destroyed the great Library of Alexandria, thus losing all of the accumulated knowledge they plundered from other nations, in a catastrophic act of vandalism and a waste of human resource. It is likely this information was destroyed to bury Roman iniquity.

Part of Constantine's task in life was to keep order in his empire and, the emergent Christian community was gaining in strength and power, so he either had to amalgamate, or defend against it. Amalgamation was the result, of a Christian faith emerging quietly out of a corrupt Rome.

As Christian numbers swelled in the east, there were factions in various segments of the Christian church and this signalled trouble ahead. Constantine was asked to deal with it, to bring some conformity to the practice of the Christian faith.

Theology in Christian terms was still in the making, and much of the population was unable to read the sacred Jewish texts; clearly the Christian following was a faith that many recognised as moral.

The New Testament was a later arrival, for the Gospels were written some years after the events they record. Constantine, having met with senior figures in the emergent Christian movement had decided what he thought were acceptable writings and had the first version of the Creed written down and distributed to the clergy, to end disputes on matters of doctrine, but he certainly took advice and certainly scrutinised what he wanted to place on the matter before committing anything to parchment. So are all the texts by his command, believable?

It is apparent the Romans could not conquer Britain entirely and so enslaved and brainwashed part of the nation they had under their control, in order to hide their evil and depravity.

If the Romans had any plans for the British Islands, it was to take anything of value that was to be found here. We know that slaves were valuable to the Romans, and we also know that British technology and skills were worth having. The islands were a rich source of minerals which was being mined for thousands of years, and that was also an attraction for the Romans to invade.

Note: You will recognise that I am evidencing from one period and to another to span at least 24,000 years; this is to evidence something in time which relates to an earlier time to show where certain items and/or conditions evolved from, or not, or that other peoples assertions may be incorrect.

Chapter 7

Beware the Roman invaders and the Roman deception that has lasted for at least 2,000 years

When the Romans invaded, the British nation was well established. What was it like to be under attack? How did our ancestors arm themselves and how did they defend? From a Caesar's description BC and of which can be deduced from the epic poems and tales that have been passed down through the generations, I imagine a possible scenario for this British strategy as follows: - "With no fear of death, frontline warriors went into battle with their bodies and shields covered in elaborate geometrical patterns, painted on with their blue-dye war paint. Their first arrow wave would have been followed by a spear and sword attack, with hornpipes trumpeting their advance. They forced open a passage through the enemy's front line, to enable the main thrust of chariots to forge through the opposition's middle ranks, opening them up and forcing them to disperse, in order to drop off their outriders into preferred locations of battle, while an armoured infantry of warriors advanced from behind, with skirmish attacks from the sides, culminating in a pincer movement, with the chariots moving through and then circling round to pick off from the outside, any enemies in retreat, leaving their option to move in with chariots to pick up their outriders, in order to recoup, or to defend at other strategic points of battle".

Question: How did invading Romans enter Britain with such a defensive sea barrier to overcome?

Amongst the reasons why the Roman forces were so easily able to enter onto the southern shores of Britain is the one that claims perhaps treachery, which lay behind Roman success. Like all stories, there is a ring of truth about this one. First of all, it is necessary to know that some southern "leaders" were conspiring with the Romans and were probably promised kingdoms as a reward for their treachery. This may have been a result of Rome terrorising and enslaving members of these leaders' families in forcing them to conform. However, it is documented by historians, particularly Tacitus, that there were certainly two leaders colluding with Rome at this time, thus giving them an attachment to Rome.

The Britons in the course of their expanded trade had provided the technology and arms that were used against them by their enemies. The British had not stopped to consider they would be betrayed by some of their own chieftains, for whatever reason. And as history portrays we cannot blame the normal people for what they may have been forced into at knife point; this is terrorism.

There is little doubt about it however, there is one phase of history that left our British ancestors vulnerable to what happened and they were simply betrayed by a leader who had connections with Rome. If the southern clans had held true to Britain, then patriotic Britons would have been better prepared to resist the Romans (and following Saxons and Normans, will be referenced later). Firstly, let's put to the test the many historians' comments through the ages, to say "the British were ignorant barbarian heathen savages", please read following to compare and consider:-

Britain had its own form of religion long before the Romans tried to invade Britain; and before Jesus of Nazareth was teaching in the east. Britons were worshiping "Iesu Grist" (Jesus Christ) before 30 AD. They respected the laws of nature of which encompassed the deities of one supreme God when progressing into their own Christianity up to and after 500 BC, and their religious ceremonies indicate a belief in the afterlife. Bodies or ashes were offered back to the mother earth, a lake, or a sacred tomb. These religious practices were performed in a belief that the spirit could be released into the afterlife and into the presence of their supreme God.

When Jesus (who was called "King of the Jews") was crucified, he said to one of the thieves being crucified with him, "Tonight you will be with me in paradise". He was releasing the man's spirit into the afterlife and into the presence of his Father in Heaven. After His death, Jesus' body was placed in a tomb. This shows similarity of beliefs and practices between Judaism and the British rites. It is not a matter of fact that there had been any early connection between them, but that cannot be ruled out and it does reinforce what we know of the human need for a Supreme Being, someone to whom we believe will save us if certain events overtake us all.

People in time have fought to possess religious artefacts including some alleged remnants of the original, "Crucifixion Cross". It is only important in that it demonstrates the fact that mans' beliefs in certain events have always played a part in a human need and greed, to posses a fragment of Jesus' past, which may somehow give them supreme powers.

Ancient Britons placed their offerings into lakes and burial tombs, which should be possessed nor plundered by no man, they should be returned to their resting places as a mark of respect. It is from these certain artefacts we can piece together the whole picture of the British Isles.

Most invaders malign their victims as heathens or savages, no matter what they understand of their victims. Do the Britons, described so far in this book, merit the description the Romans and some following historians placed upon them, as being ignorant savages and heathen barbarians? Let's compare and put this myth to rest:- Let's reflect on some Roman principles and the time when Roman depravity and slavery and the tax men were arriving in Britain. Augustus Caesar was made Emperor of Rome, 17 years before Jesus was born. Augustus wanted to tax the world. In the *'descriptio orbis'*, a Roman circular, he sets out how much tax had to be raised and how it was to be used. Can you notice Caesar's legacy of taxing the populace in certain places today? Do any hard working-class people ever achieve their true worth? Are any hard working-class people ever able to leave anything much to their family after they die? Are governments in place to live off the populace, or should they be in place to work for the populace? We know a reliable source of income is from keeping slave labour in continual poverty and debt (as any loan shark will agree) and this is why certain institutions move their assets to 'any country' that employs it, to the exploit demise and demoralisation of nations, to be enslaved, or absorbed into a Roman type regime, or annihilated.

One has to understand that this is the Roman way of life and administration, from making each new tax law, to giving the best education to their favoured, and titles to their Lords and Duchy's etc, to creating new Senate buildings with countless departments, where generations of aristocracy exist; to be funded by the slave classes. Romans have also taken over nation's technologies and businesses (and banks) in order to place their Barons and the likes with a comfortable profit-making device, to keep their workforce to exist as slaves; and have also absorbed other migrant slaves as they wished. Notably, retired Roman Senators were given an enormous pay off and a large residence with slaves, with a good pension to retire on (successful or not). This is not a book about modern politics, but it is sometimes useful to see how certain threads of history stretch back into the mists of time, and yet remain as strong as ever they were. As one industry is exported, so another slave industry emerges and takes its place, to the demise of nations.

Also consider the paedophile Tiberius Caesar, the son-in-law of Augustus, who was a disgusting sexual pervert who forced his licentious unnatural sexual practises onto innocent people. He collected young men and women to be made to copulate before him to excite his vile lust. He also trained little boys for his vile criminal obscenities, he called his little 'minnows', to lick and nibble him between his legs; he also used innocent suckling babies to suck at his breast or groin. He further had an incestuous relationship with his mother. He also caused young men to be castrated so that he could take them as lovers to satisfy his unnatural homosexual vile lust, of which his practices are documented.

One must ask, are these immoral acts the perverted conditions of all megalomaniac rulers alike, for it is certainly prevalent in most? Can this Tiberius child abuse also be linked to the Roman bathhouse of Ashkelon in 37 BC, where recently, hundreds of babies were found in a sewer system below the bathhouse were bludgeoned to death. Most were males, and we do know the Romans disposed of female children as they wished. Were these male children used for the same deplorable acts as Tiberius Caesar used children? Dr Helen Scott described this act as infanticide. This must be wrong, how could hundreds of mothers have done such awful deplorable deeds to their own children, over many years, cannot be a sudden mass hysteria. Some skulls had at least three deathblow impact fractures on them. Was it therefore cold murder in each instance, perhaps after some deplorable child abuse, likewise that practised by the Roman, Tiberius Caesar.

Are there echoes of the same Roman depravities creeping through the churches, governments and establishments of today? Is it a fact that some churches protect perverts and do little to protect children who fall victim to abuse. Why have Governments lowered the age of consent, which allows perverts to prey on the young legally, for perverts will undoubtedly trump up the consent card to any perverse act they can groom any youngster into over time.

Are these Roman traits what some historians say is how the Romans civilised Britain? Apparently it is open for moral people to live in line with the natural laws of God, so is it the test to reject depravity in all of its forms; can governments and the church institute moral principals?

Ruthless and calculated was the Roman might, but civilised they certainly were not. In any Roman Colosseum, men, women and children died in the name of 'sport' for Roman entertainment. The Roman Empire rampaged across the face of the earth putting to death by fire and the sword millions of innocent people for no other reason than to rob them of their worth, to place them into slavery, or worse. Rome imprisoned innocent victims; men women and children would expect to be stripped naked to be crucified or impaled, or appallingly used for Roman entertainment, to be herded into the arena of the Colosseum with wild beasts, where frenzied Romans watched them being torn limb from limb, eyes burnt from sockets with white hot pokers, tongues cut out at the roots, and old and young disembowelled, all in the name of 'sport', praising "Hail Caesar"! By this very appalling disposition of the Roman Empire, this would disqualify it from being morally civilised by any account. Why are these murderous acts dismissed?

What is not understandable is why some historians have been so willing to accept the myth of Britain's primitive condition, as portrayed by the Romans, to agree with the Roman comment "it was the Romans who civilised the British".

Nazi crowds shouted 'Hail Hitler' in the same frenetic manner as those Romans who came to watch the torture of their victims and, in each incident these Roman and Nazi people and associates' had made their own choice, it is unlikely that all were terrorised to follow their vile leaders in their horrid acts of genocide, which was not for revenge or protection, but just cold genocide, in order to enslave the world for their own benefit.

It is alleged that Hitler perpetrated his crimes in the name of 'revenge', Can you comprehend the slaughter of innocent helpless people old and young, or the appalling deathly experimentations on babies by the named "Angel of Death" Doctor Josef Mengele? These Nazis' allegedly were intelligent people; actually, they were habitual sadistic murderers. Some that were brought to trial after the Second World War would not apologise, nor did they show any remorse in their crimes against humanity. How anyone could say these incomprehensive immoral acts were perpetrated in the name of revenge or in any pledge of honour is inconceivable.

Nothing was too vile to appeal to the Romans who regarded their vile acts as a sporting spectacle of entertainment; for under the stands of the Colosseum there were also private viewings of naked women being raped to death by animals. Now let's ask here, who are the ignorant barbarian heathen savages?

Caesar certainly needed to spin any story, to try to conceal Roman vile acts, as did his successors. His need to denigrate the civilisations of his victims was in order to portray Rome as the civilised empire. Any Roman description of the British was a calculated defamation, which has wrongly been accepted as valid for nearly two thousand years, but it is a fact of history that any predatory race will malign its victims.

It is unfortunate that most past written history is at least fifty years after any actual event. Authors copy authors and by repetition what is an aged hearsay account of history is taken as 'fact' even to the extent whereby photographs etc, have been altered to convey whatever false message anyone wishes.

Other events that we assume to have happened are recorded in chronicles of an earlier age and might well be the product of one person writing down what happened to him and what he thinks happened elsewhere in the same event. This sometimes lack of a bird's eye view of events, which accounts for considerable distortion in the assumptions made by certain authors and monks and some historians alike. So we must ask - why do some historians write these distorting reports and elude to cite the true issues of matters of fact; surely this is all Roman propaganda?

The Soviets and many other dictating states have been known to alter books of history, to support political opinion and to give an altogether different impression of what really happened. Many books have been burnt, destroyed or misplaced by any deceiver who wants them gone. The pen is mightier than the sword so to speak, unless the writing is carved in stone, with carbon-dated evidence of course; of which incidentally a lot of the archaeological evidence in this book is from.

It is worth mentioning here that the Egyptian *Book of the Dead*, that was discovered in Luxor, Egypt, in 1887, by Earnest Wallace Budge, who worked for the British Museum, raises a time-line issue. The ancient parchment that Budge found predates Moses by several hundred years; it is dated to about 1,230 BC. The parchment is an account of Egyptian early religious beliefs and a description of the ethical behaviour needed for someone to lead a virtuous life on earth, in order to enter the afterlife; it actually describes most of the rules of conduct given in the Ten Commandments; which Moses received from God, but years later.

So, were all of these moral precepts of the Ten Commandments recited to the Egyptians by their God of the Underworld, Osiris? Or were they recited to Moses by God and burnt into stone, several hundred years later? The logical explanation lies in the fact that social living requires rules, whereby selfish or harmful behaviour is strongly discouraged and kindness and caring are encouraged. The prospect of a happy-ever-after is the promise; eternal damnation is the alternative. The fact remains that if the Ten Commandments were recited to Moses by God and burnt into tablets of stone and placed into the Ark of the Covenant after the Egyptian account, and then is this a second hand account? Did God pass these commandments on two occasions? Did this author recall this from some earlier knowledge? Either the author is wrong or Moses was misunderstood; or is it a hearsay account?

In both the latter citations, the ethics of the Ten Commandments are morally good. Do these Egyptian commandments pre-date Moses and if they do, then it is possible that these ethics were imparted from a land outside Egypt. British envoys were travelling the known world before the birth of Christ in Bethlehem, as Strabo documented. Is it feasible to make a direct connection from one and to the other? It is interesting that all these ethics are relative to a customary moral code. Is it likely that these ethics came out of a moral Britain and were acknowledged in the east? Is it also possible to have a picture of any Briton? To get this, we have to turn to the recorded writings; firstly the Greek geographer, Poseidonius, who described the Britons of the second century BC, on the lines following: -

'... Were startling in appearance, wearing colourful tartan cloaks, and trousers they call *braceae*. Their armour includes a full length shield decorated with personalised art and, were wearing bronze helmets. Their forthrightness and high spirited temperament must be added to their pride of boastfulness and love of decoration. They wear adornments of gold torcs on their necks and bracelets on their arms and wrists (such torcs of BC have been excavated throughout the length and breadth of Britain) while warriors of high rank wear dyed garments of woven thread, like sprinkled gold.'
Incidentally, Strabo also described a British envoy who was an astronomer of his time, BC. There are also the recent finds in Chin-Jung China dated at 2,000 BC as aforementioned, and the burials of the Boscom Bowmen near Stonehenge, are all in support of a British culture.
There is also a misconception that the early British people were made up of a mixture of European races. In reality the British had developed their technologies up to and through the Stone, Flint, Tin, Copper, Bronze and Iron Age; they were independent and defended their British shores from any invaders. There is no evidence of major inward migration into Britain at this time.
Caesar's record supports the belief that Druid learning moved into Europe from Britain. It is also evidenced the British taught astronomy and apparent that the British with this knowledge designed and built Stonehenge?
Let's look at what Caesar said for it is well documented that when Caesar landed in 55 BC, he described the people thus: - 'The population is extremely large and the land scattered with farmsteads, closely resembling that of the Gaul's. Cattle are numerous".

Caesar also wrote: - "The British Druids are the head leaders over religion and public duties. They hold office of tribunals and give decisions in disputes and order fines and give instructions and duties. The Druid doctrine is believed to have been founded in Britain and spread to Gaul and those who have learnt it generally studied it in Britain. British students must learn and memorise vast numbers of verses which usually takes a study of 20 years to achieve, they also study astronomy and the Druids instruct the young men in all these subjects." (I ask here, was Jesus taught in Britain and are these 20 years the missing Jesus years; it is possible).

The latter evidences that Druidism was a product of Britain and Britons taught trained and influenced the European Druids. Is this the reason why Caesar wanted to destroy this British culture entirely, was to obliterate the memorised knowledge of the head-leaders; a typical Roman waste of knowledge. Caesar acknowledged and wrote that "the British had no fear of death and so would never divulge their knowledge, even under torture," and this is probably the reason why Rome wanted to destroy the British Druids and this living library of memorised knowledge, (and evidence of the Jesus missing years?)

It is understandable that British technologies were copied or commissioned by allied foreign traders and chieftains, in order to advance their own industries. We know there was a continual contact through trade out of an independent Britain, from whence ideas, equipment, engineering, woven and pressed fabrics, metalwork and even the method of breeding and training hunting dogs were exported; and once a technology is learned, self sufficiency will follow.

Up to early AD, Britain was a free Nation; however as history portrays, British southern leaders, Tincommius and Dubnovellaunus, and later, Adminius were conspiring with and came under the protection of, Emperor Augustus of Rome. In 42 AD, Verica conspired and pleaded with Emperor Claudius for his protection, and Rome invaded Britain again, in 43 AD.
Once the Romans had gained a foothold into Britain, it was the Roman ploy to try to enslave the whole population, to provide them with mineral wealth and a slave workforce to supply their vile needs. Britain must have been seen as a breeding ground for slaves to export to Rome and to use for the Romans' every immoral need, including their so called sporting entertainments in the Colosseum.
There is some evidence of slave chains having been used. One was found at Lyn Cerrig Bach, on Anglesey, and another in Kent, but these may simply represent the suppression of certain warriors in single shackles, not chain-shackles such were used for lines of slaves; indicates that the Romans were chaining Britons. Britain used to be called the workshop of the world; apparently it became the slave-shop of the Roman Empire, as the British King Caradoc predicted, of which I must reference here for you to fully understand, as follows:-
In the first invasions of Britain by the Romans they were repelled, so it is evidenced the British stood together. In the later Roman invasion, it is written that Verica a southern clan leader defected to Rome. These southern clans may have been press-ganged into this strategy however we must go along with written reference here to the three Roman invasions as is described following.

As in Victor Dunstan's book "The Invisible Hand", he describes "The Greatest Hoax of all Time", I elaborate: - On 5th August 55 BC, Julius Caesar sailed, with two legions, from Calais, France, and landed on the southern British coastline near the Clans area of the Atribates. And so, the deception of denigrating the British as barbarian heathen ignorant savages began, that has lasted for about 2,000 years. Just 55 days after the Romans landed, they had advanced no more than 7 miles inland, to the place where Caesar was actually humiliated by defeat. Under cover of darkness, the Romans retreated to the safety of the French coast, with their tails between their legs. They came, they saw, they scarpered!
On May 10th 54 BC, a second Roman campaign was launched. About a thousand ships relayed at least five legions, with thousands of mercenaries, to land on the southern shores, but the Romans were unable to penetrate more than 70 miles inland. This second Roman invasion lasted until September 10th, when peace was negotiated at St Albans, so apparently the Romans were again defeated and pardoned. A storm had damaged the Roman fleet and whilst the soldiers repaired their boats, Caesar spent hours writing a description of the British people: - 'All the Britons indeed dye themselves with wood (his cross Latin interpretation of the word woad) which occasions a bluish colour and thereby have a more terrible appearance in fight. Most of the inland inhabitants do not sow corn, but live on milk and flesh and are clad with skins' (Note: Is it no coincidence that this bluish colour camouflage has been used by the British army ever since).

Can you believe that Caesar gained knowledge of the entire British nation in a few weeks, without getting any further inland than 70 miles? And so, the deception of denigrating the British began, that has been repeated by one historian after another for about 2,000 years. Why did Caesar bother to record this unless he had an ulterior motive, was it to denigrate the British for all posterity.
Caesar's descriptions have come to be accepted as fact, and yet, belief that civilization in the British Isles commenced with the Roman occupation has been based on the word of a defeated man, who had only been in Britain for a few weeks. Caesar was able to fool the world into believing that the British were warring, painted, ignorant barbarian heathen savages and, that it was the Romans who civilised Britain. What basis of the latter encourages historians to believe this Roman trumped up flight of imagination, which bogus stories of the British morality has been falsely witnessed?
Caesar also wrote that the British King Caswallon (Romans named Cassivelaunus) was warring against the southern clans for their betrayal of siding with Rome, but on Rome's arrival in Britain, the southern clans in turncoat fashion, appointed the mighty Caswallon as their commander for a joint British campaign to try to repel the Romans (prior to this Caswallon had killed certain British kings who had defected to Rome).
The fact is, Caswallon was actually uniting Briton's against Rome, however on the arrival of more reinforcements from Rome and, during an attack, the south-eastern clans in their same turncoat fashion betrayed Caswallon and defected back to Rome again, and Caswallon was forced to surrender.

It is written that Caswallon commanded squadrons of infantry and 4,000 chariots with at least two outriders, indicating that the British had not only trained armies, they also had a vast company of charioteers. Caesar had not encountered this force before, because his description following is clearly new, otherwise he would have referenced it before this time, Caesar interpreted: -
"On the main charge, they disperse in all directions, hurling spears. They succeed in displacing the lines of their opponents into confused disarray, by the fear caused by their charging horses and the whirring sounds of the wheels. They interact through the squadron lines of their own mounted cavalry, whereby the chariots' outrider-warriors would disembark and fight within the ranks, whereby the charioteers withdrew a short distance from the attack position in order that their warriors could be retrieved and replaced at particular strategic fighting positions, or for a swift retreat to lines of defence, with the mobility of cavalry and the strength of infantry, training daily to become very efficient to negotiate the steep slopes and could control their horses at mid gallop, check and turn them in a moment, run along the pole to control the horses or fight from the yoke and get back to the chariot with incredible speed".
Clearly, this chariot strategy Caesar described was devised and perfected in Britain. The Britons did not learn all these tactics in one fleeting moment, because to develop and firstly use the wheel and then the chariot, to attach horses to train them to draw and run must have taken thousands of years to perfect. Perhaps this is the strategy that the Romans copied into their chariot races of the Colosseum.

Caesar also said at the time of this battle, the Britons talked and shouted in riddles, which clearly evidences that ancient Britons were still the residents of Britain and were still speaking their native tongue at this time, which was confusing the Romans. It is clear that Britons were the residents in Britain before and at this "very time", this supports the argument that the British must have learnt other languages besides their own, in order to trade abroad.

Later reference is Greek eye-witness Diodorus, he observed (Welsh) Britons speaking their own tongue, playing their ancient game called Knappan (Rugby) played between adjacent Clans; this rugby progressed to be played with an oval chunk of yew wood; and this was nineteen centuries before that English public school.

The Romans are praised for building straight roads and were dedicated soldiers, this should not detract from what the Romans did to enslave nations, for the Nazis particularly the Waffen SS did the same, and indeed copied the Romans to establish a 3rd Reich, are the same Roman despicable traits that crop up through history.

Rome was as corrupt as the Nazi's and all other megalomaniac rulers alike, in their same genocide slaughter, and oppression of the people they invaded.

The Colosseum today has become a respectable Roman great 'sports' arena tourist attraction for celebrating the achievements of the Roman Empire; therefore will Belsen and Auschwitz also become respectable tourist attractions celebrating the achievements of the Nazis? I categorically think not, for certainly the same degrading and agonising human suffering took place in Belsen, Auschwitz and other such dreadful places.

Britain and their allies have a humane moral understanding and respect for these horrific places as graveyards of victims of oppression, and they are also a remembrance of the misery and degradation which all these fanatical vile rulers, executed, of which we must not brush under the carpet or hide it amongst the architecture. We must know and remember these places as being used for the wrongs against humanity. All these places must be made cenotaphs, memorial graveyards in respect of the innocent people who were murdered.
In the 3rd invasion of the Romans in 43 AD, King Caradoc led the British into battles against the Romans on the Medway and Thames, where his brother Togodomnus was killed. Caradoc retreated to one of his ally Siluri fortresses from which he led at least a seven year campaign with great military decisive precision and tenacity against the Romans, tactically moving into the west and north when pressure came from the Romans.
Tacitus wrote: "Caradog and his chieftains moved amongst their forces, encouraging them and telling them that the outcome of this battle would be the beginning of the recovery of their freedom, or else bring them into 'everlasting slavery,' Caradoc was reminding his warriors of the bravery of their ancestors, whereby they defeated and repelled the Romans twice in the past in 55 and 54 BC. Caradoc's warriors swore to fight to the death."
Caradoc and his warriors must have been a great force in their fight against the Romans at this time; for the Roman Emperor Claudius had to take personal charge of his legions to organise to send for more reinforcements from other parts of the Roman Empire.

Claudius had to swiftly gather most of his legions in Rome and bring them into Britain, despite there being three of Rome's most famous generals already on the southern shores of Britain. These were Aulus Plautius; Vespasian, who was later to become Emperor, and Titus, the general who later destroyed Jerusalem. Caradoc faced the Romans in his last battle, at or near "Fort Caradog" (Caer Caradog) in the region that is now known as Shropshire (which indicates that the Silures "Welsh" region extended eastward). This fort was one of the many British camps throughout Britain at this time.

Caradoc's warriors fought courageously, in the face of these overwhelming odds. During Caradoc's last battle, he sheltered with Cartimandua the Queen of the Brigantes, who cowardly betrayed him while he slept, and he and his family were placed into chains and taken to Rome in about 50 AD.

I mention here that Tacitus also wrote about the British: "Once they owed allegiance to kings, but now they fight amongst their own clans, which help us more, in fighting against this very powerful nation, than their own inability to stand together. It is but seldom that two or three kingdoms unite to repel a common danger; thus, fighting in separate groups, all are conquered". He later wrote: "Britons think they had been brought into civilisation, when in reality it is a feature of their own enslavement"; (writing about the southeast I assume)?

The latter suggests that if all the Britons had held true, the Romans would not have entered into Britain, as Caradoc conveyed in his speech that their ancestors had defeated and repelled the Romans in 55 and 54 BC when they all proudly fought for their lands and freedom.

Because of Caradoc's fame and leadership in his many battles with Caesar's legions, the Romans acknowledged him as a nobleman. He was allowed the privileges of a Chieftain King by being permitted to address the Senate, as Tacitus recorded Caradoc's speech, of which Caradoc may have made in Latin (As Strabo also evidenced such British knowledge of Latin), interpreted as follows:-

"Had my government in Britain been directed solely with the preservation of my hereditary domains, or the aggrandizement of my own family, I might long since have entered this city an ally, not a prisoner; nor would you have disdained for a friend a king descended from illustrious ancestors and the dictator of many nations. My present condition, stripped of its former majesty, is as adverse to myself as it is a cause of triumph to you. What then? I was lord of men, horses, arms and wealth; what wonder if at your dictation I refused to resign them. Does it follow, that because the Romans aspire to universal domination, every nation is to accept the vassalage they would impose. I am now in your power, betrayed, not conquered. Had I, like others, yielded without resistance, where would have been the name of Caradoc, where your glory? Oblivion would have buried both in the same tomb. Bid me live. I shall survive forever in history; one example at least of Roman clemency".

Caradoc's speech is that of a civilised, proud, educated man, it is couched in the language of a king of illustrious ancestry, a ruler of many nations. His speech could measure up to that of any of today's most eloquent speakers, of any King, Queen, President or Prime Minister.

Caradoc's speech was not of an ignorant 'barbarian' or 'savage', it was the speech of a highly civilised British King. Caradoc was addressing people who knew of him and his British nation. He could not lie to them, nor could they dispute with him, for what the Romans encountered in their battles with Caradoc is what they got. Caradoc's speech was true to fact; otherwise the Romans would have treated him with contempt and would undoubtedly have ridiculed him, as they had ridiculed and "crucified" any would be King. Such was Caradoc's fame in Rome, as was written by Roman circulars at the time, "Tens of thousands of people crowded the streets to see the mighty Briton". I note that the fate of any foreign king captured by the Romans was usually certain death, either by being dragged behind a chariot through the streets of Rome or the Colosseum, or being impaled, disembowelled, crucified, or worse; however, Caradoc was pardoned. This can only mean that Caradoc was a mighty chieftain who was respected as a warrior King.

Caradoc fought for at least seven years to defend Britain against the best Rome could put in the theatre of war. Caradoc's perfect speech can only represent an intellectual of a highly civilised British Nation, whose culture was in place before any interference from Rome. To mention here, the Silurian Britons never yielded, and continued to defend Britain constantly.

Perhaps Rome was terrorising the south-eastern clans, in order to establish a gateway into Britain; but this was not the first time that treachery led to the southern Clans' conquest, for the Saxons and Normans did the very same, you will read following.

For many years, Caradoc and his family lived in the Roman building known as the 'Palace of the Britons', probably as an icon, evidence of Roman success against a mighty Briton; nevertheless an unlikely habitation for a painted heathen savage, don't you think? Caradoc's sister, Gwladus, married the Roman Commander, Aulus Plautius, for what reason I do not know, perhaps he fell in love with her or, she was forced into it, or it was for her own self preservation. Gwladus, (who could speak Greek and Latin fluently) was arrested and accused by the Romans of being a Christian. When Gwladus married, she took the name Pomponia Graecina Plautius. The description of her by the Roman recorder Tacitus, he wrote:

"Pomponia Graecina, a woman of 'illustrious' birth, and the wife of Plautius, who, on his return from Britain, entered the city with the pomp of an ovation, was accused of embracing the rights of a 'foreign superstition' (Christianity)."

Gwladus was set free, and later, her husband Plautius, the Roman Commander, became a Christian. None of what Tacitus wrote about her in any way describes the British as painted ignorant savages of which most recent history books reference regarding these times. It is written that Caradoc had a government in Britain and had hereditary domains; he was a king descended from illustrious ancestors, ruler of many nations, and able to speak at least three languages; evidenced by the Roman recorders of this time.

We must wonder why the British are so often dismissed as barbarian ignorant heathen savages. Why is there this incessant denigration of such an advanced nation?

The Roman Emperor Claudius offered the hand of his daughter, Venus Julia, in marriage to the British King Arviragus and they were married in Rome. Would proud Romans have associated in this way with a people that they considered being in any way inferior? In most Roman accounts the British are degraded, but here they are elevated to commander's wives and Royalty, is odd?
Caradoc's sister Gwladus (according to Tacitus) was converting Romans to Christianity, and so it seems that the British had cultured their recognised beliefs of nature and one God, to become a form of their own Christianity with a highly civilised British society intact, which Caradoc's sister as a captive, took with her to Rome. It is said that some Popes will admit that the British Church was one of the "first".
It was easy for Britons to continue the worship of Jesus because they were worshipping a Jesus for many years before Jesus was teaching in the east. In many Welsh Chapels you would hear a minister preaching about 'Iesu Grist', is Jesus Christ. Did the Romans AD progress to try to conquer Britain entirely, in order to annihilate any evidence of British Christianity and civilisation, or perhaps of Jesus' missing years?
Britain must have posed a threat to the Romans because of Britain's alliance and Druid connections abroad, as Caesar referenced, European Druids were taught in Britain, it is possible that Ambiorix and Vercingetorix chieftains of the of the European Eburones and Arverni Clan were taught in Britain. This must also relate to earlier connections with these nations, so why is it so hard for some historians to contemplate an advanced British nation in place before any Roman invasion?

As it arises here, I must now put into context, the Roman strategy at this time was to firstly destroy the European clans, and then go onto their invasion of Britain, to plunder, and try to expand their enslaved territories, and conceal any evidence of Britain's own Christianity and moral civilisation into obscurity.

After the death of Jesus and the early spread of Christianity across the Roman Empire, the Romans began to take religion in the conquered territories more seriously; they possibly regarded this as a worldwide threat to their security for the Christian following was growing into what they must have seen as a great force.

The Romans could not conquer Britain entirely, so they built garrisons in the south and as far north as they could, to try to control the Clans, in their effort to subjugate the Druids and chieftains and to enslave the British Nation. When this failed, they built walls across the island, to try to keep the unconquered Clans at bay. The Romans marched from London with 10,000 troops including Saxon and Spanish mercenaries to destroy the fortifications of Anglesey, to try to subjugate the Britons of the western part of Britain. What was so important about pursuing the British into this area? The Druids were the Pen-dragons, the keepers who held the knowledge of their religion, metallurgy and mining and who governed and controlled for the benefit of the clans in a once free nation. The British Druids would never yield to slavery, so the Romans tried to subjugate them all and take charge of the whole of Britain and their mines and foundries etc, for themselves; and possible to destroy any remembrance of Rome depravity, and British connections with Christianity in the east.

The British retired to highly defendable positions, such are now called Anglesey, Isle of Man, Ireland, and Isles of Scotland, and Wales; to obtain strategic positions to defend or attack from and, it is evidenced, the Silurians and allies, campaigned ceaselessly to free all Britain.

At about 60 AD the Romans needed to cut the Druids off from the rest of Britain to try to destroy them, hence the old saying cut off the head and the body will fall, or the Roman strategy of "divide and conquer,". Or was this a British strategy, for it seems that it was a coordinated strategy of the Druids who clearly had true connections with Boudicca, who were dividing the Romans in order to conquer; for some of the legions were manoeuvred to march north to try to destroy the powerful Druids. The latter strategy allowed loyal British Clans under the command of Boudicca, the Queen of the eastern Iceni, to destroy the Roman held Colchester and most of the 9th legion, to then erase London and the Roman Tax-Lords; and then St Albans (Verulamium) from the face of the earth. Boudicca was reaping revenge in the east because the Romans were greedily taxing the British and taking over her land but, more disgracefully, the Romans subjected Boudicca and her children to deplorable savage acts in an open public spectacle of vile rape and torture, defiling these princesses to preclude them from their pure religious rites.

This clearly shows that most Britons were in joint campaign in trying to free all Britons from Roman rule and vile Roman depravity. The Romans allegedly, eventually defeated Boudicca, but they did not defeat the western and northern Clans entirely.

Later, the Romans started to build a huge fortress at Chester, North Wales, probably as a garrison for the troops who were to pursue the Silurians into Anglesey or to what is now called Ireland and Scotland. The fortress at Chester was called Deva; it was abandoned at least twice, and fell into ruin in about 122 AD, probably as a result of the attacks against it by the British. Historians say that Deva was later reduced to rubble by defecting rebel Romans, who were defacing masonry with Roman inscriptions, and there is very little left of the masonry of which the fortress was constructed. It is also claimed that these defecting Romans finished off the Britons. However it takes little thought to work out that if the might of the Roman Empire's Legions could not finish off the British, then it is very unlikely that a rabble band of defecting Romans could have done so. It is more understandable to think that the British obliterated Deva from the 'face' of the earth, just as they had done to the Roman fortress of Calleva Atrebatum, in Silchester, whereby the Romans had built over the foundations of the British fort of the Atrebates; where apparently nothing much exists above the soil there either.

The latter was a cleansing of the earth ritual, for at the excavated site of the Atrebates, there is evidence of them trading with Rome in the first century BC. It is also documented that Caradoc's uncle, Epaticcus, defeated the Atrebates in early 40 AD, possibly because the treacherous Atrebates King Verica was conspiring with Rome; he had fled to the new Emperor Claudius, and this was the pretext for Rome to invade Britain in 43 AD. These are very good reasons why the British removed both these sites from British soil.

While on this subject, I explain: - The Romans extended Calleva to have looked like a mini Rome, the layout reminiscent of the remains of the Roman town of Dougga in North Africa, to note here: - The Roman General Scipio in 146 BC destroyed Carthage by fire and the sword, in a holocaustic attack on this refined nation, plagiarising their unique ideals and written works on agricultural systems, to claim it in their own Roman texts. They assimilated the remainder of these African people into being Romanised slaves, absorbed into diluted obscurity, forced to continue working in their rich lands to supply food for Rome; and Carthage became known as the breadbasket of Rome.

Note: The Romans could not plagiarise any writings of the British, for there was no knowledge written down. This is one good reason why the British did not commit their knowledge to parchment. Nor could the Romans assimilate, absorb or dilute all of the Britons into obscurity, of becoming another Romanised slave nation entirely.

At Calleva in Britain, excavations show that loyal Britons were attacking this Romanised city, before and after the Romans left, and later obliterated it from the landscape in a cleansing of the earth ritual, for there is not a lot remaining above the soil; nor any evidence of the stone used elsewhere. Is it no coincidence that most Roman remains have been scarcely left above the topsoil in Britain, to realise why reminders of Roman invasion is scattered or buried?

Chapter 8

Britons were not alone in their fight to keep their freedom

As mentioned, Caesar stated that the European Druids were being taught by British Druids, so let's analyse this here: - Caesar tried to invade Britain in 55 BC and 54 BC but failed. In a winter of 54-53 BC Ambiorix commander of the peaceful European Eburones, possibly with Vercingetorix, rebelled against Roman invasion, and defeated the Fourteenth legion that was under the command of Quintus Titurius Sabinus. This was a major blow to Caesars strategy in Gaul and, it is suggested that if Ambiorix had gone on to deal the death blow to Caesar, and then this would have been the end of the Roman Empire. However Ambiorix showed mercy to Caesar and his legions, to let them return home.

The revolt of Vercingetorix of the Arverni, an ally of the Eburones started in 52 BC, against continual Roman invasions into their territories, whereby Vercingetorix defeated Caesar at the next major battle of Gergovia inflicting heavy losses (possibly knowing that the British defeated the Romans in 55 and 54 BC after which, the British also allowed the Romans to return home). What was left of Caesar forces could have been utterly destroyed, but Vercingetorix allowed them to retreat from Gergovia, was another act of clemency. Four times Rome was given clemency, what a grave mistake that was. Rome did not forget these embarrassing defeats and instead of honouring these moral acts they prepared to annihilate Vercingetorix.

Julius Caesar replenished his forces and pursued the Arverni in a genocide siege attack on Alicia in September 52 BC. Of those who were not slaughtered, he gave to each centurion as a slave. Vercingetorix was imprisoned and then murdered by Caesar to be publicly beheaded as part of Caesars triumph, in 46 BC. What a vile coward Caesar was, to behead the man who showed him mercy. Caesar died two years later.

The Romans did not try to invade Britain again until AD 43.

I must also mention here another Roman genocide act: In 106 AD, the Roman Trajan took 13 legions and slaughtered the European Dacians. The Dacians were mining white gold, opals and diamonds, in what they called their metal mountains. Trajan exterminated this nation to satisfy Rome's greed. There are at least 400 gold mines scattered throughout these regions. I note that the British were actually using gold coins in the 1st century BC and were trading with the European Celts who were learning British technologies and sciences in Britain, as Caesar described. These Druid connections possibly influenced the Dacians in their mining and metallurgy projects. It's possible the British had interests in the technology they passed to the Dacians? Is this why the Romans came to Britain, to steal this British wealth?

The heartland of the British Druids was Anglesey in Wales, an area rich in minerals. The Romans failed to defeat the British entirely, for the British would have retreated to what is now called Wales, Ireland, the Western Isles and Northern Scotland, if they had found themselves hard pressed, for it is evident that these British are still in residence now.

In about 400 AD, the Huns forced the Vandals off the Baltic. The Vandals moved south, and proceeded to ravage parts of Rome. Rome had expanded its Empire to such an extent that it no longer had the resources in manpower to control and defend it. When the very heart of the Empire began to feel threatened, legions from all over were recalled and the Romans left Britain in 410 AD, hurrying back to defend Rome against the Huns and Vandals and other marauding European tribes, such as the Germanic Franks, Lombards and Saxons. In about 430 AD, the Vandals moved south to southern Spain and into North Africa, where they took Carthage from the Romans, thereby cutting off what historians say was Rome's breadbasket, for as previously referenced, Carthage became one of the main food suppliers to Rome.

Attila the Hun was also plundering Rome from the east, and the Vandals plundered from the west. Rome, at this time, came under the rule of a new type of Emperor, the Catholic Pope Leo, who agreed to meet Attila's demands. I mention here, that although the Pope was allegedly Christian, the depravities and slaughter of Christians in the Colosseum continued. Pope Leo was in no position now to protect Rome and was forced into bargaining with Attila. He probably wondered how long the remnants of the Roman Empire could survive. The Vandals in 439 AD plundered Rome, and Rome crumbled. The Pope Maximus then ruled, and Rome came under the Papal Roman Empire.

After the Romans left Britain in 410 AD the Britons started a clean up of the regions that was once under the influence of Rome.

At this time, some southern Clans in their same old mistake enlisted the help of Saxons in order to try to take control over the southeastern regions again.
Archaeologist Francis Pryor says there is an obsession with the idea of a Saxon invasion, with no credible evidence of this. Although, Saxon burials are found alongside British burials, it might be better to speak of Saxon collusion, for Saxons were invited in by the southern clans as mercenaries, but turned on their hosts, to gain control of the southern clans and, took over the eastern side of the country, to call it Angle-Land (England). Never learn would they!
Pryor says that the castles built on the south coast were placed there for export and import and not for defense. He says there is no evidence of these castles defending against the Anglo Saxons.
Archaeologist Dominic Powlesland excavated at least 49 acres through the Thames Valley, of pre and post Roman settlements, which he calls his ladder excavations. He has made at least 35,000 finds which show a continuance of a thriving complete way of life in peaceful times, which are primarily of British people. There were no gaps or changes of pattern whatsoever, evidencing these were Britons who continued with their normal lives. He did not unearth any evidence of any Anglo Saxon invasion.
Geneticist Paul Budd's examination of the oxygen isotope found in teeth enamel extracted from some British burials, concluded that the majority of these skeletons were of people originating from the west side of Britain. A few other skeleton of women, were possibly from Scandinavia (kin relations perhaps?).

It is noted the British mined vast amounts of metal; this propagated the growth of villages into towns and towns into cities. Through the archaeological finds of hundreds and thousands of years we can see good evidence of a continuing and expanding cultured Britain.
Pryor maintains that England did not exist before a Saxon monk known to us as Bede invented it about 1,296 years ago. Bede in (AD 673-735) was alive a few short generations after the Angles or Saxons infiltrated what is now known as Jarrow.
Historian Colin O'Brian says what Bede wrote is hearsay, for he never left the Jarrow area. Was Bede misrepresenting that every person in the place he invented as England, were Germanic Angles or Saxons? We know we have Saxon regional names now, but nevertheless it must be understood that true Britons are not Romans, Angles, Saxons, nor Normans. Was it Bede's attempt to remove any knowledge of the British in this invented region for some reason? Admittedly the aristocracy could be Roman, Angle, Saxon or Norman, who did not mix with the British who they perceived to be un-free inferior 'commoners' and pathetic little Brits.
Powlesland clearly evidenced that the majority of the people in what Bede had invented as the English Region, are not Germanic Angles or Saxons but are mostly British. This infers that each mercenary ruler gained a Royal standing within Britain to brainwash and enslave British kin-peoples into an army of Anglo Saxon, or Norman farce; to make them into an invented English race apart from the British, probably brainwashing or press-ganging Britons of the English regions into fighting the British Clans who held true.

The evidence which Powlesland has unearthed shows that the Saxon population was miniscule, a minority integration of foreign people coming into Britain; so Anglo Saxon and England must be a manipulated invention by Bede.
Recent finds of the TV Time-Team at Sedgefield is of a Pre-Roman British settlement surrounded by 20 enclosures of British farms and agriculture, centred about a pottery kiln, and a mint where they were die-striking Roman coinage. They also found a Roman bronze helmet handle, dated around 300 AD. This shows evidence of enslaved Britons producing their fine engineering for the Romans, for I certainly don't think they were free spirits producing armour to kill their own people.
Archaeologist John Franklin suggests that Tintagel in Cornwall was a harbour fortress, with evidence of post Roman imported pottery from the Mediterranean, and an inauguration stone suggests a royal citadel; so life simply went on there.
Britons of the English regions suffered severely from the invasions and, as much as the aristocracy have tried to subdue the rest of Britain, most Britons are still here and their language and culture has survived.
The Doomsday book of 1085 shows evidence of the Super Landlord, the "Tax man" and it is this aristocracy which took over from where the Romans had left off. These were the Kings, Nobles, Lords and masters over the downtrodden British eastern and southern Clans, enslaving them again, to become serfs and peasants. They were placed into a life of hard labour, to provide their slave masters with wealth and a good living.

This slave trade is shown from evidence of strip farming and field systems. In times of starvation, if they were caught hunting the King's deer, they would be hung. There is also evidence of slave-shackles for these enslaved Britons.
So if you look at it all realistically: - rather than these invaders transporting slaves, it seems they came in to try to take over and enslave a nation, but only managed to enslave the southeastern Britons and their lands.
As mentioned, the Roman Tacitus wrote on the lines "Britons assume they were civilised by Rome, but in fact they are slaves of a Roman system".
When the Romans left Britain in 410 AD, this period following became known as the "Dark Ages". Did the Romans turn the light off when they left, or did it burn brighter? Pryor suggests that the use of the term "Dark Ages" is nonsensical; Britain was in economic decline once the Romans withdrew, but the Britons had a strong society and a lasting culture, remnants of which exist today. He says that Britain would have recovered quite quickly after the Romans left, as can be seen from the hill fort of Cadbury Castle in Somerset, with ramparts and five-metre high walls, showing a continuation of building and re-building.
In the Saxon invasion it is said that three ships arrived on British shores, this seems bizarre because this numbered at most to about 20 men per ship was 60 Saxon men. Surely this was an advance invite, a ploy, to allow the main force in to take over this region? By this southern clan leader trying to enlist the Saxons, he unwittingly initiated their demise, by being taken into slavery by the Saxons, just as the Romans did to them previously.

At this time the British King Emrys, and possibly a chieftain called Arthur, were pressing the Saxons hard. It is also evidenced that Emrys and Arthur defeated the Saxons at Mount Badon (Bath).

King Arthur may have been a genuine leader in Britain, for there are an enormous amount of poems and stories written of him. The best evidence that he was British is the fact there is no written evidence of it in his time. British history was in a library of memory, which was recited in poetry, and if there had been any "written" evidence, then King Arthur would probably have been other than British, for it would have been documented by people who 'wrote' historical facts, for I am sure they would certainly have documented any Great King of theirs.

Did the Saxons get the names wrong, for the words for "Marvellous King" in the ancient British tongue is "Brenin Aruthr" this may have been misinterpreted for King Arthur by moving the letter u three places to the right. Another possible Saxon mistake of "Aruthr" which extended means "stranger" and the Saxon name Welsh is sometimes interpreted as "stranger". So it is possible that "Brenin Aruthr" was a "Marvellous King" from the Western Clans of Britain which region is now called "Wales". The first written mention of Arthur is in the *Brittonum,* attributed to a monk called Nennius, who records that Arthur was killed at the battle of Camlan at about 515 or 539 AD. The stories of *Mabinogion,* written later, have many references to earlier oral legends of Arthur and his Knights, of a great British warrior who led the Britons against the Anglo Saxons and won many victories.

Excavations in Wales have provided considerable information that there was such a leader as Arthur who came out of what is now known as the Saxon name Wales. These two references both *Brittonum* and the *Mabinogion* talk of Caerleon (which incidentally was one of Caradoc's Silurian Fortresses') in South Wales, as being the site of King Arthur's court.

Other candidates which have been put forward for Arthur are: - Caradoc's line; or Caradod Freichfras 470 AD who held lands in South Wales and the Gower and on both sides of the channel. Mealgwn ap Cadwallon 480-547 AD was king of Gwynedd. Owain Ddantgwynn "the Bear" which translates (Din Arth)" ruled Rhos and Gwynedd in the fifth century, he succeeded is brother Cadwallon. Athrwys ap Meurig (Morgan) 645-655 AD, who held lands in Glamorgan is another candidate.

Without proven evidence concerning the exploits of Arthur, he has entered the world of myth and legend, allowing later writers to interpret him as they wish. For this reason, little credence can be given to writings on the subject. It has been alleged that Emrys was King Arthur, but this cannot possibly be correct, because he would have been a 70-year-old man at this time. King Arthur was a young warrior king and possibly one must look for a young British King of this time, who fits the bill. The relevance is that a British King reigned at about this time, and he was defending Britain against the Saxons.

The 'Dark Ages' is a term that is really only applicable to the alien historians who wrote about the Britons. They were 'in the dark' about the exploits, religion, culture and innovations of our talented ancestors.

According to folklore, the clans were re-established under Excalibur, "the sword drawn from the stone". This metaphor is possibly a representation of something that actually happened. Our ancestors had an oral history, which they passed to their descendants in songs and rhyme; as exampled following for bronze casting.

"From the earth's life veins mix copper and one tenth tin, out of the furnace flows blood metal to a stone cast sword within; unto the lady of the lake to be tempered in brine, then honed on blue pennant and polished by time".

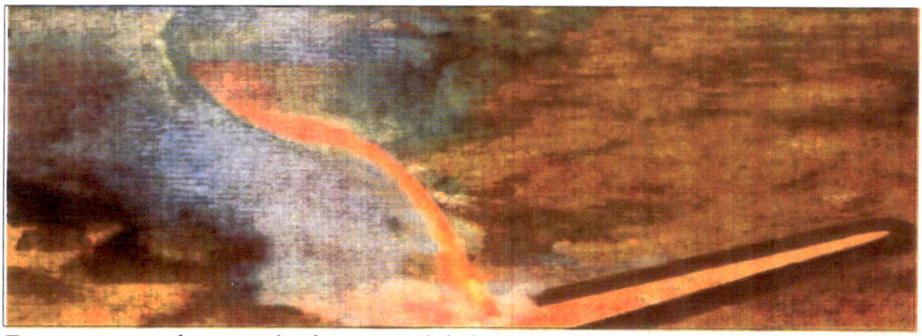

Bronze casting techniques which remain unchanged since BC.

It is written that the sword was returned to the Lady of the lake upon the death of a leader, whose body was sent out on a burning float to the Isle of Avalon, in a manner that makes it akin to a religious offering. The Romans adopted to copy this rite from the Britons, so must have accepted this as a superior rite? Is it a coincidence the ancient British name for Apple is "afal", Merry is "llon", and grove is "llwyn", in combination with "afal" is sounded Avalon, which means "merry-apple" or "apple-grove". The Romans destroyed the sacred apple groves on Anglesey, so is it possibly this is the Isle of Avalon?

Swords, spears and certain personal items were cast into water as religious offerings. Historian Jo Hamberley has studied artefacts found in the Wytham Valley, through the fens and up as far as Lincolnshire, usually beside causeways leading through the marshes to islands, with evidence of fourteen abbeys lined up on them; some built on earlier British foundations.

It has also been revealed by Francis Pryor that Fishbourne Palace is a Pre-Roman British residence, which covered a larger area than Buckingham Palace, so we can assume that Britain was cultured and had links with parts of Europe before any invasion by Rome, Saxon or Norman. From the site of another burial dated to sometime BC, at Colchester, it has been verified from bronze work and other items found there, the Britons were trading with Italy and Spain pre and post Roman. Francis Pryor says that the Romans did not change Britain's soul.

There is evidence that after the Romans left, the British Clans re-opened ancient trade routes and continued trading with Europe and the east. Archaeologist Mark Whyman, excavated coins, pottery and ceramics near York, which originated from the eastern Mediterranean, which included Byzantine pottery and ceramics, evidencing the trade routes were reopened.

Archaeologist Ken Dark inspected Byzantium pottery found on Caldy Island in Wales, to say it was proof of British trading with the east; and this trade evidently gave rise to a continuation of the exchange of ideas, diplomacy, and a spiritual ideology between these trading partners.

Theologian, Jonathan Wooding, examined his finds and he also felt obliged to say that the Britons were not illiterate people but were cultured and refined in the arts. They were the scholars of the time, with normal contacts between other intellectual nations before the Roman invasion, evidencing that Britain was a refined nation.
Historian David Hewlett says that the inscriptions carved on ancient stones show learning and a co-operation of minds, demonstrated in these arts. He also says that modern Europe was invented in Britain, the inscriptions when read backwards, contained a clever version of classical Latin poetry. This portrays continuity in intellectual life, in an extraordinarily creative time, with solid British foundations. He also cites poems of an early chieftain, found at Wroxeter, were dated after the Romans departure. Archaeologist also excavated a huge building at Wroxeter, which was built after the Romans, confirming that Britons were still actively building and re-building.
Also, near Hadrian's wall, at the site of Camlan where King Arthur reputedly fought his last battle, the Britons built huge buildings with enormous wooden halls. Granaries were also excavated there, and all these buildings were post Roman.
Excavations at Tintagel Cornwall prove that tin was being traded with the east. Other excavations have found wheel made pottery, which originates in Turkey; so sea transportation is evident of a vast trade route to the east.
On a dive in a Devon estuary, tin ingots have been found that were 99.9% pure, which indicates a continuation of trade. Tin was extremely marketable and the Britons were also trading in tin in pre and post Roman times.

Beach excavations on the southern coastline have turned up hearths and charcoal deposits, with encampments attached to trading ports, clearly a flourishing trade was continuing; so why the term Dark Ages?
The western and northern Britons were a great force and impossible to subdue. I note here, the Saxons in 453 AD offered to meet with defending Britons at Stonehenge, in order to discuss peace terms. In honourable tradition the British disarmed to attend the peace gathering, but the Saxons had hidden their 'Sax long knives' about their person, and when inside, slaughtered all of the unarmed British. This event is recorded in history as "The Night of the Long Knives". It should have been recorded as "The Night of the Cowardly Saxons". Having shown themselves in their true colours, the Saxons had progressed to take what are now called Kent and up as far as York, including the eastern coastal areas. By 700 AD most all of the east of Britain was enslaved again.
The Vikings invaded in 870 AD by taking York, so this apparent slave industry of the eastern British must have been a highly valued prize, well worth taking over. The Saxons remained in control of the southeast.
The inhabitants of what is now called Ireland, Scotland and Wales were true to Britain, and have always been free to a great extent.
In 870 AD about 817 years after King Caradoc's sister Gwladus had converted Romans to Christianity, the Saxons were still European Pagans in Britain, sacrificing their British prisoners to their Pagan Gods and placing the remainder into slavery; so about 70% of the eastern Britons were placed back into slavery. Civilised Christians, the Saxons were certainly not!

After 870 AD, some Saxons must have converted to Christianity, they must have progressed and adapted to learn and absorb British principles and moral ideals and use British resources and skills to learn other languages and to educate their children, just as the Romans had done before them.
The Normans did the same when they came in, but took another 300 years to make any headway in their invasion into Wales.
In about 1175 The Princes of Wales were successfully keeping the invaders at bay and were invited to Abergavenny Castle to a Christmas feast, to sign a treaty between Wales and England. In honourable tradition the Welsh left their arms at the front door; but when inside, their hosts called their soldiers to arms and slaughtered them all (another 'night of the cowardly long knives'). These cowards then hunted down to his death, a surviving Prince called Cadwaladr; he was a young boy of seven years of age. In the 1400's the Welsh Prince 'Owain Glyndwr' destroyed Abergavenny and other castles held by these aristocratic Barons.
Let's summarise the latter: - British envoys were travelling the world to teach astronomy BC. Caesar identified Britain with at least 40 establishments (Universities) with 60,000 students, (involving religious instruction) post 55 BC. The British were preaching about a Jesus Christ (Iesu Grist) early AD; and up to about 43 AD the Britons had defeated Rome on at least two occasions. After 43 AD Caradoc was defending against the best Rome could place in the theatre of war, by which Caesar had to send for more reinforcement to help the three generals already here.

Caradoc and his sister could speak at least three languages. Rome allowed Caradoc the right of a British King to address the Senate in Rome, where he gave an exceptional speech and was pardoned. Rome gave Caradoc and his family a 'Palace of the Britons' to reside in. Caradoc's sister Gwladus was accused of practising her foreign superstition "Christianity" and she married a Roman Commander and converted him and other Romans to Christianity in about 53 AD.

Now let's analyse who was civilised or not, for there are many opinions on the matter. However it is appropriate to know exactly what we mean by civilised; do our present day definitions of civilisation apply?

One definition of several to be found can be used to justify the view of those who claim that the Romans brought "civilisation" to Britain. The other is by which the Romans described the British as ignorant heathen barbarian savages. Firstly, there is the one that refers to civilisation pertaining to a certain type of culture and society and, the Romans' civilisation fitted this definition.

The other refers to intellectual, cultural, material, and moral development, as seen in the Druid arts and sciences. This definition usually includes written records, that will not be found in early British society, however you cannot rule out the living memorised library of Druids and their rules of counselling were real signs of political and social institutions, of which civilisation does not support the assertion, the British were ignorant heathen barbarian savages. I think the correct description for Britain should therefore be "The British were morally civilised". The Romans were not.

Caesar should have respected the fact that Ancient British innovation culture and artwork is the first and finest in the world, a product of a moral civilised nation, who were independent and undeniably brave in battle. The British were a moral people who looked after their young and old, and cared for handicapped children; and whose women were of equal status, by the fact that women rose to be leaders of Clans.
It is recorded that the Romans, discarded their infirm children and adults onto the rubbish dumps outside their city walls, baby girls were disposed of at birth and, ordinary women were second class citizens below their husbands and rulers.
I note: The Greek explorer and geographer, Strabo (63 BC to AD 24) wrote of the visit to Athens of a Briton, who was as he put it, an *astronomer of his day*:-
"He came not clad in skins like a Scythian, but with a bow in his hand, a quiver hanging over his shoulder, a plaid wrapped around his body, a gilded belt encircling his loins and, trousers reaching down from the waist to the soles of his feet. He was easy in his address; agreeable in his conversation; active in his dispatch and secret in his management of great affairs; quick in judging of present accuracies, and ready to take his part in any sudden emergency; provident withal in guarding against futurity; diligent in the quest of wisdom; fond of friendship; trusting very little to fortune, yet having the entire confidence of others, and trusting with everything for his prudence. He spoke Greek with a fluency that you would have thought that he had been brought up in the Lyceum; and conversed all his life with the academy of Athens".

Strabo's graphic description does not give the impression of an illiterate ignorant barbarian savage Briton; nor does the Tarin Basin finds; the Boscom Bowmen; nor the description by Poseidonius of the Britons BC. Does it become clear that some historians are deliberately maligning the Ancient British in their own, or perhaps a Roman agenda, that has existed for over 2,000 years?

The time span up to and from 30/24,000 BC of the Paviland Red Man's existence surely evidences a pure British bloodline to present day, this knowledge gives some certainty about our first ancestors.

Some historians suggest that Britain was conquered, probably towards the end of the Bronze Age around 1,200 BC, by Germanic Celtic invaders. However the evidence of archaeology has shown that British culture and art were in the British Isles before 3,500 BC as aforementioned. Britons were cultured and on the forefront of technological advancements, with a religion in place, and there is no such extensive similar archaeology or religion in Germany from 3,500 BC.

We do not know how far the British influence had spread by 1,200 BC but it must have gone out of Britain, not entered. There is also Caesar's reference of European Druids learning in Britain and also his references to Britons speaking their own languages when fighting to repel Caesar in 55 and 54 BC and the invasion of 43 AD. The British clans must have progressed over thousands of years to be mining copper before 3,500 BC and were trading out from the Great Orme at this very same time.

The evidence is that the British had strong connections with and traded with Europe and beyond BC.

Caesar certainly referenced that European Celts were being taught in Britain; this alone must have been a great influence on European Celts. Also, excavated near Stonehenge is the "Amesbury Archer" dated at 2,300 BC, and from the evidences of artefacts found with him, it is quite possible he was actually trained in British metalworking. It is also possible that Britons opened mines in Europe and set up metalworking there.

The mists of time can be penetrated by archaeology and historical writings, and we have to build on the tiny glimpses of the remote past that we get when new sites are discovered and investigated, even though most of the evidence left behind by our forebears has been lost to wind, weather, grazing animals and new buildings, but the remaining evidence should be read correctly. The Romans left us the most tangible reminders of their occupation, but they helped to obliterate many traces of the peoples they enslaved in the south and east and, without British written records, we must logically use what we see and have found in the living landscape. Britain was a leading civilisation of moral peoples, for the evidence strongly supports this. I fervently suggest that the immoral facts of the Roman, Saxon and Norman past must not be written out of history, or lost in the architecture, or brushed under the carpet, for we must pin-point and identify all the wrongs through the ages in order that we can reject it entirely.

Genuine friendly peoples have come into Britain through the ages, which have been welcomed and, in some instances have proudly joined with Britons to live by moral principals, just as Britons must respect other nation's values when they enter their lands?

We know that in any invaders directive, their agenda was to enter in order to terrorise, slaughter, plunder, immorally enslave and, to live off the British nation. The fact remains that Britons are first in Britain with their own bloodlines that extend into the mists of time (just as other nations in their lands). We must identify who we are and where we come from, to understand our aims going forward, as being genuine free spirits of a certain moral British Nation, which should never be taken over, enslaved, destroyed, or given away, to the loss of "British Lands and Freedom".

From here on, I would like to support my own British region, which is now called Wales, to name some good Britons and particularly those who pioneered to the Americas in the 16th and 17th centuries. This was again probably an unwitting rejoining of the clans, and I am sure the British - Cornish, Scots, Irish, Manx and English, can also relate and may realise the same.

The Welsh reside in Williamsburg, Virginia, Carolina, Dover, Pittsburgh, Goochland (taken from Welsh Cochland is Redland) and many Welsh names are prevalent there. The Welsh flag in Pennsylvania is called the "Star Spangled Dragon". In fact, nine American presidents are of Welsh descent. Hilary Clinton, first Lady, who also ran for the presidency and is in power now, is of Welsh descent and was originally from Scranton. The town of Scranton, Pennsylvania, is called "Mini Wales". The population is predominantly of Welsh descent. The Welsh of Scranton, Pennsylvania are mining experts and ironmasters. The Welsh also settled in Patagonia and they retain their Welsh heritage and language to this day.

Famous Welsh innovators in America are: Pierpont Morgan (banking magnate). Howard Hughes (pioneer of aviation). Howard Stringer (innovator and automobile pioneer). Oliver Evans (steam engineer). D W Griffiths (architect). Charles Jenkins (pioneer of radio and TV). Elihu Yale, founder and benefactor of Yale University. Ben Evans (rancher and meat entrepreneur). Robert Owen (visionary and founder of the cooperative society and world renowned education system). Frank Lloyd Wright, Gerry Lee Lewis, Sam Phillips, Treat Williams, Robin Williams and Tommy Lee Jones are all proud to be of Welsh British ancestry.

Interestingly, another connection is the Parys Mountain on the Island of Anglesey, which was mined for the abundance of copper there, using coal to power the mining machinery. Copper ore from Parys Mountain supplied almost three quarters of the worlds copper. It was smelted in the Towy valley and shipped down river to Swansea, which was called "Copperopolis" at this time. From here it was shipped all over the world, in long haul ships. These ocean-going ships such as the *Cutty Sark* were copper-bottom-plated; as was Nelson's fleet, to give superior manoeuvrability, in his "Victory".

Swansea mariners were known as "Cape Horners" (master mariners) the crew were "Swansea Jacks" is taken from "Jack-Tar" which is the slang word for a sea merchant and, coincidentally Cornishmen are called "Cousin Jacks" is this relative to an ancient link?

Mercantile vessels sailed from Swansea to the Falkland Islands and Chile, the journey usually taking up to 110 days. The fastest Welsh record for a voyage to South America stood at 96 days.

The Welsh also sailed to San Francisco, Statten Island, Santiago, Cuba, and Valparaiso, where as many as 50 copper-carrying ships would be in the harbour at one time. Many of these places have street names reminiscent of Wales, such as Aberavon and Llanelli. These long haul ships also sailed to Africa, India, Australia, and the rest of the world.

In the doorway scene following is a Welsh lady, repairing fishing nets. In the background of the picture (allowed by the courtesy of the Pembrokeshire Tourist Information Centre) you can see long haul ships.

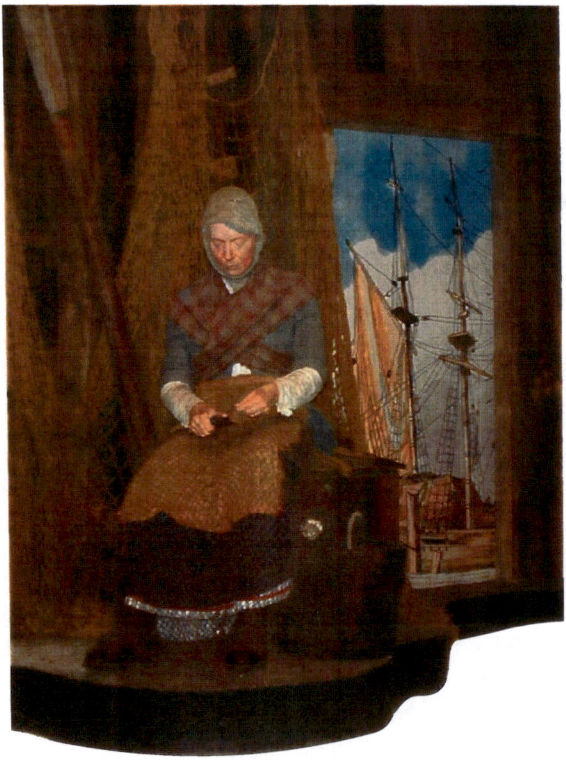

Swansea was once the capital city of Wales. "A lovely ugly Town," Welsh poet Dylan Thomas once said of it and, perhaps, it was the very first lovely ugly town, for the Red Man's people set down their roots here up to and after 30,000 BC. Fishing boats from many ports along the Welsh coastline cast their nets far into the oceans.

Notably, there were Welshmen who penned some of our ancient verse around 800 years ago, making a permanent record of the facts contained in the oral tradition. The *Black Book of Carmarthen* is one of the oldest known documents to tell of our Welsh Kings including one called Arthur. It seems that the English under Norman rule were at the Welsh borders, when this unnamed Welshman took up his quill, in a brave endeavour to prevent some of our Welsh history from being wiped from all records. And it is the realisation of subsequent Welshman such as Sir J Price, R Vaughn, W E Wynne, and Sir J Williams, President of the National Library of Wales at Aberystwyth, who have now protected these valuable writings for posterity, in the first book of Wales, known as Penyard 1.

In the 19th century, Iolo Morganwg (1747-1826) from Glamorgan, travelled throughout Britain, gathering and documenting Druid – Welsh stories and poetry. It is alleged he was dishonest in claiming that some of his own work was written by the medieval poet Dafydd ap Gwilym. He claimed that the Bards of Glamorgan used a metre that had disappeared from all other areas of Wales. He also declared that they would gather together in an elaborate ceremonial event that he called the Gorsedd (Eisteddfod), claiming the tradition had continued unbroken in Glamorgan since before the birth of Christ.

In 1792 Morganwg persuaded a number of London Welshmen to hold a Gorsedd at Primrose Hill. However, there wasn't much interest in the Gorsedd until 27 years later, when Morganwg made links with the National Eisteddfod that was taking place in Carmarthen. Some historians debunk Morganwg's work as drug induced; but perhaps these historians should not be too harsh for he was "prescribed" laudanum for his depression and, we do know that governments have "knighted" certain individuals who have openly used and may have promoted drugs in their verse. Some of the documented evidence Morganwg found was from far and wide and was intellectually sound, but because of the ensuing misjudgments of his refined works, a lot of his valid information of the Druidic movement in Britain has been dismissed to a certain extent, however has helped in its existence. Iolo Morganwg's research was sound, and so the Gorsedd of the Bards may be descendant from British Druid originality, which possibly goes back to the rituals and assemblies of Stonehenge.

I do not think it is helpful when TV presenters such as in the article "The Making of a People" imply that the Welsh are diluted into being English and that England made Wales? This is the fallacy that continues, for if you look at the facts of the evidences, all Britons are from the pedigree of the Red Man. It was also suggested that Offa's-Dyke was built to keep the Welsh out of England. I prefer to believe it was built to keep the Barons, Dukes and Tax-Lords, out of Wales. Another presenter said that England absorbed Wales into being English, is this comment a bit short sighted?

No matter where we look in Britain today, we can see many traces of the ancient Britons. The medieval castles are simply a modified design built on what existed long before. Drover roads and track-ways are often so antique that only the footprints of the Red Man's people can be found there.

Britons have joined with many peoples of the world, but true Britons know that a diluting of any nation is not really possible if the majority remains - and it looks as if the majority is far greater than anyone imagined. It is also stated that the Saxons replaced 50% of the men of the eastern and southern Clans. Let's analyse this: - 50% of the men of the eastern and southern Clans are about 10% of the British Isles men replaced; conceivably the other areas of the British Isles remained relatively as Britons. So if the Romans or Saxons intermixed with some British women of which seems unlikely for they named them ignorant heathen barbarian savages, who were perceived to be of an inferior race. It is therefore likely these invaders would have brought their own women with them. If not, the offspring would be half mix to 5% of the population of the British Isles. The Normans also probably brought their own women with them, so all we are talking about is a possible 5% dilution or less of Britons' DNA, which ultimately would have been replenished by the majority of interrelating British, so the majority must be of near true British blood in any event.

Britons have been free to some extent and have never yielded to foreign power entirely and will always admit to being the true noble descendants of the ancient Britons, as any rightful Briton's heritage must always be.

Britons should not ask any foreign factions to apologise for what their ancestors did, for that time is not theirs and has passed into history and, if Rome, Saxon and Norman had never invaded the British Isles, then Britons would have survived alone and, looking at all the evidences to the greater extent, the British have prevailed. True British have never lost their integrity, no matter who invaded here; but it has left some deep scars on British soil though.

Chapter 9

The last true Princes and Kings of the Britons

The Draig Goch (Red Dragon)

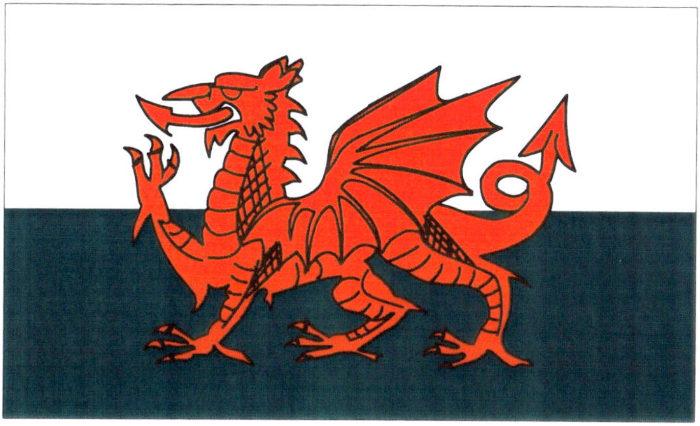

The *Ddraig Goch* (red dragon) flag is the national flag of Wales. The dragon image has its origins far back in time, but it is sometimes taken to be associated with the Tudor dynasty, perhaps on its Welsh side, for King Henry Tudor was of British Welsh blood. The white-over-green field, some historians say, is in the livery colours of the Tudors, with a large red dragon passant. It is also said it was brought to Britain by the Romans, who had copied it from the Parthians; which dragon was used by both English and Saxon Kings. But in reality, as the ancient Preseli outcrop sleeping dragon outline depicts, it is the true ancient image of the Welsh Dragon of the Britons, from many years BC.

Apparently, the Red Dragon is one of the most ancient emblems associated with the Preseli bluestone outcrop, the Great Orme (and Viking connection) and many other small islands around the coastline of Wales, which dragon became the Welsh battle emblem. The banner was allegedly used by a King called Arthur. It was also the standard of Cadwaladr, from whom the Tudors were descended on its Welsh side. Henry VII took it into battle and when he became King of England, in 1485, he decreed that the Red Dragon should be known as the official flag of Wales. The Welsh will not thank him for that, because actually, it always was.

In earlier days, the Welsh fought against Edward 1st and suffered the loss of their King Llewelyn the Last, in 1282. Llewellyn was a Prince of Gwynedd and, leader of Welsh resistance to Edward. Llewelyn wanted to regain complete Welsh British identity and see off the English King and his Barons. Henry III was on the English throne when Llewelyn came to prominence. Meanwhile, Simon de Montfort was also making life difficult for his monarch, by inciting the Barons to rebel. When he overpowered Henry; de Montfort made overtures to Llewelyn, whom he formally recognised as Prince of Wales. That was not the end of the story, for Henry soon regained control and under the terms of the Treaty of Montgomery, allowed Llewelyn to be known as Prince of all Wales, but at a price. Llewellyn had to "promise" to pay the crown £16,666, a huge sum at this time. Bizarre, a true Prince had to promise to pay the aristocracy for his rightful heritage! Llewellyn's family were not amenable to him bearing the title for which he had to pay a fortune and, run into debt.

Like all men of power, Llewelyn had to face opposition from all quarters for one reason or another and, later, Llewelyn saw Edward take the English throne. Edward was not interested in treaties signed by his predecessor, especially one making Llewelyn Prince of all Wales. As things went from bad to worse, the Welsh had to take a stand against Edward. In October 1282, during a skirmish at Menai, an English soldier allegedly engaged Llewelyn in hand-to-hand battle and killed him, unaware who his victim was.

The wild daffodil is the British Welsh National Emblem.

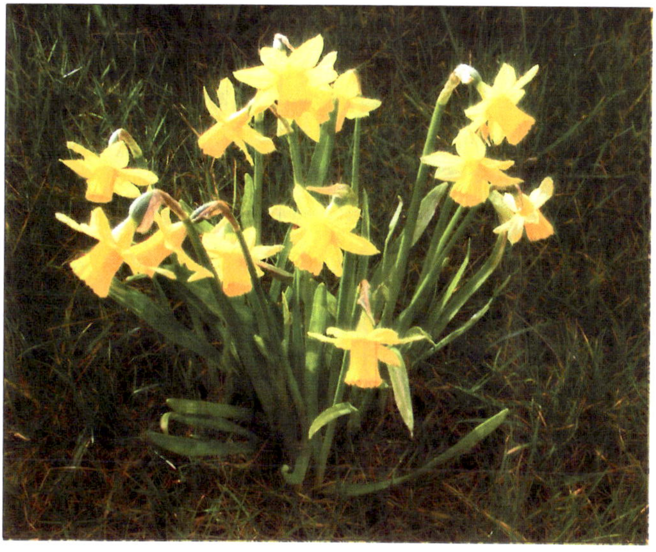

Edward built 12 castles throughout Wales to keep the Welsh British suppressed, and to keep some of the powerful Barons occupied at a healthy distance from London. A lot of Castles to keep the Welsh at bay!

Some historians say that Edward made the Welsh wear yellow felt tags, to identify them as second-class citizens in their own land. Little did he know that the Welsh proudly wore their Welsh wild yellow daffodils, to show everybody that they are first class Britons in their own land. The daffodil is now worn on St David's day.
The Welsh were exploited once more and certain rebellions ensued. The aristocracy was once again trying to take what they wanted from the Welsh in their attempt to enslave the British, but the Scottish, Irish and Welsh would not yield.
By 1349 the British Celtic divisions into Ireland, Scotland and Wales were well established by the English aristocracy. At this time, Owain Glyndwr had risen up against the trespass, exploit and abuse of Wales by the English aristocracy, particularly in the years following 1398. Glyndwr descended from the royal houses of Wales, an heir to Cadwaladr, a bloodline which extended directly from the Princes of Powys and Cyfeiliog. On his mother's side he was descended from Deheubarth in the south of Wales, making his claim *as Prince of Wales* a rightful one, which the family had fought for Llewelyn ap Gruffydd in the last war and regained their lands in North-East Wales. The deplorable life under the aristocracy in the Welsh lands was certainly a good cause for rebellion. Glyndwr quarreled with a neighbouring landowner Reginald de Gray, Lord of Ruthin, who was a close friend of Henry IV, over common land which De Gray had stolen. Owain Glyndwr could get no justice from Henry or parliament and was dismissed with insult and malice. This contempt of Glyndwr advanced to a war for the Britons' freedom.

Owain Glyndwr contacted other oppressed Welshmen and raised his standard outside Ruthin on 16 Sept 1400; from the very beginning he was proclaimed Prince of Wales. The response was great and the rebellion began. Henry dispatched troops and rapidly drew up more laws, outlawing Welsh-language, bards and singers; were these aristocrats trying to destroy all evidence of the Britons by these laws? Battles raged, with Glyndwr capturing lands back for Wales, up to 1402.
By the end of 1403 Glyndwr controlled most of Wales. In nine more years he had relieved the English of their isolated castles throughout Wales. Glyndwr and his allies defeated each of Henry's forces' all but annihilating them. It was a re-joining of the Clans which grew into a patriotic force who put their lives on the line for their land and "freedom".
Glyndwr defended Wales against the aristocracy for 15 years, which ended in about 1404; this remarkable feat of patriotic strength and willpower shows what grit and determination the British are truly made of.
Owain Glyndwr assembled a parliament out of all the major communities in Wales and signed treaties with France and Spain. Glyndwr was crowned king of a free Wales and his parliament was progressing to divide Britain into three allied British Kingdoms, however the English army enlisted mercenary reinforcements and stopped this happening.
In 1408 Aberystwyth and Harlech castles fell to the aristocracy and Glyndwr's family were taken as prisoners. Up to 1409 Owain Glyndwr, his son, and some of his best men kept up their skirmishing throughout Wales for some years.

Henry offered a pardon, which Glyndwr knew from the past deceits of the aristocracy, this pardon would have ended in demoralization and certain death. From thousands of Patriotic Britons at this time, came a loyal army one-twelfth the size of the English, up against two Kings and numerous armies for about 15 years. Owain Glyndwr was a true British Prince and a King who was never betrayed by his own patriotic Britons, who kept his whereabouts secret even in the face of their own deaths. Caradoc defended against Caesar and his three famous Roman Generals for at least 7 years; and Boudicca all but beat them. The Silurian Britons fought-on ceaselessly, winning many battles. Is why the British Welsh Nation is represented by the Leek, is a sign of a people with feet firmly planted on their own British land; is a statement of rights and Freedom.

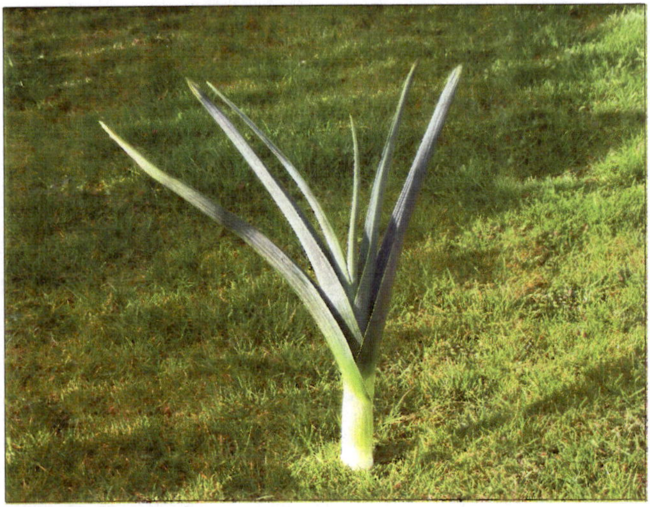

The Welsh Leek

Owain Glyndwr died in about 1416 AD, and must inspire all Britons to stand proud.

There many books and the Internet is another useful source of further information about all the subjects raised in this book. The Ancient British were amazing people; particularly from the time of the technological achievements since the RED MAN's footprints in the stone, to present day, is to remind my fellow British what an enduring legacy our early pioneering ancestors left us.

Following is research of recent TV documentaries in the order they were broadcast. I briefly comment on what was stated, to analyse and refute, following:-

"Decoding Stonehenge"

It is suggested in this TV documentary that many Britons, over thousands of years were travelling to Stone and Woodhenge at least twice a year, at midsummer and midwinter solstices, to a great banquet.
It was also evidenced that other Britons resided in a village of at least 1,000 houses near there and, other Britons visited to honour their ancestors, who are assumed to be the stones themselves.
It was also stated that ordinary people cast their dead relative's ashes into the river Avon. Six huge post holes were excavated on a ridge overlooking a track way, of which it was suggested they held three platforms to place the dead upon to rot in the sun; with ritual killings also acted out here.

Can the latter be true, as we are told that the entire ancient monuments throughout the British Isles are burial places; then why carry dead bodies or ashes and all the rigmarole to Stone or Woodhenge?

Strabo, Poseidonius, Caesar and others suggest that the Britons were a proud refined nature loving nation who dressed in fine plaid clothes, with gold hair-braids and elaborate waxed hairstyles; with neck and armband jewellery and artistic designs displayed on their bodies and fineries; so apparently were not morbid fanatics.

Caesar wrote that the British could use their chariots with great skills, with trained hunting dogs running alongside (that were bred and trained over thousands of years) so was the 3 platforms or one huge stage on 6 posts possibly for overseeing any games, or 3 separate podiums.

Why do some archaeologists have an unhealthy obsession for incessant morbid death explanations, for it is well documented that Britons cared for their aged, young and infirm; and then surely any event at Wood or Stonehenge was possibly for a seasonal fair or games entertainment, in very much the same way as the festivals and athletic events are the traditional venues of today; "rather than any morbid twice yearly funerals" over thousands of years.

The Britons could have raced chariots (called trotting today), coursed hares, raced horses or dogs, archery, or entered into any number of entertaining competitions. (Did other countries copy this event)?

Possibly thousands of Britons and invited Europeans came to partake at this magnificent complex, culminating in the magnificent sights of the rising and the setting of the Sun; with the Moon playing its part perhaps in fertility or wedding rites.

It was estimated in this program there was 1 death every two years over thousands of years, with one injured archer; suggesting these were ritual killings?

How can the latter be ritual deaths; and some fights would have broken out, usually for the love of a beautiful British woman, surely are normal incidents of death?

The Amesbury Archer burials were also said to be linked, with new pots and a bit of gold brought in by him; and another skeleton said to be his family member, that was evidenced he originating from the Wales area, contradictory don't you agree?
Can you compare the mining and smelting technologies of the Britons on the Great Orme, to simple clay pots and a little gold, to say that one European is the source of it? Is it possible the likes of the Amesbury Archer came to Britain to learn their skills or to attend at Wood and the Stonehenge arenas?

"The Great Druid Massacre"

In this documentary, a grave was excavated in Stanway on the east coast of Britain, of a Druid doctor and his possessions of medicinal pots, fine surgical instruments, and metal rods; of which it was said he used to throw onto the ground to create shapes for divining the future (surely this is a bizarre comment)?

In my opinion, these grave finds of this Druid doctor of finely manufactured surgical instruments, metal cauterizing rods and various medicinal pots, evidence that the Druids were a well educated people indeed?

It was also said in this film that the Romans asserted that the Druids sacrificed people to cut out their entrails to forecast the future. It was also noted "there is no evidence of this" so what is the point of citing this unfounded speculation?

It was then suggested that 150 individual skeletons found in a sink-hole crevasse in Alveston Gloucestershire, was a Druid single event ritual killing of these Britons, to the Gods, which would give them the ability to massacre thousands of Romans (is another bizarre comment)?

When a cracked thigh bone was found, it was said it was evidence of cannibalism.

A beautiful British bronze figurine of a greyhound was also produced to relate to a Dog God?

These TV presenters then suggested that these were Druid ritual killings of 150 Britons, in order that thousands of Romans would die in battle, is an off the wall tactic to presume don't you think?

Logically, it would have been more sensible for these Britons to have fought against the Romans, if they were able.

There is good reference that the Britons cared for their aged, young, and infirm, so why would they massacre their own beloved people and obedient dogs?

Is it possible these 150 individuals were the old, very young and infirm who were hiding out, and it was the Romans who massacred them and their dogs and then dumped them all into the sink-hole crevasse? Also, how can it be established out of thousands of bones which had been hacked, bludgeoned and battered by the well know practice of the Romans of stoning people to death, that one cracked thigh bone was the evidence of cannibalism? Does the finder of the this one cracked bone, think that one Briton survived this single event, or crept down into this stench hole, cut the flesh from this one thigh bone and smashed it to extract the marrow, why, with all the flesh about; and then left that one bone in the cave after eating the marrow, and then crept back out again?

Evidently, the beautifully crafted bronze figurine of a greyhound dog has absolutely nothing to do with these killings at all, for it is from another site. But surely the figurine does evidence a highly educated people who had the ability to produce fine (lost wax moulded) bronze work, and had trained greyhound type dogs; perhaps this beautiful bronze figurine was a prize for winning a greyhound race, or hunt?

It was then alleged, because the ritual killing of 150 Britons did not work, and the Romans were still marching to Anglesey, the Druids ritually killed a high status Briton (Lindow Man). It was also said that this was a 3 death ritual killing, because Lindow Man was bludgeoned, garrotted and had his throat cut; and also had 4 mistletoe pollens in his stomach.

Is the latter TV presenter's three death ritual theory of Lindow Man realistic or any other theory for that matter?

Accordingly, should the Druids have killed 3 people? Or is it a better explanation that this high status Briton was tortured by the Romans?
The evidence is, he was smashed on the head twice (is not any Celtic 3) then slowly torque garrotted, with his hands tied behind his back, possibly to gain information of the Britons whereabouts and strengths, and when nothing came forth, the Romans cut his throat for good measure and tossed him into the bog.
The presenter's mistletoe theory is also suspect, why 4 grains of pollen (why not the Celtic 5)? Is it simply possible that this pollen was used in a medicine preparation, or a fruit brew, or cooking procedure, which Lindow man had for lunch?
Are not 150 bludgeoned individual Britons who were killed and dumped in a crevasse, which had numerous bone fractures, a little more than 3, so why do these TV presenters always suggest a Celtic 3 death ritual, when logically more than three incidents are usually evidenced in any torture or massacre? Surely it was only one death this man encountered?

Why is there this never-ending hum-drum morbid tripe to try to portray the British as barbarian heathen (cannibals), savages and peculiar mystics? What is the presenter's evidence that proves that the British threw metal rods onto the ground to forecast the future?

Why would the British frequently ritually kill their family and friends, to place them onto platforms to rot in the sun, or pull out their entrails to forecast the future; or strip the flesh off their thighs, to crack open the bones to eat the marrow. Is this disingenuous TV reporting and to what outcome does this sort of deception try to achieve? Is it all in order to degrade the British?

It was then alleged, the Romans marched up to Anglesey (with their especially made boats or made them when they arrived at the Menai, it was not indicated which) crossed over to Anglesey and massacred all the Britons there. And then cut down all the Oak and Apple groves. It was then suggested that finds in a Lake of buckled swords, and bones etc, evidence that the Britons were offering expensive items and performing ritual killings, to the Gods.

Let's consider the latter TV reporting: -

Did the Romans carry their hundreds of sea-going boats with them on their backs, or pull them along on trolleys on their very long march?
Did they ferry at least 10,000 heavily armed legionaries across the Mighty Menai Strait? How long would it have taken to execute this gargantuan dangerous task?
Lord Nelson is an authority on the Menai Strait which he describes as one of the most treacherous areas of sea in the world, with rock-bottoms from 30 foot, in some instances raising directly to within 3 feet, with whirlpools, eddies and tides running to at least eight knots, of which the Britons would have known about.

It is not an easy passage to go through or across the Mighty Menai at anytime, and this is a commonly well-known fact by the amount of ferries and boats that have been lost there.

Let's do the sums for a minute: -

Did the Romans make their boats and march with them from London to Anglesey, and not to forget they were fighting along the way?
Well, at least 10,000 men divided to, say about 20 men per boat is 500 boats; a lot of large boats to make near London and carry them all the way to Anglesey, and a little bit conspicuous, that would suggest where they were going I imagine, so we will rule out this strategy.

If the Romans did make their 500 boats at or near London, then surely they would have boated around the coastline and up to Anglesey?

Did the Romans make these 500 boats when they reached the Menai? Well, given the fact that the Romans would have taken some considerable time to make 500 sea going boats to carry 20 men in each, to safely cross the Mighty Menai, I don't think the Britons would have hung around until they did so?

If the Romans at the Menai, made in quick time, say 10 boats, this means they would have ferried across 10 x 20 = 200 divided into 10,000 equals, at least 50 times; and on the first wave, I am sure the Britons could have dealt with 200 men in 10 boats?

If the Romans made 20 boats, clearly a massive task, as at any of the latter. Also, how many boats would have capsized, with the weight of heavily armed men, in this very dangerous stretch of water and, were they all rowing, a bit cumbersome if they were? If they capsized, I don't think the Romans would have been able to swim in heavy armour, shields and weapons? If the Romans were not in armour etc, then all would have been lost to the sea, unless they could carry it while swimming. I don't think the Romans would have been allowed to land and get dressed before battle though; and how many could swim at all, we must ponder?

Surely, if the Britons were hard pressed on Anglesey, they would have just simply crossed over the island and exited by boat; in more calmer seas than in the turmoil of Mighty Menai Strait, at anytime, to exit to the Isle of Man, or into the Isles of Scotland, or over to Ireland.

It is recorded that the Romans then marched back towards London; why didn't they boat back, seems bizarre they did not? Are these "Roman" records, believable; for the Romans could not possibly march back to London to say they had been unsuccessful at Anglesey?

Why did the Romans march back when apparently it would have been quicker by boat; if they had known that Boudicca had destroyed St Albans, Colchester and London, while the Romans were up the creek without a paddle so to speak; so is the Roman account of their Anglesey campaign believable?

It was also suggested the Romans destroyed all the Oak and Apples groves on Anglesey, what a task that must have been, for most of the island was Oak and Apple groves at this time.
Britons were likely bending and buckling enemy's swords out of shape and tossing these with the slave chains, into the lake, so they could never be used against them again; and were the bones, of the enemies' skeletons?
I will admit that benevolent offerings were also made, just as we throw coins into wells today to make a wish and perhaps these benign offerings were to keep the Gods happy and on the Britons' side, to keep their enemies and their swords from ever attacking the Britons again.
Rome's depravity was mentioned in this film, but if you blinked you would have missed it.

"Stone Age Apocalypse"

In this documentary it was suggested we evolved from apes; and the human revolution started at about 75,000 years BC (not 30,000 BC, as some historians insist). It was also stated by these TV presenters that a vast area around Indonesia was wiped out by a super volcano eruption at about 75,000 BC, after which, it was stated, that most of the origins of man came out of East Africa, from a small leftover DNA pool of peoples who survived, of which we all belong. Can the latter be correct, let's consider this following?

It is known that Boxgrove man was in Britain up to and after at least 500,000 BC, who apparently, by date and location, was not effected by the lower latitude Indonesian volcano, because evidences of human existence in Britain follows these dates to present day?

If we evolved from apes, then why from 4 million years ago are the apes still aping. If evolution predicts that brain capacity gets larger, then why did the alleged first (upright) humans have a head about 30% smaller than the first apes?

All dogs came from the wolf, which apparently dogs are still the same old dogs; so is this evidence of a weakest link barking up the wrong tree of "human life"?

I do not refute Darwin's theory; nor do I think that anyone will deny we have a "human soul".

Have any scientist found the origin of the "human soul", or the DNA of it, or the natural selection process of the first humans with a "human soul" of which the soul advanced in "humans"?

"Discovering ARDI"

In this documentary a fossilized 4.4 million years old skeletal remains of a (bipedal) female, named Ardipithicus ramidus, was found in a site called Aramis in what is known as the badlands of Ethiopia.

Her teeth were small and blunt, suggesting she lived in a hominid social group, possibly partner-bonded with a male, which brought high value food to her, while she tended to the family objective.
Her hand and fingers were not that of an ape, suggesting this is a specific species of which traits the human race evolved from; of which this book predicted.

Other skeletal remains are being found in this area to be 5.7 million years old, named Ardipithicus Kaddaba, meaning ancient father.

"Timewatch"

In this TV documentary the Amesbury Archer hypothesis is televised and it was stated that Stonehenge was built as a healing centre, because the Archers' bones showed signs of healing?

Let's analyse this:-

The Archers grave is many miles from Stonehenge; so the above is a bizarre comment, without any evidenced connection?
It was also stated that the Bluestone chippings found at Stonehenge were chipped away by the sick and maimed, to be held or kept for healing purposes? But the stone chips actually remain there abandoned; isn't that contradictory?
It was also suggested that several pieces of organic material found below a newly excavated "re-erected" Bluestone, dates Stonehenge to 2,300 BC.

Surely the latter only dates the last phase of building or simply a stone replacement; for there were at least 5 construction phases previously, is 1, 2, 3a, b and c; and then of course the Bluestones would have been transported to Stonehenge perhaps thousands of years before 2,300 BC, which were apparently used in some of these earlier phases of construction; and so the monument must be thousands of years older than 2,300 BC, so is this TV Timewatch article misleading?

"How the Irish saved British Culture"

In this documentary the TV presenters could not make up their minds to name who brought Christianity to Britain, they say was in 597 AD? Surely they must know that Tacitus wrote that Gwladus (the sister of the Briton Caradoc, the Romans called Caractacus) was accused of embracing her foreign superstition (Christianity) and was converting Romans to Christianity at about 50 AD, which clearly predates any candidate of 597 AD.

"The Seven Ages of Britain"

In this documentary, in the First Age, the TV presenter speculates upon the progression of the Ancient Britons from about 10,000 BC, but fails to identify from apparent archaeology and from the burial time of the Red Man of Paviland, to highlight the Britons' superiority in astronomy and founding of the basics of mathematics, thousand of years before Pythagoras.

The presenter also fails to mention British construction techniques and following technologies and sciences, particularly in large-scale mining and metallurgy etc on the Great Orme; from which times the British pedigree evolved and exists today.

The presenter did mention the unique houses of Skara Bray. I elaborate: are the forerunners to you modern semi with drainage systems, draft-proof air conditioning, built in beds and wardrobes etc, with an on-suite indoor toilet, built before any "stone" Pyramids in Egypt.

The TV presenter then cited a Roman pay-as-you-go taxed toilet AD, to say it was a marvellous innovation, but of course it would be, for any Tax Lords.

But surely the indoor toilets on Skara Bray BC that were tax-free were a better innovation for the British?

The presenter's comments that the flint pits at Grimes Graves were excavated for the white lime tips above, because 'they were an awesome site in the landscape', is another bizarre comment?

Surely the flint was mined for the flint, and the limestone was used in kiln construction and the burnt lime by-product for fertilizing the land, whitewashing their daubed houses and not to forget, for spiking up their hair styles and; in fact these bell-pits progressed into the coal mining bell-pits of recent years, to extract coal, evidenced in most coal mining areas of Britain.

In the Second Age the TV presenter mentions that the British were feasting well and had built fine residences of the day, was correct; but then suggested they were in an arms race.

Evidently, the British metalworking was an enormous inventive secret technology that progressed from making implements for working the land, so where does the TV presenter get this "arms race" theory from, because it is evidenced that the Romans entered into Britain to gain this technology for weapons, so apparently weapons were a by-product?

The presenter then said that Lindow man was a ritual 3 killing whereby the garrotte finished him off, and then his throat was cut to gush out blood, and was laid in a bog.

Surely if the garrotte finished him then his heart had stopped, so how could the blood gush afterwards? Understandably, and logically, the bog was a lake in those far off days.

In the Third Age the TV presenter says that the Romans in 55 and 54 BC entered into Britain on scouting expeditions, with at least 4,000 legionaries (is that correct?); quite a large expensive force to bring across the channel for scouting party's one would assume.
The fact is that on these two occasions the Romans were beaten and sent packing, by the British.

The TV presenter then said that the British were trading slaves and hunting dogs; but again there is no proof of trading slaves. Slave chains were evidenced, but with no proof they were British chains. Surely the chains were Roman slave chains, because it was they who invaded Britain (and evidently other lands) by this very fact, for supplying Rome with slaves to use and rape, and kill for their entertainments in the Colosseum.

The presenter celebrates the Roman achievement and the demise of the southern British clans with glee, but fails to mention the achievements of any British Kings or Chieftains such as Caswallon, Caradoc or Emrys, why?

The presenter then mentions Boudicca, to say, only because Tacitus did. The fact is that when Boudicca's husband died, he had made a will to leave half of his British kingdom to Rome, to try to protect his family, another instance of "comply or die" for the British people. The Romans honoured his will by taking all of his land and raping and defiling Boudicca and her children in an open despicable animal like display. In fact, as Tacitus wrote, the Chieftain King Caradoc had "predicted" this in 43 AD, "that if the British did not repel the Romans as their ancestors had in 55 and 54 BC then they would enter into eternal slavery", isn't that correct?

Tacitus also confirmed on the lines, that the British think they have been brought into civilization when in fact it is a condition of their slavery; is quite a clear instruction of events by Tacitus, don't you think?

In the Fourth Age, the TV presenter infers that Britannia is exclusively a Roman name; when actually Britan and Britanishan are the ancient British names.

The TV presenter then inferred, that a chronicle that was written 450 years after the fact of about 1,600 years ago, cited that 50% of the British of the southeastern side of Britain were replaced; can that be believed?
We know the Saxons suppressed the British of the eastern side of the country, but surely they would not have killed 50% of their golden-slave-goose would they?

Just as the Vikings knew what a values existed, to want to invade in 793 AD to exploit it.

The TV presenter then stated that the Saxons taught the British to read and write English; have these presenters forgotten that the British were speaking their own tongue BC, and learnt (and wrote) Latin and other languages in order for Europe to trade with Britain, before Britain was invaded and made downtrodden slaves by Rome.

The TV presenter then stated that the eastern side of Britain are Hybrid, cannot be correct because even this presenter stated that the British people were called "pathetic little Brits" (slaves and commoners) of whom any invaders did not mix with.

It was then said that out of this became a stable England and the "Julius work calendar"; but I guess the British knew this as the "Julian slave calendar".

In the Fifth Age the TV presenter explains that the British of the eastern side of Britain are still slaves to foreign invaders, to mention the "Doomsday Book".
I guess the "British" knew as the "Doomsday slave book".

The presenter then said that the landlords carved up the land in order for the peasants to work to supply the manor houses with food and good fuel, while the peasants eat the leftovers.

It was further stated that the British were called the "un-free", who slapped horse-dung mixed with straw onto the inside walls of their homes, to dry, to then use as fuel; what a delightful existence the British had under these foreign invaders.

In the Sixth Age the presenter said that government brought in the Pole Tax of 1380. It seems nothing has changed from the Roman occupation, for the British are still under these rules.

The TV presenter then said that a commoner named William Aston married an aristocrat named Poston; but Aston failed to doff his hat to a Norman aristocrat, who then called him a churl (a peasant). Aston then sought through a friend who was a member of an "exclusive" aristocrat club (a house of lords perhaps) a Royal declaration to say that Aston descended from Norman aristocracy (was a lie).

This proves that the aristocracy does not mix with who they perceive to be "pathetic little Brit slave commoners", do they?

In the Seventh Age, the presenter cites Roman Catholic which became the new Roman Empire; and Protestant the Monarchy (I therefore guess the British religion is "The Church of God" is within you, from BC).

The presenter then said that Protestant was a break from Rome, and to the English Nation.

I must ask here, does any presenter realise a British Nation?

Does the TV presenter differentiate the British from the English, and what she is actually portraying is from her perspective of an invaders point of view and not a British point of view? Aren't all British, British?

"The Roman Invasion of Britain"

In this documentary, the TV presenter says that the British defeated the Romans in the first century BC.

The presenter then said that in 43 AD the Romans gathered at least 800 war ships on the shores of France to invade Britain; but were deliberating about crossing because the Roman legionaries were in two minds to cross for they were afraid of what awaited them.

It was then said that Caractacus (British name Caradoc) was in Britain, spoiling for war, but heard that the Romans were afraid to cross the British Channel; and so Caradoc and his warriors thought oh bother, and went home, (What a load of tosh).

But how can this TV presenter know this?

It was then stated that the Romans plucked up their courage and crossed (but the presenter could not identify the landing place) and then took Colchester (a place the presenter earlier described in this documentary as a "small" fortified village in these times).

She then said the Romans celebrated this as a great triumph for Rome (seems an odd great triumph for taking a small fortified village).

The presenter then rightly identified the Silures who fearlessly defended Britain at all times, destroying legions; but she identified some tribes (as she put it) became client kingdoms of the Romans; she seems to be confused.

The TV presenter then inferred that the British were illiterate primitive savages, ragbag tribes who were continually warring amongst themselves.

She then misinterprets to malign Caradoc's Speech in Rome, to say it was Tacitus' words. Another TV presenter likened the British to Vietnamese.
Let's analyze the latter:-

It is well documented that the British actually defeated the Romans on at least two occasions BC; of which Tacitus referenced that Caradoc recited this in his battle speech to his warriors before their campaign against the Roman invasion in 43 AD, so the British were not all that pathetic were they?

Why would the Romans marshal such a large force of at least 800 warships, to ferry at least 40,000 legionaries and more mercenaries, to deal with a small fortification of a ragbag of pathetic little Brits?

Why did Claudius have to send for more reinforcement to place under the command of at least three Roman Generals on British soil, to attack (as the presenter put it) a small, fortified village called Colchester, a bit contradictory that, isn't it?

How would Caradoc know what the Romans were thinking, across the expanse of the British Channel? (I say British Channel because there was no England, Wales, Scotland, or Ireland etc at this time and so apparently there was no English Channel)

How can this TV presenter say that the British were illiterate when there is an enormous amount of evidence to the contrary, particularly the references of, Strabo, Caesar and Tacitus?

Why does another presenter liken the British to the Vietnamese, Al-Qaeda, and infer that the Americans are likened to the Romans?

The TV presenter forgets there was a traitor called Verica of the Atrebates who let the Romans in; and it were the other Clans of Britain who attacked the Atrebates for their treacherous collusion with Rome and; the evidence shows that the true British Clans joined, to remove the Romans.

In the second article, the TV presenter trumped up (again) that Boudicca's husband had agreed to respect Roman Rule, how does she know that? Surely it was always the Roman instance of "comply or die".

It was then stated that Boudicca's husband left half of his British land and possessions to the Emperor of Rome, to protect his family. I would mention here though, the Romans respected the latter by taking all of his land and raping is wife and children in a well know Roman (Nazi type) open mob spectacle. This started another British uprising as we know.

The TV presenter then suggested that Boudicca had only fought Roman old age pensioners. Is the presenter biased?

It was then stated that the Romans built Colchester; but the "fact" is, the Romans took over any British sites to build upon them; and also built over British paths and drover roads.

The presenter then inferred that 50% of the British became romanized? Does she mean 50% of the southeastern Britons? Does she mean 50% of what she suggests was the peasant's of the southeast, of which she says the Romans called "pathetic little Brits" were romanized? Seems misleading of this TV presenter to suggest that 50% of the whole British nation was replaced, don't you think?

The TV presenter then mentioned Minerva in connection with amalgamating Roman and British religion 50% 50%. Well we know that the Roman Constantine took the British faith to be superior to his own, to amalgamate, but we know that was a ploy to stop the Christian uprising which was a real threat to Rome. So surely if what this presenter states as matter of fact is true, then clearly these were Roman ploys to try to brainwash the British of the southeastern part of Britain, because the Romans had no real control over the rest of Britain.

It was then mentioned by this TV presenter that the Silures were formidable foes (is the presenter speaking on behalf of the Romans). The Silures defeated the Romans on many occasions and had destroyed legions; but again the presenter did not mention the Mighty British King Caradoc who was allied to the Siluri. A single stone was then mentioned which was found near Careleon (which was a British Silurian fort before the Romans took it over) with a Siluri name on it, to suggest as a matter of fact the Siluri bowed down to Rome and became Romanized

The latter cannot be true because the Silurians fell back into the depths of what is now known as Wales, Anglesey, Ireland and Scotland, of which these British clans people and their descendants are the best candidates for smashing the Roman garrison at Deva (Chester) at least twice; of which their descendants routed the Romans from Britain in 410 AD.

The "British" people we now call the Celtic Britons, most all joined as one Nation at this time. Not as suggested were separates as Irish, Welsh and Scottish etc. As a matter of fact there was no English either, because this was a brainwashing idea of a Saxon Monk called Bede hundreds of years later.

Why do TV presenters distort history as a matter of fact, to try to glorify the Romans (Saxons and Normans) in favour of giving some credence to the British?

The presenter then suggests that the British became romanised and took up great British residences, is again not true because the British logically once owned such residences. The presenter is confused to identify with Roman Lords placed into British residences and who she frequently describes as pathetic little Brit slaves; who in fact are the majority of the real British people.

Another TV presenter suggested that the Roman atrocities of the British after the Boudicca rebellion were a one off. It was stated on the lines, that by enlarge the Romans were good people. Does the presenter forget all the atrocities in and below the Coliseum?

Does he forget the genocidal destruction of the Dacians; and the European Celts at Alicia? Does he forget Dougga in North Africa whereby the Roman Emperor Scipio in 146 BC destroyed Carthage by fire and the sword, killing most of the men women and children, and assimilated the remainder into being unidentifiable slaves, used for every immoral Roman depravity, absorbing these people into diluted obscurity?

These TV presenters only remember what they want to portray and will distort the rest for their own reporting to what can only be to support their own positions in their TAX funded existence.

I note here, the Romans could not plagiarize anything of the British for there was no knowledge written down, and I say this is the very good reason why the British did not commit their vast amount of knowledge to parchment. Nor could the Romans assimilate, absorb, or dilute all of the British into the obscurity of becoming another Romanized slave nation, nor should this Roman ploy ever be attempted now.

In the last showing of this documentary the TV presenter states that the Roman invasion did achieve its aim by separating the North from England in the South? What "England", there was no "England"! Can anyone imagine the Romans building a wall separating the western side of Britain what is now called "Wales", a bit longer than Adrian's wall don't you think? The Normans tried a Dyke. Or was it the Welsh who built the Dyke to keep the Tax-Lords out of Wales.

This TV presenter then said that 10% of the Roman Empire was in Britain to control what was only 4% of the Roman Empire (bit of an overkill force for pathetic little Brits don't you think), does that seem appropriate to compare with what the TV presenter describes as 50% of Britons being Romanized, either her calculations are wrong or the presenter is misinformed. Or is it a matter of fact that the British were not cowering down to Roman rule, because even the Roman Caesar had written "the Britons had no fear of death and would not willingly yield to any foe".

The presenter also mentioned that 5,000 legionaries were placed to fight the Siluri; which is contradictory of her comments of fact that the Silurians were complying with Roman rule and had become Romanized; and from the TV presenters own evidence of alleged fact, it becomes farce and is false witness!

The TV presenter then attributed the Pumpsaint Dolaucothi mines in what was one of the densest forested areas (of Wales) to Roman prospecting and "open cast mining" expertise, again cannot be correct. Firstly how did the Romans know where to go prospecting in a mountainous maze of an expanse of what is now known as mid Wales? Secondly the mines are firstly deep shaft mines and the British open cast mining progressively followed; and thirdly they are of early British mining expertise, likewise the mines on what is now called the Great Orme, up to and from at least 3,500 BC.

The presenter then said as fact that the mines were run by European miners, using British slaves, suggesting that the British were not experienced in mining? It must be asked - why do these programs mostly denigrate the British people in order to glorify any invaders on any level they can distort?

The presenter then mentions the lead curse tablet of the "native" British (are there any other type). Romans are "named on lead folded of the cursed within and sealed with a copper pin" etc; whereas the British were cursing the Romans. I do not think the latter supports the TV presenter's perception of fact, that the British were being romanized, for this is again contradictory.

The presenter then mentions (with the Roman name) Ambrosius, who we know is the British King Emrys, who defeated the Saxons at Bath, and he is also linked with a King called Arthur; well we must thank her for this British mention at least.

This TV presenter then suggested that some Britons were still fighting any invaders, is again contradictory. Does she realise that British descendants are still here?

Why is there so much disingenuous misrepresentation of the British; when in fact the Romans were no better than the Nazis, for the Romans actually tried to enslaved all the British and take over the British Isles for the mineral wealth and to keep the British alive (like animals) to exist and breed more slaves to supply the Romans for their every immoral act, to do with as they wished.

Should these TV presenters apologies for making their slanderous' remarks about the British in their own lands, to liken the British to Al-Qaeda and Taliban; when the latter paragraph is the true description of the Romans who were the indisputable despicable "terrorist" invaders of Britain.

"Britain BC"

In this documentary, I congratulate Francis Pryor for his well-presented knowledgeable unbiased report of the sophisticated Ancient Britons, as apposed to the dirty grubby history of the Romans. Although, I thought he should have mentioned Boxgrove or the Red Man of Paviland as a starting point for the identification of the British Nation. I also think there is another explanation than Mr Pryor's for Lindow Man, as herein. There is also another explanation for his Seahenge theory, for simply a tree could have tumbled off a bank and into a ditch whereby the sand blew in to cover it; and hundreds of years later the sand blew away to reveal an upturned tree stump; whereby Britons could have used this as a central pole to erect a roundhouse or make a beach windbreak.

Why do most academics trump up incessant death and misery theories of every aspect of British life, when of course we do agree that the British had no fear of death, and we could reasonably place a few good words to describe the British, rather than being labelled as religious fanatics, such as following:-

How about the status': Honourable, Chieftain, Brave-heart, Warrior, Esteem, Champion, Winner, Defender, and these are the very same principals the British, particularly our British Soldiers have today, and likewise Francis Pryor suggested, we should raise a glass to thank them one and all.

<u>"Britain's real Monarch"</u>

In this documentary the TV presenter exposed a farcical British monarchy, whereby a chap called Michael Hastings now living in Australia, by divine right of succession, is the rightful King of Britain. It was suggested that the current Royal family line are murderers and thieves who concealed the rights of Mr Hastings.
I wonder if the presenter informed Mr Hastings that by his new found knowledge, he may only have 3 years by the "governments" Limitation Act in order to pursue his claim; however it seemed that Mr Hastings thought the monarchy was a sham and were pretenders who can never be true British Kings, Queens or Princes, by the fact they are not "British".

<u>"Seven Ages of Britain 2nd showing"</u>

The TV presenter describes a statue (as seen at the website – Aphrodsias -) of the naked Roman Claudius about to deliver a deathblow to a half naked young women, the presenter names Britannia (of which I say depicts Boudicca or one of her young daughters being raped in an open public spectacle by the Romans).

The presenter then goes on to glorify this statue to demonstrate the defeat of Britain. Well I must say that the British actually defeated the Romans on at least two occasions and Britain was not defeated entirely, and I cannot see what bravado there is in Claudius raping and killing a defenseless young lady half his size, can you?

Nor should these TV presenters glorify the vile homosexual and child molesting acts of Tiberius Caesar, or the child murders and possibly child abuse at a Roman bathhouse in Ashkelon. Or the atrocities carried out in and below the Colosseum in the name of sport. Under the Geneva Convention these Romans would have been tried for their appalling crimes.

Claudius and his historians apparently labelled the British as ignorant heathen barbarian savages, clearly was to hide the evidences' of Roman depravity, which deception by Claudius has lasted for nigh on 2,000 years.

"Dark-Matter"

In this documentary it references dark-matter, although there is no evidence of it; but I must ask: are we held in a "superior force" of the actual-matter we are in, by which all galaxies and all the universes' are held?
I will try to explain this as: if a being could only live near the middle bottom of the ocean, it could not establish or identify that the water was held in place by the force of the earth's basin-sides and gravity and that there was anything beyond it.

Likewise, our planet could be held in place by the gravity of a "greater orbital density", and when our universe has expanded from the big-bang, or my collision, or vortex theory (of which example you can see is the Jupiter-great-red-spot) to be an equal (perhaps lesser) force, and then it could merge back into the greater orbital density.

The latter would explain why it is thought that universes collide to form a super-universe. Or in another analogy such as water eddies can collide to form larger eddies that will allow debris to be pulled into a whirlpool to be later dispersed into the greater-expanse. This can then explain why black holes are wormholes that can pull planets in, to be dispersed into the greater orbital density and to another position.
Did the Mayan experience such an event in the past, of which they predicted would happen again in 2012 regarding the black hole in the middle of our Milky Way?

"Wales and the History of the World"

In this documentary the TV presenter is misinformed (or this may be what his colleague references as brainwashed pathetic little Brits).
Clearly, the British are of the multitudes the indigenous people in the British Isles and abroad, and I am offended by what seems to be a racist remark in this TV program, to be called multicultural. Of course we have welcomed foreigners and many fine decent people have actually joined our British Nation (not the other way round).

But it must be realised that we are mostly of existing British lineage which evolved from many thousands of years BC; evidently with our red dragon image and passant. Our huge British Nation has not been absorbed into any multicultural faction at all (of which is an old Roman ploy to suggest, and it is evident that the British actually avoided that part of the Roman scheme) for the British Nation exists.

"Finding the Hoard"

In this documentary there are evidences of 1,600 pieces of "Saxon" treasure found in Britain.

Does this program suggest it is all Saxon, or is simply from the Saxon period?

Clearly it is Celtic British designs and workmanship, and why would Saxons be dismantling their weapons to bury the precious metal in this area alone?

Did the British relieve the Saxons of what were once British artefacts, to make use of the blades and bury the precious metal for later use?

I must also evidence here: From British mines up to and after 3,500 BC are wherefrom British technologies craftsmanship and designs were being produced. The British taught and remembered in verse suchlike my example for Bronze:-

"From the earth's life veins mix copper and one tenth tin, out of the furnace flows blood metal to a stone cast sword within; unto the lady of the lake to be tempered in brine, then honed on blue pennant and polished by time".

As evidenced, the British advanced and evolved up to and after 3,500 BC to have progressed to astronomy, mathematics, and in mining for metals such as gold, silver, lead, copper, tin, etc, and to the sciences to exact the combination of metals to produce bronze and so on. The British also founded and developed in some of their own specific sciences of inventing the furnace, to metallurgy and smelting and moulding, and all this did not happen overnight, did it?

"Stonehenge Atlantis"

This documentary is of the Mesolithic period, of finds of refined artefacts' found on the seabed around the British Isles recently. These areas are dated from around and after 30,000 BC were flooded by glacial ice melt along with glacial rebound, which lowered the southern land to be submerged. The TV presenter stated that the archaeological world would have to take a U-turn on their thinking, that these middle stone-age peoples were ignorant hunter-gatherers.

I note here that very intelligent British people were at this frontline point and settled on the land at and across the ice-shelf, particularly at the catchment area of the Gulf Stream running into the west coast of Britain and up against the ice-shelf, bringing in superb fishing etc.

In this area and particularly on the Gower Peninsula there is ritual burial evidence of the Red-Man of Paviland, provisionally dated at about ,30-24000 BC, which evidences that it is these people who pioneered along this latitude. It seems that my findings and format are now being utilised by certain archaeologists, which is the old Roman filch Ploy.

"Britain's Drowned World"

In this documentary (regarding the latter) it now seems that the "Time Team" also takes up this story:-

Clearly the human bone finds by the Dutch, in what they call "Doggerland" are evidenced to be that of the short thick-set Neanderthal, which supports my theory's that the British from Boxgrove-man who was at least six foot tall, dated at about 500,000 BC; and up to the Red Man of Paviland who also had modern human features, dated at about 30 - 24,000 BC resided in front of Neanderthal; which is further corroborated with human bones found on Caldy Island West Wales, also dated at about 30,000 BC, who are our true ancestors.

I also note that the British had progressed from the flint knives, and arrowheads, which were found in great quantities near the Paviland Caves, to use the discarded microlith chips for small hand knife-like blades, by using up these smaller chips from the actually making the arrowheads.

These hand-knives were better suited for carving up the meat, or for harpoon design; and logically because these microliths were readily available it was a much easier innovation for novices to utilise these than make a full blown knife or arrowhead point from one piece of flint; which undoubtedly many fractured or snapped. So it was wrong for the TV presenter to insinuate that the British were poor innovators to make microliths into blades, to further note that they were not found in Europe, to try to suggest that the Europeans were somehow superior to the British, is apparently incorrect.

I must also remind the TV presenter that the British progressed into astronomy, mathematics, mining, smelting and stone and lost-wax forging of combinations of metals, progressing from 30,000 BC and up to 3,500 BC and thereafter. Here again in these TV programs you can see the use of the format of my book, for I theorised all of the latter pre these programs.

"Great British History"

In this documentary about "King Arthur's Round Table Revealed", clearly the table was not revealed, and what has the amphitheatre at Chester they trump up got to do with any round table; so why this continual disingenuous speculation? I must ask here, are we British taxpayers paying some academics to brainwash the British, which academics clearly despise and racially call the British ethnic, Taliban, Al-Qaeda, barbarian ignorant terrorist savages?

Apparently from the evidence it can be extrapolated that the Roman fort of Deva in Chester, (was once a British site) which was raised to the earth at least twice by the only candidates to do so were the "United British" up to 410 AD.

Likewise the British obliterated Calleva Atrebatum in the south, possibly in a cleansing of the earth ritual in both instances, to destroy any Roman remnants from British soil. Including the burying of the Roman "slaughter" tether stone the TV presenter cited.

Evidently, anywhere the Romans cowardly killed and crucified the British, the British erected shrines in those places in honour and remembrance of the brave Britons who died for Britain.

I see these academics cannot refute the many graves of the invading Romans and Saxons that were wiped out by the British, who were actually allowed honorably burials by the British. It was not so for the many British who died at the hands of Romans or Saxons though.

As historical evidences predict, the possible best defense areas of the British at this time were in their areas in and around the Silurian, Dumnonii, Brigantes and Cauci regions, which are in the areas of Britain of which the Saxons named Wales, Cornwall, Scotland and Ireland, using all the "original" British drover roads and systems.

Possibly, a British King called Arthur was from the Silurian area, within a mostly United Britain in his time.

Apparently the Romans could not keep the British at bay in certain regions up to 410 AD, and then I am sure that no defecting Roman rabble or Saxons could have after 410 AD, as TV presenters suggests.

The TV presenter insinuates that the Celtic Dragon was a Saxon or Parthian icon, but the evidence is paramount that the Celtic Draig Goch extends from the many named islands and the sleeping dragon image of the Preseli hills outcrop of many years BC, and was also a feature of the British hornpipe (and Viking connections).

"Treasure of the Anglo Saxons"

In this following documentary, It seems the TV presenter fails to realise that the British existed through any period, and that the main reason the Romans and subsequent factions invaded Britain was to try take over the British technology's, mining, metallurgy, agriculture and wealth etc, and most importantly to create their "golden goose" slave nation in the southeast of Britain.

The Romans knew the British did not write anything down, and so wrote anything of British historical value as Roman innovation, as the Romans had evidently done at Carthage.

Logically, the Saxons (and Normans) invaded Britain to inherit a Roman setup of an in-house slave nation to bend to their every immoral need and to use the British to make weapons and finely crafted metalwork and art etc.

This TV presenter then referenced a field at Stafford, but this reference actually evidences that the Saxons must have been defeated by the British, and the (British) steel of the these weapons etc was thereafter used again for British swords and they buckled the gold and silver to bury for later British use. So in reality the metalwork the presenter talks about was in fact British metalwork with Saxon designs incorporating the far superior British Celtic designs within. Understandably, designs and art progressed and work was copied and improved, so to say that any Saxon work was far superior to British work is a misconception, particularly when it was the British slave craftsmen that were producing it. If you own a dog you do not bark yourself, just as detestable people that controlled a slave nation would use the enslaved to produce their metalwork and for their "every" immoral need.

The presenter then said that St Augustine (the so called missionary of 597) viewed Angle slaves in the Roman slave market, to comment they were Angels not Angles. However at this time they would have been British slaves in a despicable Angle (Saxon) slave market, which Augustine must have condoned.

Augustine did not ask that these British children be freed, did he?

It is no wonder that the Saxons Vikings and the Normans invaded after the Romans, wanting a piece of this golden goose slave setup for themselves. And you would not kill all of your golden geese, would you?

"The God Delusions"

In this documentary, firstly I do agree with the TV presenter who stated that science is the best evidence of evolution (is of nature). Just as the British of BC realised that the natural courses of life are of nature. To respect the Sun as the Father the Moon as the Seed and Mother Earth, is an analogy of 'Man with Woman and Child as Family' is apparent throughout nature.

Yet the presenter actually refutes evolution by saying that our life on this earth is all there is, but surely he must agree that there is a soul, or should I say an intelligence that is separate from the flesh that can evolve into a higher power or condition.

The TV presenter then suggested that homosexuality is an accepted practice. But I must say that I have highlighted the Roman (Nazi) 'unnatural homosexuality and paedophilia' of which apparently British morality did not accept.

The presenter suggested that these unnatural practices are now rife in the Catholic Church (is the Papal regime of which Constantine had apparently high-jacked Christianity for "Roman Catholic" use) which is not so different from most factions the presenter cited which also preach hell and damnation in order to brainwash (meme) control to live off the masses.

"Digging for Britain"

In this documentary this TV presenter at last cites that people resided in the British Isles in front of Neanderthal at about 800,000 BC, but wrongly added that we are not descended from them because they would have been wiped out by the ice age. How can this TV presenter be so categorically sure of her comment when apparently the indigenous North American Indians retreat to a temperate climate, from their ancestral homes, when it got "progressively" colder at certain times "over many thousands of years". More than possibly the indigenous British did the same.

The TV presenter then cited what she described as the oldest rock art in Britain at Creswell Crags, of a deer and a bird dated at about 12,000 BC; but the presenter again failed to cite the Paviland caves on the Gower Peninsula in South-West Wales. The latter warm Gulf Stream location is possibly where the British also retreated to in a more temperate clime; where the skeleton of the "Red Man", with tangible items of flints arrowheads and sculptured artefacts' of drilled periwinkle and fox incisors adornments and mammoth teeth are evidenced that he resided here, dated up to and after 30,000 BC.

The presenter said the Creswell Crags people were hunter gatherers, but this presenter failed to recognise that the British Isles was partly covered by the ice shelf at this time, with the Gulf Stream running into a catchment area of land and ice-shelf near and above the Paviland caves area where they has settled to reside.

Understandably at these times, the hunting and fishing would have been very good indeed, which allowed the pioneering British people to have settled here, for they could not go any further north, but from this ideal settlement area could work behind and across the ices shelf west and east.

The TV presenter rightly evidenced there were people on the Orkneys making pottery, growing barley and herding sheep and cattle at about 4,000 BC, but failed to grasp the fact that it would have taken about 26,000 years for the ice shelf to have retreated from the area of Paviland, to the Orkneys.

The presenter identified mundane beaker pottery was made throughout Britain at about 2,500 BC and said the British people were very mobile. Surely children could have made mundane pottery, and logically these people were mobile, so why state the obvious?

The term Beaker People (of the mundane pottery) is another academic misconception to suggest that the British are German; and I must say that the names Ireland, Scotland, Wales and England are Saxon names, for the British name for the British Isles was Britan or Britanishan with many British Clan regional names.

The presenter cited British finds at Sercombe in South Devon which yielding tin-ingots, iron-ore and refined gold work, possibly for export dated at 2,300 BC; so why do they contradict themselves later, to infer that anything good is Roman or Saxon?

In Forteviot Scotland a burial was described as a Celtic Chieftain, which turned up a magnificent crafted dagger, a dog skeleton, with the tender act of placing flowers, for the presenter to say a complex society developed. But the presenter failed to relate all this to the British technology's and sciences and of the industrial mining and smelting on the Great Orme from at least 3,500 BC. "British Made" artefacts are not Roman Saxon or Norman are they?

The evidence is that the British were first to domesticate and train the dog; and the 4 headed dog ring the TV presenter exampled in these finds from 3,500 BC 'which represents protection from all quarters' can only be of British workmanship; as evidenced above was made by the British.

"The Incredible Human Journey"

In this documentary, again the evidences are misread, for clearly the British finds dated at 980,000 BC, and Boxgrove man from at least 500,000 BC, and the cave burial and associated finds of the Red Man of Paviland on the Gower Peninsular dated to at least 30,000 BC, is evidences of a specific front line British Nation.
This Nation would have exclusively settled in a fruitful landfall to ice-shelf Gulf Stream catchment area, in the farthest habitation northwest. Going further north was not possible up against a 100-meter thick ice-mass that was not accessible by any person or animal.

One “academic” said that the Chinese were a specific species. Perhaps correct, because DNA evidence only proves that people mixed, and by the passage of at least 980,000 years of mixing DNA I do not think you can prove a person is from an original specific species out of Africa; as the “TV presenter” said you could.

The latter is evidenced by perhaps British whites (not out of Africa) pioneering east to mix with darker skinned people along this latitude, as the presenter suggested these brown colour people possibly pioneered north; and perhaps travelled the coast around Alaska to colonize down the west coast of America, in a more recent temperate climate. The relevance the TV presenter misses is that British people evolved or were first in the British Isles areas, who are the only candidates to have pioneered west; and also east on this latitude from at least 20,000 BC.

Black people it seems remained behind in Africa and possibly pioneered east by a different lower latitude route. However the TV presenter suggests that it was only black people that came out of Africa, she said had turned white because of a vitamin "D" deficiency, and had arrived in the British Isles area, and that cannot be correct. I say the latter because rickets would have wiped out all whites and no rickets have been detected in any British skeletal finds. Or from being so weak would have been wiped out by beasts. I cannot imagine a vast Nation evolving from black people with a vitamin D deficiency or Rickets, to remain white and healthy, can you?

It is possible that the British colonised the British Isles from where they originated or had migrated.

I suggest the latter because Pangaea as we know had dispersed from its magma epicenter, of which academics say was Africa. If the latter is so then of course the outer regions of the Earths crust from the baron magma epicenter are where humans could have first originated and evolved, whence vertebrates first ventured from sea to land from about the Silurian period. Thereafter people could only have migrated back into Africa.

When the Americas plate separated from the British Isles perhaps it was below sea and had not developed any substance for human evolution, because no human evidence have been found there yet as I know of, that is older than about 20,000 BC.

It amazes me that some TV presenters and authors always present their theories as a matter of fact when clearly it is not.

"The History of Ancient Britain"

This seems to be a copy of the format of my book.

Surely British history should mainly feature in any teaching of the British people in order to acknowledge the magnificent "British" early achievements up to and after the Roman and following slave masters. The Ancient British are sometimes called "The Lost Nation". Is the correct description - "The Hidden Nation"?

Other interesting sites: I list a small amount of other sites to visit, you may find more from other sources, such as I have suggested herein and in the Museums I have also listed following:

At Llanwrthwl Church, Powys is a font which is carved with four heads projecting from its round bowl, and this is considered to be an echo of the British cult of the head, a possible link back to the Pendragon (Head-Leader).

At Garn Fadron, Gwynedd, covering an area of approximately 5,500 square yards, is an Iron Age hill fort. The main ramparts enclose some 1,000 square yards of the hilltop, and inner defences enclose foundations of round huts.

Garn Boduan, Gwynedd, is a large hill fort, which lasted until the 12th century. There are remains of 170 round huts within this area of approximately 1,500 square yards

At Old Oswestry, Shropshire is an impressive Silurian Iron Age hill fort in the Marches.

Castell Odo, on the Lleyn Peninsula, Gwynedd, is a Bronze Age to a 300 BC Iron Age settlement with double bank defences and round huts.

Din Lligwy, Anglesey, is a British settlement with round and square stone huts and workshops with walled defences.

Ty Mawr, Anglesey, is another Iron Age settlement; remains can be seen of about 50 circular huts. Archaeological evidence from this site proves that Britons inhabited it before, during and after the Roman occupation of Britain.

Caer y Twr, Anglesey, is an Iron Age hill fort on the summit of Holyhead Mountain.

Britons' sacred wells are also prevalent in Wales, such as the Gwynedd and Fawr healing wells, dating back to the 6th century, on the Lleyn Peninsula.

St Winefride's Well, Holywell, Flintshire is the most important holy well in Britain and has been a place of pilgrimage before and since the 7th century. The story of Winefride and the healing properties of the water from this well is likely a continuation from its earlier use by the ancient Britons.

At Knocknakilla, County Cork, there is a 5-stone circle with 2 stones approximately 4 ½ yards high.

Bohonagh, Cork, has a circle with stones in line with the solstice.

At Drombeg, County Cork, there is a stone circle in line with the midwinter solstice. Here is evidence of two hut circles and cooking activity. A central pit held the cremated bones of a youth.

Lettergorman, Cork, is a four-stone arrangement.

At Ballynoe, County Down, there is a large stone circle with double portals and outer layers; with a mound containing cists and cremations from the Bronze Age.

At Grange, County Limerick, you will see 2 tall stones and a raised bank circle of about 50 yards in diameter. Nearby are remains of a small and a large circle.

At Lios, County Limerick, there is an approximately 60 square yard embanked circle with two tall stones, perhaps used for sighting the solstice degree.

Beltany Donegal is a circle with standing stones in line with the solstice.

At Pobull Fhinn, North Uist, Outer Hebrides, is a stone circle, overlooking lochs and moorland, aligned with the solstices.

At Beaghmore, County Tyrone, there are seven stone circles with cairns between them. Burial cists found here contained pottery, charcoal, flints and broken skull fragments, dated to about 1,500 BC.

Callanish, Lewis, on the Outer Hebrides, is a small circle with a great central pillar with a passage-tomb added to it, dated to about 2,750 BC.

Skomer Island, Pembrokeshire, is covered with the remains of huts and walled cultivation sites dating from the Bronze and Iron Ages.

Nash Point Fort, Llantwit Major, is a Silurian hill fort with 4 ramparts and ditches.

Tre'r Ceiri, Gwynedd, is one of the most impressive hill fort sites in Wales; there are remains of at least 50 huts and the site is topped by a Bronze Age cairn.

Caerleon, near Newport, is known for its Arthurian connection and it is said that King Arthur lived and was crowned here, the place where his knights gathered at the round table assembly.

Tredegar Camp, Newport, is a Silurian Iron Age hill fort with ramparts, which later became surrounded by a medieval motte and bailey.

At Ruthin, Denbigh, in the Clwydian Hills, there are four Iron Age hill forts.

St Eliseg's Pillar, Denbighshire, is an approximately 3-yard-high pillar, erected in the 9th century by Cyngan, in memory of his great grandfather, Eliseg, a king, who annexed Powys from the English. The earlier cairn on which it stands was found to contain remains of a British chieftain; his skull was gilded as a sign of respect to an ancestor of the Powys line, Fynnon Gybi, Llangybi.

At Conwy Mountain is an Iron Age hill fort with at least 60 round hut foundations surrounded by a rampart. Clearly the British Isles had progressed to a nation of regional status of educated Britons who could manage their own areas, just as we do today.

Pen-y-Corddin, Conwy, is one of the major Iron Age hill forts in North Wales; it sits on a coastal rock mass, protected on three sides by sheer cliff, with several remnants of huts.

Pen Dinas, Ceredigion, is an Iron Age hill fort, which has twin summits, individually fortified and protected by ditches and lower walls.

Craig Rhiwarth, Llangynog, Powys, is a British Iron Age hill fort site with the remains of many stone huts.

Pen-y-Gaer, Powys, is a small hill fort with the remains of an outer stone wall defence.

Pen-y-Gaer, Conwy, is another hill fort.

Strata Florida, near Lampeter, Carmarthenshire, is an area that was taken over by the Cistercian monks in AD 1,164, but the ruins there today are of the 12th-century church, which for 200 years was the religious, political and academic centre of Wales. It was here that Llewelyn the Great gathered the assembly of Welsh princes in 1,238, to swear allegiance to his son Dafydd. This area was occupied from at least the Bronze Age.

At Craig Gwrtheyrn, Carmarthenshire, above the river Teifi, is a hill fort surrounded by stone defences.

The Clwydian Hills are lined with four Iron Age hill forts.

Carmarthen's Welsh name is Caerfyrddin and, legend has it that Merlin (Myrddin) was born here; he was the grandson of a king. A priory once stood on the site of St Peter's church and it was also here that the Black Book of Carmarthen, the oldest existing manuscript in Welsh, was written in the 12th century. This document is now in the National Library of Wales, Aberystwyth.

On the south side of Snowdonia, at Beddgelert, is the hill fort of the Royal Chair, held by Emrys.

At Llanbedr-y-Cennin, Conwy, is the hill-fort of Pen-y-Gaer, which has three ramparts and two areas of sharp pointed stones in the lower defences. These hill forts are, conceivably, the forerunners of many of the strategically built defences we see today, for you can see the remnants of these early building strategies used in later defensive constructions.

Near Llangollen, in Denbighshire, is Castle Dinas Bran, initially a Bronze Age site, then later an Iron Age hill fort.

At Machrie Moor, Isle of Arran, are seven stone circles and cairns.

At Balnuaran, Inverness, are two Bronze Age tombs with passageways aligned to the midwinter sunset.

Aviemore, Inverness, has a cairn with the remains of a stone circle.

Cothiemuir Wood, Aberdeenshire, has a stone circle; near the centre is a cist, with cup-marks on the outer face of the main stone.

Glenquickan, Kirkcudbrightshire, has a circle and a standing pillar that is approximately 2 yards high.

Croft Moraig, Perthshire, is a circle of 12 stones, with two more forming an entrance to a half circle of tall stones.

At Easter Aquorthies, Aberdeenshire, are more stone circles.

At Grey Croft Cumbria, is a 12-stone circle.

At Sunhoney Aberdeenshire, is another stone circle.

At Loanhead Daviot is a stone circle with ring cairn and a cup-marked stone. The main stone, which is in line with the southernmost moonset, may be consistent with the 19-years' moon phase, inline with the midwinter sunset.

At Goatstones, Northumberland, is a four-post cup-marked tomb about 5 yards square, showing a habitual theme found throughout the British Isles.

Castlerigg, Cumbria, has a stone circle with an entrance to the north and a tall pillar to the south, in line with the Candle mass sunrise in early February.

At Grey Croft, Cumbria is a 12-stone circle of about 30 yards diameter, with a central cairn, with evidence of cremation and finds of flint microliths and a jet ring.

At Arbor Low, Derbyshire is a stone circle henge.

Avebury, Wiltshire, started as two small circles; it was further expanded on the same lines of design as Stonehenge and is the largest of all stone circles.

The Sanctuary, Wiltshire, has the remnants of a ring, which it is said may have been a Neolithic burial chamber. The site lies near several Bronze Age round barrows.

At Boscawen-Un Cornwall, is a circle of stones with a central pillar.

Brisworthy, Devon, is a stone circle henge.

At Down Tor, Devon, is a stone circle and cairn. There is also evidence of huts near this site.

At Fernworthy, Devon, is a circle of 30 stones.

Stanton Drew, Somerset, is a stone circle of about 120 yards across; there are two smaller rings nearby, with avenues leading down to the river Chew.

At Grey Wethers, Devon, are 2 approximately 30-yard diameter stone circles.

At Kergonan, Brittany, is a huge, approximately 90 by 60 yard site aligned to the midsummer sunset.

At Kerlescan, Brittany, is an approximately 90 by 60 yard avenue aligned to a huge 240 by 240 yard horseshoe arrangement.

At Menec, West Brittany, is a stone-arched arrangement covering approximately 90 by 60 yards, with a 90-yard avenue of stones running to it.

At Crucuno, Brittany, is a rectangular tomb perfectly aligned with the solstices.

At St Just, Brittany, there are 2 megalithic rows of stones and a four-post passage-tomb; there is also a small cromlech and other archaeological items.

The Isles of Scilly, which were once also joined to mainland Britain, are also known as the Isles of Samson. Archaeological investigation here made finds dated to about 2,050 BC; with Bronze and Iron Age artefacts and ancient field boundaries.

Quite evidently, the British exist!

MUSEUMS TO VISIT

Cyfarthfa Castle Museum Merthyr Tydfil

Museum of Welsh Antiquities, Margam

Scolton Manor Country Park Museum, Swansea

National Museum of Wales, Cardiff

St Fagans, Welsh Folk Museum, Cardiff

Royal Institution of South Wales Museum

Oriel Museum, Newport

Brecknock Museum in Shire Hall Brecon,

County Museum Carmarthen

Tenby Museum

Llandrindod Wells Museum

Grosvenor Museum

National Museum of Wales, Bangor

Margani Stones Museum, Chester

Powysland Museum, Llangefni, Anglesey

Royal Museum of Scotland, Edinburgh

Rowley's House Museum, Shrewsbury,

British Library, London

National Museum of Ireland, Dublin

Trinity College, Dublin

Ulster Museum, Belfast

Index

Authorities and Authors

Bibliography

There is a lot of written material about archeological finds and historical events in books and on the Internet just type in a good keyword and that should link you up. Some books are listed following, which will link you to other books.

Prehistoric Britain by James Dyer ISBN 0571098835.

Prehistoric Britain by R R Sellman (Methuan's & Co Ltd).

Prehistoric Stone Circles by Aubrey Burl ISBN 0747806098.

The Astronomical Significance of Stonehenge by C A Newman (Moon Publications).

The Church of St. Brynach NEVERN Pembrokeshire. E L Jones & Son, Printers, Cardigan.

Bronze Age Copper Mining by William O'Brien ISBN 0747803218.

The Bronze Age in Barbarian Europe by Jaques Briard (Book Club Associates London).

Iron Age Britain by Barry Cunliffe ISBN 071388395.

The Inca Trail by Richard Danbury ISBN 187375664X

Celtic Wales by Pitkin Guides ISBN 0853727988.

Celtic Britain by Lloyd Laing ISBN 0586083731.

Later Celtic Art in Britain and Ireland by Lloyd Laing ISBN 0852638744.

The Invisible hand by Victor Dunstan ISBN 0946922004.

In Search of Wales by H V Morton (Methuen & Co Ltd).

Heroes and Warriors BOUDICEA Warrior Queen of the Celts ISBN 1853140023.

Searching for the Silures an Iron Age Tribe in SOUTH-EAST WALES by Ray Howell ISBN 0752440144.

A. WALI

CW01640382

COLOUR-MUSIC

THE ART OF MOBILE COLOUR

PREFATORY NOTES

BY

HUBERT VON HERKOMER

AND

W. BROWN

Elibron Classics

www.elibron.com

Elibron Classics series.

© 2005 Adamant Media Corporation.

ISBN 1-4021-2612-3 (paperback)
ISBN 1-4021-2611-5 (hardcover)

This Elibron Classics Replica Edition is an unabridged facsimile of the edition published in 1912 by Hutchinson & Co., London.

Elibron and Elibron Classics are trademarks of Adamant Media Corporation. All rights reserved.

This book is an accurate reproduction of the original. Any marks, names, colophons, imprints, logos or other symbols or identifiers that appear on or in this book, except for those of Adamant Media Corporation and BookSurge, LLC, are used only for historical reference and accuracy and are not meant to designate origin or imply any sponsorship by or license from any third party.

COLOUR-MUSIC

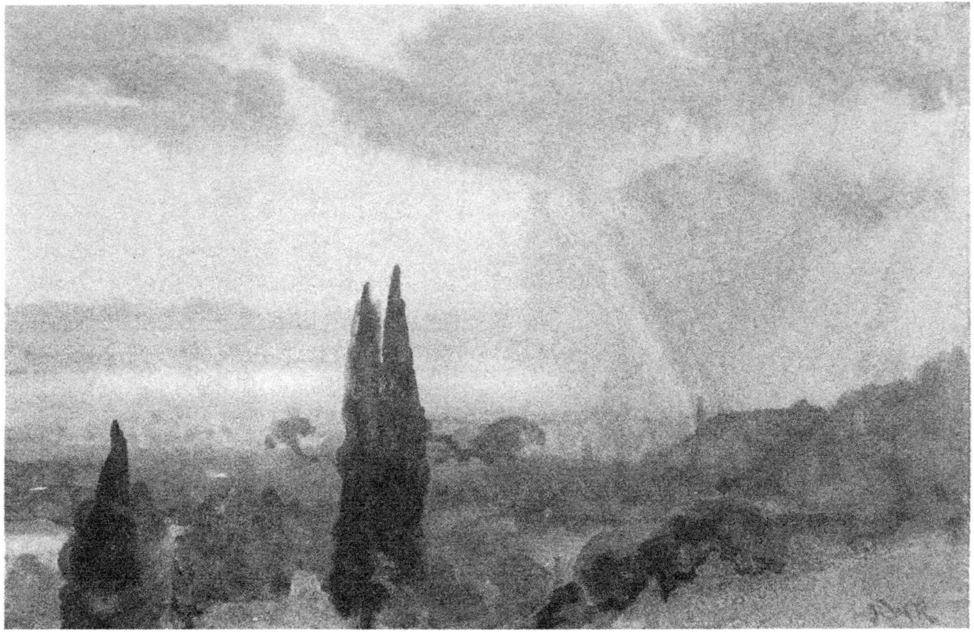

NATURE'S COLOUR SCALE.

Frontispiece.

COLOUR-MUSIC

THE ART OF MOBILE COLOUR

BY

A. WALLACE RIMINGTON

A.R.E., R.B.A.

PROFESSOR OF FINE ARTS, QUEEN'S COLLEGE, LOND.

WITH ILLUSTRATIONS

PREFATORY NOTES

BY

SIR HUBERT VON HERKOMER, R.A, M.V.O.

AND

DR. W. BROWN, King's Coll., Lond.

London: HUTCHINSON & CO.

Paternoster Row 1912

AUTHOR'S PREFACE

THE interest aroused in the whole subject of Colour-Music seems to have become so widespread, and I have received so many inquiries with regard to it, that a short volume giving a brief description of the present position of the new art, and replying to some of the questions that are frequently asked about it, may perhaps not be unwelcome. Hitherto it has hardly seemed advisable to publish a book upon the subject, because fresh experimental work and frequent modifications of the instruments used in the production of Colour-Music have carried the art further and further into the field of the untried, but some statement of what has been and is being done should perhaps not be further delayed.

In writing these pages I have felt myself to be addressing two classes of readers, namely, those who know something of the art of

Mobile Colour, its past history, its hopes and its aims; and others who have never even heard of the subject. To the former, including, as it does, many of those who have followed and assisted in the experimental work carried out by me for a good many years past, I would take this opportunity of expressing my thanks for the keen interest they have shown in it, and the many excellent suggestions I have received from them; and, from the latter, I would ask for as open-minded a consideration of the subject as they can give me, more especially in view of the difficulty of placing it before them without being able, at the same time, to give practical demonstration of some of the points dealt with.

Upon a subject so new misconceptions are sure to arise again and again; but in the present statement of the case for Colour-Music, I have used my best endeavours to guard against them, and, discarding much more that might have been said from the artistic and technical standpoint, to write as clearly and simply as possible. I make no claim to absolute originality of conception with regard to the whole matter. Since I first took up the question of the need for, and possibility of, such an art as Colour-Music, it has come to my knowledge that even from very early times—perhaps prior to the Christian era—the possibility has been alluded to by various writers, and, in the sixteenth century, it took somewhat more tangible form in the mind of a Jesuit, Lewis Bertrand Castel. It was also referred to in an eloquent passage by the late Mr. R. H. Haweis, which I have quoted, with regretful memory of the author, in the Appendix, Mr. Haweis having afterwards become one of the warmest supporters of the forms given to the new art.

Starting from my original belief in the need for and the importance of such an art, which, when I first conceived of it, I supposed to have been hitherto unthought of, my personal part has been to devise instruments for bringing it into practical being and to develop, through a long series of experiments, some of the principles upon which Colour-Music compositions can be produced. This has demanded the expenditure of much time and thought upon the construction and reconstruction of successive instruments and experimental apparatus, and I have been tempted further and further in the direction of fresh modifications and improvements which have necessarily meant long delays. It took centuries to evolve an instrument like the pianoforte, and therefore no excuse need be made for the amount of time which it has required to produce the Colour-Organ and its allied instruments. Others will, I hope, in their turn, improve the forms and powers of these, and build upon the foundations I have laid. The development of Colour-Music is not a commercial undertaking, and I have no wish to exclude rivals, but rather to welcome them.

I should wish to express my indebtedness for valuable advice and assistance—or personal interest in the experimental work—received from the late Sir George Grove, Sir Wyke Bayliss, Capt. W. B. Marling, Mr. W. Basil Wilberforce, Mr. De Vere Barrow, Sir Hubert von Herkomer, and Professor Gregory, amongst many others; also to

Professor Silvanus Thompson and Dr. W. Brown, who have made suggestions as to the chapters of this book dealing respectively with the physical and psychological aspects of the subject. The notes contributed by the latter and by Sir Hubert von Herkomer will, I am sure, be read with special interest.

Whatever may be the divergencies of opinion as to how far the analogies between colour and sound extend, one thing at least is certain, namely, that Colour-Music opens up a new world of beauty and interest as yet, to a great extent, unexplored.

A. W. R.

INTRODUCTORY NOTE

BY

SIR HUBERT VON HERKOMER, R.A., M.V.O.

THE analogy of music to colour has occupied many minds, but, so far as I know, no attempt has been made before to bring it within the scope of physical demonstration; therein lies the great value of Mr. Wallace Rimington's pioneer work in this fascinating field of thought. Although he calls his chief instrument, for the present, a "Colour-Organ," he does not propose to prove by means of it that certain waves of light have their exact parallel in certain waves of sound. He uses the musical keyboard merely as a convenience, and has, for the same purpose, split up the spectrum-band in accordance with the musical octave, but he does not necessarily base his general contentions upon any such division.

One of the instruments with a musical keyboard, which the author has designed, and by means of which he projects his colour on to a screen, can be either mute, or made to produce musical sounds simultaneously with the colour.

It has been denied by some that colour suggests musical sounds, and that musical sounds suggest colour. But it is safe to say that a psychological affinity *is felt* by artists and musicians between sound and colour, hence the use of common terms of expression between them. The painter speaks of a *note* in a painting, and a musician of a *tone picture.*

Amongst other claims put forward by the author is that of providing a new source of pleasure—a new art appealing to the mind and the senses—by means of colour alone, without form. But I see something besides all this in it—I see in it something "medicinal" for the painter, a "tonic" for the colour-sense of the artist, a suggester, a corrector, and a purifier.

Most painters in their career pass through several colour phases in their work that are difficult to account for. If there is such a thing as habits of thought (and we know there is), one may declare that there is such a thing as habits of colour in the painter. These habits of colouring will enable the spectator to spot a certain painter's work at a glance, and I cannot see that a painter's work can keep fresh and vigorous if he plays on one "note" of colour throughout his life.

Let me here say that the colour-sense is by far the most sensitive and delicate of all the faculties that go to the making of the artist's brain. The sense of *form* is far more robust and can bear severe handling. For instance, a painter can, by pegging away from a model, get his drawing right in the end, that faculty having something physical in it. Not so with colour; no pegging away can make colour good in a picture. Hence the painter surrounds himself with all manner of richly coloured rugs and hangings, in order to stimulate his sense of colour. I can, therefore, see clearly that an invaluable *tonic* could be given to the painter's colour-sense by means of Mr. Rimington's instrument for the production of mobile colour, even without necessarily laying stress on the affinity to music.

To sit at this instrument and improvise for half an hour whilst watching the ever-varying combinations of colour on the screen produced by the playing is not only an unspeakable delight, but of real health-giving effect on the sense of colour. How much more valuable as a stimulant is mobile colour than the fixed colours of a rug, which the eye gets accustomed to, and which thereby act no longer *as a tonic.*

Perhaps the author has in some measure overstated his case; but much allowance must be made for the enthusiasm of the pioneer. It may be questioned, for example, whether the contemplation of formless colour will call forth such great pleasure in the majority of people as the author believes; whether the close analogy of colour to music will hold good in as many respects as he also claims. In fact, many questions of doubt may arise in the reader's mind. But there is so much in the author's experiments, opening out such vistas of possibilities, that the whole matter should be carefully investigated before judgment is given. Without holding a brief for the author, I, for one, believe in the potentialities of his new departure.

An introduction such as this must necessarily be short, therefore I cannot enter into the thousand and one ramifications that surround this fascinating subject. But to sum up briefly, Mr. Rimington's mobile colour system seems to me a method to enable one to *see sound* and *hear colour.*

BUSHEY, HERTS,
July, 1911.

NOTE

UPON THE PSYCHOLOGICAL ASPECTS OF COLOUR-MUSIC

By DR. W. BROWN

CONSIDERED from the points of view of the psycho-physics and psychology of visual and auditory sensations, a colour-music art seems full of promise. The analogies existing between these two realms of experience are numerous and, in many cases, very close—probably even closer than the majority of psychologists have hitherto been ready to admit. Too much stress should not be laid on the discrepancies between the quantitative stimulus-relations in the two cases, since the question is primarily a psychological one, and such discrepancies are not sufficiently pronounced to detract from the significance of analogies arrived at on purely psychological evidence. The emotional influences of colour, as those of sound, are obvious and beyond dispute, and the scheme of introducing rhythm—i.e. the time relation—into colour combinations opens up an entirely new field of investigation which psychologists will not be slow in exploring. Whatever the future of colour-music may be on the plane of æsthetic production and appreciation—and it seems to be exceedingly hopeful—the theory cannot fail to be of the greatest importance and productiveness for future research in the domain of the psychology of colour.

King's Coll., Lond.,
July, 1911.

CONTENTS

ILLUSTRATIONS

COLOUR-MUSIC

CHAPTER I

A MOBILE COLOUR ART

HITHERTO there has been no pure colour art, that is to say, no art dealing solely with colour for its own sake as music deals with sound.

Colour has held a secondary position in all the arts into which it enters, or has only been used jointly with other means of appealing to the senses or the emotions—and it has always been more or less associated with form. We are accustomed to see colour, if it is used at all, combined with form, and employed chiefly to emphasize and explain form, or to add interest and beauty to it, as, for instance, in painting and architecture, in decoration, and in other arts, and we can hardly realize its existence apart from form.

But though, in the case of sound, the great art of music has been created, no such art with colour for its main object has yet been built up. There is, however, no reason why this should continue to be so, or why a great colour art analogous to the art of music should not be developed.

Colour-Music, or the Art of Mobile Colour, is the art which fills this gap, and which after some years of the experimental stage now seems to call for further statement of its claims for consideration. That the development of a pure colour art of this kind has been so long delayed in the history of the world has probably been due, in great measure, to the fact that, although colour is capable of providing almost as much pleasure and interest as sound, and, as I shall hope to show, has quite as great, or even greater, power of appealing to the emotions, it is a far more difficult matter to devise an instrument suitable for the production of colour, and for placing it under the control of an executant, than to construct one for the production of musical sound.

It is, in fact, hard to imagine, and still more

so to design, any such colour instrument; whereas in the earliest periods a reed or a conch shell has been easily converted into a means of producing music, and almost every race has devised its own musical instruments at an early stage of its civilization.

The non-existence of a pure colour art has from time to time been more or less recognized and commented upon, but, owing probably to the difficulties just referred to, nothing has come of it.

Within the last twenty or thirty years, however, a desire to study and enjoy colour for its own sake has sprung up, and the art of painting has tended somewhat to devote itself to the production of pictures in which colour is the chief factor, and Whistler and others, with some appreciation of musical analogies, have gone as far as to call their pictorial works "harmonies" and "symphonies." But in most pictures colour has necessarily remained subservient, to some extent, to their subjects, and in any case a picture cannot give more than one colour scheme, or the solution of a very few problems in colour within the boundaries of its frame. Once painted, moreover, that scheme, harmony, symphony, or whatever the artist may call it, remains fixed and unaltered. At most it is a chord or two of colour, or a single colour-phrase, even though much may be sacrificed in expression of the subject of the picture, or even in truth to nature, to make that chord or phrase harmonious and interesting.

But the desire for a more developed colour art is at the root of these attempts to force painting to do almost more than it can legitimately or successfully attempt, and to sacrifice subject and much else to obtaining beautiful quality in colour, and an attractive colour scheme. Something, no doubt, has been gained, and the demand of the impressionist for interesting and beautiful colour at all costs is in great measure a just one ; but the result of the attempt to make painting do what it is only possible for a mobile colour art to achieve has been to cause it to abandon many of its means of appealing to the artistic faculties which we cannot afford to lose, to narrow its scope, and weaken its position.

On the other hand, an art like that of colour music devoted solely to colour gives us what the finest impressionist or expressionist—even Turner and the greatest artists—can never give.

Experiment has moreover shown it to be certain that such an art has the power of appealing to the emotions to an extent which it is difficult for those to realize who have never seen it, and is capable of giving somewhat similar æsthetic and emotional enjoyment to that given by music, but appealing to and developing a different sense.

It may be said, with a show of reason, that pleasure and mental refreshment are not sufficient foundations for a new form of art; to which it may be replied that, even though the art of music rests mainly upon them, it is not contended that they are entirely so. The other practical advantages of a pure colour art will be dealt with later on.

Let us first see whether there is not only room for an art of this kind, but a great need for it, whether its absence under certain conditions of life does not account for some present-day tendencies towards artistic degeneration, and whether it is not worthy of our serious consideration as an influence in civilization. I propose also to show that it is not merely possible—a mere theoretical dream—but how, after some years of experiment, it has been brought into actual existence and is being further developed, and to give some description of the forms it has at present taken.

The instruments used and the results arrived at will also be described, various criticisms and objections will be replied to, and the future possibilities of the new art will be briefly foreshadowed.

CHAPTER II

THE USES OF COLOUR-MUSIC

LET us, in the first place, consider whether there is likely to be any real use for an art of the kind referred to, and what is the present position with regard to the general feeling for colour.

It may safely be said that hitherto, and especially in modern times, the colour sense has in a very large proportion of people been allowed to lie dormant, and their appreciation of colour in nature and art is extremely limited. This is probably due to there being so few means by which their attention can be directed to colour, apart from the interest it gives to the form of the objects around them. There is, in fact, a general insensitiveness to colour which we will consider more closely farther on.

Supposing an art with colour as its main object were in existence, its other advantages and uses, apart from any æsthetic pleasure and satisfaction it might give, are therefore not far to seek.

If any art is practised it tends to develop the faculties upon which it depends for its existence, and a pure colour art would thus help to restore and develop the colour sense. Experiment confirms this assertion.

If the colour sense were stimulated and developed, all those arts into which colour enters would benefit. If the painter had a more sensitive eye for colour, his pictures would be better ; the architect, with his colour faculty increased, would deal with colour to more artistic purpose in his buildings ; the craftsman would produce better colour patterns in his fabrics, his wall papers, his combinations of decorative tints, his enamels or his glass. If there were better and more harmonious colour in all the arts, the world would at least have gained something. Here, then, apart from its possible artistic and emotional value, *per se*, is a practical side to a pure colour art and an object for its existence.

It is probable, for various reasons, that at

the present time any widespread advance in the feeling for colour can only be arrived at by increased special cultivation of the colour faculty, and increased knowledge as to harmonies and contrasts and other qualities of colour; and this cultivation in its wider sense, it is contended, can best be developed by some form of mobile colour art, such, for instance, as that I have called, for want of a better term, "Colour-Music."

Apart from this, there is the increased need of such an art at the present time, because not only has there been neglect of the cultivation of the colour faculty, but because there has been an evident decay of it in most Western nations. Here and there is to be noted some slight revival of the feeling for colour, but in the main there has been a tendency for good colour to disappear from our surroundings, from costume, and from fabrics, from architecture, and from other decorative arts.

This can hardly be denied, and it would almost seem as though an advancing material civilization were inimical to colour, as Nordau and others have asserted. Be this as it may, amongst large sections of the population in many nations it is no exaggeration to say that any real feeling for colour has died out. As instances of this, take the working classes of most modern cities and even the peasantry of many European countries, amongst the majority of whom there is no evidence to be found of any real love of colour, and where enjoyment of it, except in its cruder forms, appears to have perished.

This is unquestionably a great loss, and we are only just beginning to realize its consequences and also how much the presence of good colour in our surroundings has to do with our enjoyment of life and even with our mental health. The whole subject of colour as a factor in our lives has been so neglected that its influences are not in the least realized, and it has come to be looked upon by the majority of people as concerning chiefly or solely the painter, the architect, or the decorator, and otherwise as of little importance. The extent to which colour in nature and in art, in its capacity for giving pleasure or pain, in its value for all kinds of delicate observations in science, in its artistic and emotional power, and, I might also say, its ethical influence, has been overlooked and neglected is almost beyond belief.

Perhaps this can scarcely be better shown by a single example than by the fact that the *Encyclopædia Britannica* contains no article upon colour, except from the purely optical and physical standpoint, or as a means of assisting protective devices in animals. There is hardly a word about its uses in art, or upon theories of its harmony and contrast, or those obscure questions of quality, texture, or luminosity, which are so interesting to the artist; still less anything as to the range of its action upon the mind and the emotional faculties.

It is with this emotional side of the subject that the new art of Colour-Music is chiefly concerned, and it is especially through such an art that it is possible to study the influence of colour upon our senses and upon our minds, and, through them, upon our lives.

CHAPTER III

RESEMBLANCES BETWEEN MUSIC AND MOBILE COLOUR

SOME of the contentions put forward on behalf of a mobile colour art will, of course, be questioned, if not altogether disputed by some people—especially by those to whom the subject is new, and, perhaps, not infrequently by those whose chief interests are centred in music or in science.

They will be further explained and defended as we proceed.

Meanwhile, for the sake of argument, let us assume that there is something to be said for them, and let us endeavour to make the whole question clearer by examining more carefully the points of resemblance between music and colour, and seeing what grounds there are for using the term "Colour-Music" in speaking of this new colour art.

First, let us ask ourselves, what is the place of music amongst the arts, and as an influence in modern civilization ?

If we look at the matter dispassionately, I think we shall come to the conclusion that the whole use and influence of music rests upon its power of stimulating the emotional faculties. Whether the emotions aroused by it are identical with those of our ordinary life and experience, or whether, as some philosophic writers think, they are of a somewhat different and special kind, belonging, as it were, to a higher plane of feeling, matters little for the moment. The fact remains that music interests, refreshes, invigorates, saddens, or makes us glad through its action upon the emotional side of our nature, and is a language without words, through which the mind of the musician can speak to the mind of the hearer.

For instance, it is used almost universally to stimulate religious emotions and aspirations. It helps to put the mind into an attitude for receiving religious impressions and assimilating religious truths. As it fills the vaulted roof of the cathedral and echoes through its aisles, we feel the better able to understand the thoughts and realize the faith of the builders expressed in the very stones around us.

In the concert-room, is not the mental refreshment, the keen interest aroused, and the pleasure we receive mainly due to the emotional effect of music upon us? Our admiration for the technical dexterity of the executant, as also our interest in the personality of the composer's methods, counts for something; but music which consists only of dexterities, not based upon a theme acting upon the emotional imagination—music which expresses nothing beyond mechanical perfection—surely takes a very secondary place in our estimation.

Music, again, finds another use, as Plato remarked long ago, in stimulating the military spirit, in maintaining the soldier's courage and making him forget his exhaustion.

In a word, emotion, of one kind or another, is always called into play by music, whether it be of the kind which is aroused in the concert-room or the church, in the ballroom or on the battlefield.

The foundations of music, therefore, as

has been said, rest upon this capability of arousing emotional feeling, and it seems very remarkable that so great an art, and one which makes so wide an appeal to the human race, should have been thus based and built upon these subtle psychological sensations.

The action which colour has upon us in its harmonies and contrasts, its varying strength and delicacy, its power of giving joy or pain, is also, to a large extent, an emotional one ; and if a mobile colour art be attacked because it rests upon this appeal to emotion, music must be attacked on the same grounds.

If, on the other hand, we frankly admit, as I think we must, that emotional appeal is at the root of all art, then it may well be profitable to go on and examine the further points of resemblance between a mobile colour art and music.

CHAPTER IV

THE COLOUR SCALE AND MOBILE COLOUR

COLOUR, like music, is both precious for its own sake and as an educative influence. It also can stimulate the imagination and develop other mental faculties ; can give pleasure and refreshment to the mind, and increase the responsiveness of the sense to which it appeals.

Let us, then, begin to clear our path through the jungle of untried possibilities, which prevents our seeing clearly how to use these attributes of colour in a mobile colour art somewhat resembling music.

They are so striking and so significant that, in devising any form of such an art, we can hardly escape from them.

As most of us know, according to generally accepted scientific theory all colours are produced by varying frequencies of vibration of the ether acting upon the retina of the eye, and all musical sounds by varying frequencies of air vibration acting upon the ear. Both colour and sound, as we perceive them, are due to vibrations which stimulate the optic and aural nerves respectively.

This in itself is remarkable as showing the similarity of the action of sound and colour upon us, for within the variations of frequency of these two sets of vibrations are contained all, or nearly all, the impressions we receive of pleasure and pain, beauty or ugliness, interest or dullness, both in colour and sound.

If we go a little farther we shall find a second, and perhaps almost equally remarkable, point of resemblance, though I have no wish to lay undue weight upon it, and if it could be successfully disputed, it would not in the least weaken the position of colour-music as an independent art.

All music is built upon the octave. Western nations have mostly divided it into twelve intervals or notes, and Eastern ones into more; but the octave is and must be the foundation of the division. And it is so because our ears demand it ; because we cannot escape from it ; and because for some reason of which we have no certain explanation it is in itself an inexorable psychological necessity. No sound without vibrations ; no musical notes without selection of certain definite rates of vibration carefully related to each other ; no such selection possible without reference to the octave. What, then, is the octave, looked at from the musical standpoint ?

Take any audible rate of regular air vibrations and you have a musical note. Consider it as the first note of your octave. Double the speed of its vibrations and you have the first note of the next octave above it.

Turning now from sound to colour, what do we find ?

If we experiment upon colour with suitable scientific instruments and split up colours of all kinds into their components, we arrive at the fact that all visible colours can be resolved into proportionate mixtures of those we see in the spectrum-band or the rainbow, both of which contain all the primary colours.

White light can be divided into its constituents, as we all know, by passing it through a prism. If we allow a ray of sun-light, or a beam of light obtained from an arc-lamp, to traverse a prism, after passing it through a lens and a narrow slit, and arrange the prism at a proper angle, we shall obtain a series of colours which, if received upon a white screen, spread themselves out into a long band, and range from a deep red to a very tender violet. This is the spectrum-band.

Below the red and beyond the violet are other rays, or other colours, which our eyes cannot see; but confining ourselves to those which are visible, and comparing this band of colours with the musical octave, we shall find at least one very remarkable point of resemblance.

If we get the physicist to measure the speed of the vibrations of the ether at the red and violet end of the band respectively, we shall find that, as in the case of the last note of the musical octave, the latter has approximately double the number of vibrations. The octave of colour is in fact practically complete, and a counterpart of the musical octave as regards the range of vibrations which produce it. It does not extend to the first note of the octave above it, but it constitutes one nearly complete octave in itself.

To make this quite clear let us place the two scales one above the other.[1]

Of course the selection of the note C as a starting-point of comparison is purely arbitrary. All that it is wished to show is that, recognizing the musical octave as the physiological basis of music, there is a corresponding octave of colour with its lowest and highest points also separated by a proportionate increase of speed of vibrations.

This is a very remarkable fact, and would seem to point to some common foundation or organic basis in nerve structure, or in mental constitution for receiving both colour and musical impressions. Its significance may, however, easily be exaggerated, and too much stress should not be laid upon it.

It is possible that it is a coincidence, and nothing more, but it suggests, as I have said, that there may be laws connected with the

[1] See Appendix.

nerve impulses of eye and ear, and their action upon the mind, which we do not yet understand.

There is, however, a remarkable and significant point to be noted which tends to carry the analogy a step farther.

Taking the last note of the colour-octave from the spectrum-band, namely, violet, if we examine it carefully we shall see that as it approaches the dark spaces beyond it into which our eyes cannot penetrate, it tends more and more towards becoming purplish before it finally fades into a dark neutral tint. In other words, purple being a mixture of blue and red, it has more and more red in its composition. This suggests as a possibility that if our eyes could see more of the dark rays falling on the screen beyond the blue and violet, we should again receive the impression of red. If so, this would be a repetition of similar notes in a succeeding octave as in music. Sir J. Herschel remarked upon this in the following passage: "I cannot persuade myself that they could fail to recognize a certain redness in the colour of the violet, which Newton appears to have had in view when he regarded the spectrum as a sort of octave of colour, tracing in the repetition of redness in the extreme refrangible rays the commencement of a higher octave too feeble to affect the sight in its inferior tones."

An examination of the red end of the spectrum also, I think, reveals a tendency towards carmine before it fades away into darkness, which means the presence of a small proportion of blue in the red, and perhaps suggests a return to the violet of an invisible octave.

It is of course evident that in the case of the musical scale there are many octaves, but in that of colour we have only one, and one which is not quite complete as to part of its last note. This is, however, from the mobile colour point of view, compensated for by the far greater variety of combinations possible in colour than in sound, and the immensely greater sensitiveness of the eye to minute differences of "pitch" as compared to the ear, as I shall show later.

This brings us to a further resemblance.

As with colour, so with sound; there is a

long range of vibrations below and above the first and last visible colour and first and last audible note, of which we are unconscious.

The invisible rays beyond each end of the spectrum-band can be photographed and made evident in other ways, and it is extremely probable that various animals and insects are visually affected by them, though we are not consciously so. Similarly, there are many air vibrations which we cannot hear, but which other creatures are sensitive to, though to us they are beyond each end of the audible musical scale. In both cases it is only a limited range of vibrations that can act upon our senses, which have, as it were, selected this range for their own purposes.

The question now arises as to whether there are discords and harmonies in colour as in music, and what points, if any, of resemblance there are between the action of these respectively upon our senses. This is an important point, because if an art of mobile colour is to be developed and we are to obtain any assistance from the example of the methods of the older art of music, harmony and discord and intermediate stages between them must play a great part in its construction.

All musical compositions depend largely upon the approach to, or the divergence from, what is thoroughly pleasant, namely, harmony or concord, or what is thoroughly painful, namely discord, and even the lightest music is more or less dependent upon this undercurrent of pleasure and pain based upon concord and discord.

Turning from sound to colour, there can of course be no question as to the broad fact of the existence of discords and harmonies of great power and wide range. Everyone realizes this more or less. Most people are pleased by the decoration and furnishing of a room if it is harmonious, and displeased by a glaring discord in a picture or a wall-paper, a dress or an advertisement-board.

Those who have a highly developed colour faculty feel these discords acutely, and those whose colour sense is weak somewhat less, but few are quite unconscious of them.

To appreciate subtle harmonies in colour as in music requires a trained sense, and to reproduce or create any series of refined and beautiful harmonies in either requires an educated and sensitive eye and an artistic mind. In fact, we all admit the existence of discords in speaking of crude colours and vulgar contrasts, and there are certain juxtapositions of colours which almost everyone feels to be painful. And, in referring to contrast, it should, of course, be added that it plays so great a part in the relative pleasantness and unpleasantness of colours, that as soon as any individual colour is placed side by side with another its beauty is either diminished or increased, or altogether destroyed.

Here, then, we again have a characteristic of colour which is extremely like what we find in music, when the simultaneous sounding of two notes each pleasant in itself may produce a discord.

Elaborate experiments have been carried out in Austria and Germany with the object of finding a basis for determining upon scientific grounds which colours should be regarded as beautiful and which as ugly. It has been found that with single and isolated colours there is a certain unanimity of opinion as to the beauty of certain tints, amongst several hundred persons taken at random from all classes and submitted to the same tests ; and physiological theories have been put forward by Professor Exner and others to account for this. But he and other investigators all admit that the influence of contrast, both as to tint and as to intensity, overrides all these calculations when they are put into practice.

In other words, all decorative arrangements of colour are dependent for their effect and their beauty upon properly adjusted contrasts and harmonies as in music.

In the latter art, as just pointed out, if we sound a single note, beautiful in timbre and pure in quality, we can instantly make it intolerable by another, also beautiful and pure in itself but discordant when sounded at the same time. And exactly in the same way, a colour exquisite in itself can be made painful to the educated and sensitive eye by placing another beautiful but discordant colour side by side with it. Every artist learns this with the *a b c* of his professional work.

It cannot, further, for a moment be denied that the ranges of beautiful harmonies in colour, as in music, are almost infinite. Even if we take the harmonies producible by admixture of the various colours of the spectrum in one degree of depth or luminosity, millions of such harmonies are possible. And, when we consider that the eye is capable of appreciating a vast variety of degrees of luminosity of each colour, we see how difficult it is to assign any limits to harmonious sequences of colour; and this applies of course also to discords and partial discords.

We have, therefore, in colour, as in music, both discord and harmony, wide in their scope and mutually dependent. We can in both produce series and sequences of harmonies differing in their degree of pleasantness. We can change them into discords and resolve them again into harmonies, we can, in fact, use colour as we use musical sounds, and we know that, although the physiological laws which govern the effects of both upon us may be obscure, they exist, and in some respects are common to eye and ear.

In music, after centuries of experiment, we have ascertained much more about them than we have as yet succeeded in doing in the case of colour, but the art of colour-music is now enabling us to pursue the subject much farther than has ever been possible before, as will be shown later on.

Passing on from this broad statement as to the general analogy, the next question may well be whether there is any close resemblance in detail between the musical scale and the spectrum-band in respect of harmony and discord—whether we can divide the range of visible colour into intervals like those of the notes of the octave, and whether, having done so, we shall find the same relative discords and harmonies.

There are great difficulties in making this comparison, as we shall see, but we may begin by pointing out one remarkable and perhaps significant resemblance.

If we strike the first note of the musical octave—say the middle C of the pianoforte, and also the last note, the seventh—we have a peculiarly disagreeable combination of sounds, a discord in the strongest sense of the word.

If we take a patch of red from the red end of the spectrum and place it side by side with a patch of blue-violet, we also have for most people a most unpleasant and crude contrast—a discord in colour for the educated eye—and if we combine the red and the blue, we obtain a compound colour which, by fairly general consent, is a disagreeable one—namely magenta.

This, again, seems to point to some underlying physiological law of sensation common to the organs of seeing and hearing, or to some laws governing the mental impressions received through them ; but when we try to go farther we are met by various difficulties, some of them so considerable as to lead many to doubt whether there is any parallel here.

Let us go into these difficulties a little more carefully.

In the first place, as has already been said, the construction of the musical octave is somewhat arbitrary. An octave has been generally agreed upon as consisting of seven whole tones and five half-tones—seven white keys and five black keys on the pianoforte.[1]

All modern European music has been composed in conformity to this scale or to others very closely resembling it, but we must not forget that it is an arbitrary one. The Greeks had a different division in classic times, and some of the Oriental nations have another very divergent one to this day.

From time to time new and more accurately divided scales have also been introduced, but as they would have rendered obsolete all previously written music, none of them, so far, have found favour with the modern musical world. Amongst these may be mentioned the harmonic scale of Baillie-Hamilton.

If, then, we were to apply the ordinary division of tones to the colour-band, dividing it into similar intervals according to rates of vibration, we should be applying an arbitrarily constructed scale.

[1] See the diagrammatic scale by Professor Gregory on p. 122, and Note upon the defects of the diatonic scale in the Appendix.

We should have, moreover, to decide what musical note to take as the first note of our scale to correspond with the lowest tint of red of the spectrum-band.

Let us suppose that we take the middle C. We have then introduced two arbitrary conditions. First, the method of division of our octave ; secondly, its starting-point.

In drawing any deductions as to the extent of the direct analogy between the two scales of sound and colour, we must bear this in mind and remember that it can scarcely be positively asserted that an analogy holds good or that it fails.

Further than this the colour sense has been so little educated as an æsthetic faculty as compared with the high cultivation of the musical one through past centuries that, although there is, perhaps, a general agreement as to certain pronounced discords, in colour—though even that is open to question—there is not the same general sensitiveness amongst most people as to lesser ones. Hence, although there may be a general agreement as to the discord between the juxtaposition of the colours at the beginning and end of the spectrum-band, there will be less unanimity as to whether intermedi te combinations are discordant, even supposir we have divided our colour scale correctly and started it from the right point. Opinion as to what constitutes a discord in music is, moreover, undergoing a change and becoming less definite in its pronouncement, as is evidenced by some advanced modern music.

This portion of the general analogy is purely a question of opinion or of psychological investigation, and it is of little importance as affecting the main theory and practice of colour-music. In the earlier days of my experimental work, I was perhaps inclined to think it of more value as a working hypothesis in the construction of some of my instruments than I do at present, and there is, no doubt, a certain fascination about its mysterious possibilities; but I cannot too clearly guard myself from being understood to lay any great stress upon the probability of its existence. Some physicists consider that there is no evidence to support the contention, others

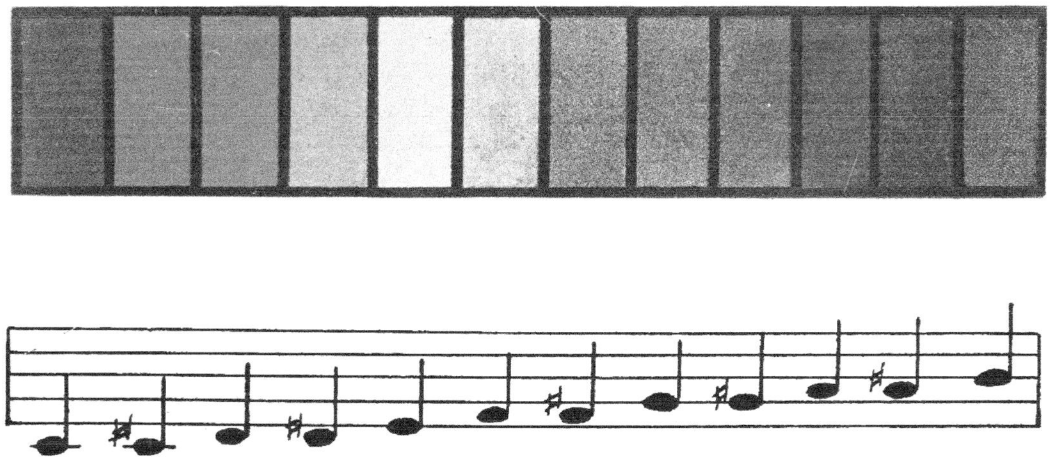

Chromatic scale in Music and Colour.
Shewing correspondence of intervals when C = lowest spectrum red.

are in favour of it; but it is really a question for the psychologist.

If it could be shown without possibility of dispute that similarly divided scales of colour and musical sounds have insufficient features in common to establish any emotional analogy whatever based upon numerical division, the general theory and the main advantages of colour-music as an art and as a mode of experimental research would remain unaffected, and the force of the chief arguments, which can be advanced in support of it as a separate and distinct art, would not be weakened in the least. The question of a possible analogy between the two scales is an interesting one, but how far it holds good is relatively not of very much importance.

CHAPTER V

POINTS OF ANALOGY BETWEEN SOUND AND COLOUR

WE have already seen that there are many strong points of resemblance between colour and music, and there are others which I shall touch upon in considering further questions connected with colour; but, as we have also seen, we must not attempt to insist upon the closeness of the analogy at all points, and for the present, until we have more facts to go upon, we must suspend our judgment as to the exact extent to which it holds good.

The points of resemblance we have examined thus far may be briefly restated thus:

1. Colour and musical sounds are both produced by vibrations acting upon the nerve terminations of the eye and ear respectively.

2. Both are limited to a certain range of

visible and audible vibrations, and there are certain numerical relationships in these which may or may not be of psychological significance.

3. Both are largely dependent for their common, mental, or psychological effect upon relative degrees of harmony and discord.

4. Combinations and sequences of notes or tints in both are capable of affecting us emotionally and giving us pleasure and pain.

5. Both are capable of adding interest to and deepening or lessening mental impressions received from other sources.

We have yet to consider amongst many others the following points :

(*a*) The musical resemblances arising when we make colour mobile and introduce the element of time into its production, or, in other words, when we make given colours and combinations of colours appear at will for a longer or shorter period.

(*b*) Resemblances in rhythmic compositions in music and colour.

(*c*) The conditions which arise when with the element of time we introduce repetition, gradation, and relatively quick or slow increases of strength and delicacy into colour.

(*d*) The emotional effects of mobile colour as a form of art upon us as compared with those of music.

In the first place—to return to a matter already briefly referred to—let us see how far it may help us if we use a similar scale to the musical one in designing an instrument by means of which we can produce colour somewhat in the same way as sound is produced for musical purposes.

Such an instrument should be able to produce all the simple colours, and, by combining them, almost any compound colours.

It should also enable us to place them side by side in larger or smaller quantities, or mingle them in one compound tint, and their production should as far as possible be entirely under the control of an executant as to their strength and delicacy, and the length of time they are allowed to appear upon the screen or other reflecting surface.

Several such instruments have been designed and constructed by the writer, and will be described more in detail farther on, but for the purpose of the argument let us merely assume the existence of such a means of producing colour.

Taking it for granted that we have provided suitable arrangements for producing delicate or strong passages of colour, corresponding to soft or loud passages in music, we shall find upon experiment that variations of strength in colour will produce the same kind of impression on the mind as in music, that delicate passages will have a quiet and peaceful effect, and strong and vivid ones will be more exciting.

We shall also find that we can take advantage of the influence of contrast as in music. Opposing colours can be used to make the action of each upon the eye and the mind more powerful, and partial combinations of divergent colours can be employed.

In music, a gradual or rapid increase in tone or strength—or vice versa—plays an important part in most compositions, and with our mobile colour instrument, or colour-organ, we can deal with colour in a similar way.

The faintest possible flush of colour can be made to swell into a full note or chord of great strength, and also to die away through a long succession of changes until it disappears.

A blaze of magnificent colour can be thrown upon the screen in a short sharp burst, or a few wandering notes can be made to flit across it, so delicate that we are hardly aware of their existence.

In the sister art, the gradual decrease of the intensity of musical notes has, as a rule, a pathetic effect upon the mind, whereas a rapidly increasing strength of tone has a joyful or stirring influence.

That the same thing applies to colour even in nature will be generally admitted.

The gradual dying away of colour in a sunset is usually more or less pathetic, and the increase of light and splendour in a sunrise has a certain joyfulness.

If we analyse our impressions, I think we shall find that this is not merely due to the disappearance and loss of the sun in the one instance and the hope of a bright day in the other, but to the lessening of beautiful colour and its final disappearance into a cold and unsatisfying grey or the gradual increase until it blends and merges into the full strength of daylight.

Experiments in mobile colour enable us to produce similar impressions.

Then, again, in dealing with colour, with the help of our colour instrument, we cannot avoid introducing the element of time.

If we strike a single note and produce a given colour upon the screen, the length of time that colour remains there before it is succeeded by another will correspond to the length of a note in music.

If we have a series of colour notes differing as to the length of time they appear, we also have something corresponding very closely to a musical phrase, and a good deal will depend upon the way in which we balance and combine the varying duration of each colour, just as in music.

To make the matter clearer, let us take a simple sequence of colours thrown upon the screen. We will say that such a phrase consists at its opening of a pale amethyst tint lasting for a quarter of a second, succeeded by a rose colour for half a second, after which the amethyst is repeated for an eighth and develops into a strong crimson for a whole second. Another short phrase may be stated thus, in diagrammatic form, and might be paraphrased by the series of musical notes placed under it.

It is quite clear, therefore, that here we have another point of resemblance between the foundations of an art in which musical sounds are used and one devoted to changeable colour under the control of an executant. Time—used in the musical sense—is more or less common to both.

This is worth noting because it is a key to some other facts about mobile colour.

It also leads us on to one of the other points of interest already referred to.

In music, as in poetry and architecture, there is always a tendency to rhythmical repetition. Passages are frequently repeated with a slight variation, and many compositions are ended with a restatement or *coda* of the leading motives which have been worked out in it.

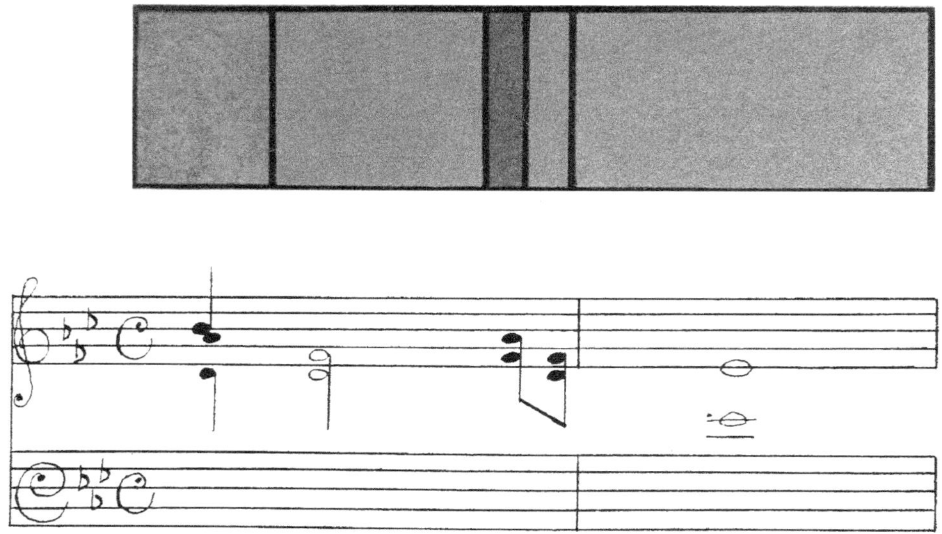

Diagram to illustrate introduction of the element of time into colour effects—the duration of the colour chords upon the screen corresponding to the musical notation.

In early poetry there are also tendencies towards repetition of ideas in echoing phrases, as, for instance, in the Psalms, and a rhyme is but a repetition of a somewhat similar sound at the end of another line.

In architecture repetition is still more formal and definite, arch repeats arch, and column echoes column, though varied perhaps in proportion or in the detail of its ornament.

We may also trace the same principle at work in the art of painting and in the pleasurable sensations we receive from nature. Intentional repetition of form with a slight alteration enters into the art of many of the great masters. It occurs again and again in the landscapes of Turner, especially in those wonderful colour dreams of his which are essentially rhythmic in their composition.

In nature it probably has much to do with our enjoyment of the inverted reflections upon the mirror-like surface of water. The beauty of the isolated stem of a silver birch, or the delicate lines of a group of reeds, is increased by their reflection in the pool of the moorland, and the campanili of Venice have an added charm when they are reversed in the wavering reflections of the lagoon.

In all these cases there is increased mental satisfaction derived from varied repetition, and we find, upon experiment, that this is also the case when we are using our mobile colour instruments, and endeavouring to produce beautiful colour sequences upon the screen. A passage of beautiful or striking colour seems to demand its echo.

Passing to the emotional effects of colour upon us, the important part that harmony and discord play in colour, as in music, has been already referred to. Much of the joy of life stands in direct relationship to the mysterious element of pain, and could not be fully felt without experience of discomfort or of suffering.

Even comedy borrows much of its joyfulness from our knowledge of tragedy, and in all great art there must be an echo of the pathetic as well as a suggestion of the pleasurable, or we feel that it is out of key with our experience of life and nature.

Here we find another peculiarity which is

common to both colour and music, and which is emphasized by a further mutual characteristic.

In literature the references to pain and to pleasure and to all the gradations of feeling and experience that lie between those two extremes are more or less definite, our interest is excited by descriptions of facts which suggest either the one or the other.

In music, however, the appeal to the emotions, except when music is allied with literature, as in an opera or a song, is essentially indefinite. With a musical composition —for instance, a Beethoven symphony—every hearer may well read a different meaning into its tender, its lively or its majestic passages. It would be difficult for a member of an audience to write a description of exactly the emotions or ideas suggested to him by a musical composition; and if two or more hearers did so, no two accounts would agree. A pastoral symphony may be in a certain sense descriptive, yet its descriptiveness is of a very indefinite kind.

In a musical work between its opening notes and its last chord there is a wide emotional field within which the imagination has freedom to wander at will. There are emotional suggestions, but no definite outlines —tragedy with no precise indications of its source—joy with no definite reasons assigned for it.

Part of the great value of music to us—certainly a great deal of the pleasure it gives —is closely connected with this indefinite quality, and its inexhaustible power in brightening, strengthening, and refining our lives, and in prompting our imaginations is largely dependent upon it.

A similar indefiniteness of action upon the mind and the emotions belongs also to colour, and experiment has shown that the art of mobile colour has for a considerable number of people, even in its present forms, the same kind of emotional and stimulative power that music possesses, though appealing to another sense.

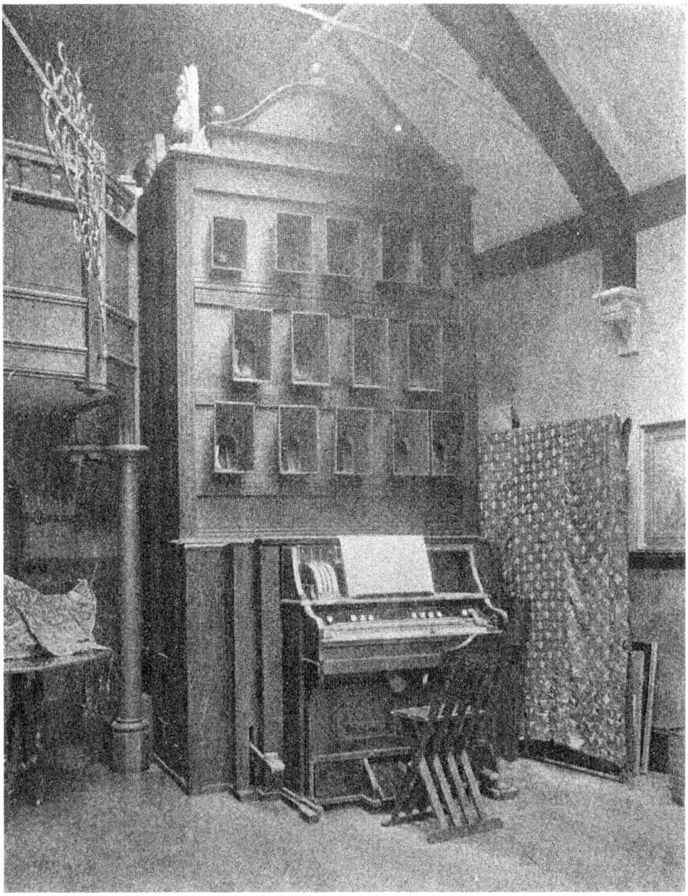

Exterior of a colour-organ.

CHAPTER VI

CONSTRUCTION OF COLOUR-ORGAN AND OTHER INSTRUMENTS

AS the qualities we have been examining are, to a great extent, common to both music and the new art, and as they are so numerous and carry us so far towards the same artistic aims and ideals, it would therefore seem reasonable to use musical precedents to some extent in laying the foundations of one form at least of colour-music.

Very possibly the buildings raised upon these foundations may, later on, be pulled down again and better ones erected in their places upon the solid concrete of newer experiences. Or perhaps, to use another figure, musical methods should be regarded as merely the scaffolding upon which the first arch is thrown across the chasm of the untried—but this matters little, they will have served their purpose and given us experience of how to build.

Almost all arts have been developed from others that preceded them, and we are beginning to see that what we supposed were absolutely new inventions in art are far fewer than we believed.

Greek architectural forms were developed from Egyptian and other Oriental styles; early Italian artists painted their Madonnas upon outlines which had come from Byzantium, and even the mediæval pointed arch may have been suggested by Arabic buildings.

We must walk before we can run, and as there is a sister art some few centuries older, perhaps it may be well for the composer in colour-music to accept her guidance to some extent in making his first steps.

Taking it for granted that something is to be gained by adopting musical methods for some forms of the new art, though they certainly will not be the only ones, let us see how this is possible.

In one of the principal instruments which

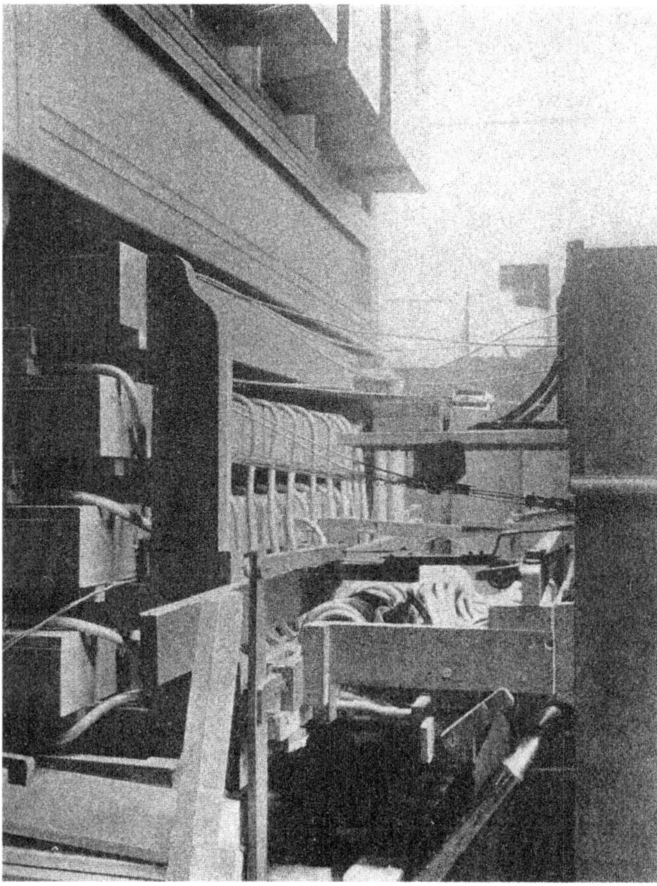

Part of the pneumatic "action" of a mobile colour instrument with keyboard.

I have designed and constructed and used largely for experimental work—which will be referred to in future as the Colour-Organ—this has been done as follows:

a. By dividing the spectrum-band similarly to the musical octave.

b. By giving the colour-organ a keyboard like that of the organ or the pianoforte.

c. By arranging for the general control of the whole keyboard by means of stops somewhat like those of the organ.

d. By providing higher and lower octaves in the colour scale of relatively paler and deeper intensity, somewhat analogous, though not strictly corresponding to, the higher and lower octaves of the musical scale, though, of course, in the colour the wave-length remains the same.

It will be well to make this arrangement a little clearer by considering, first, the division of the colour-octave.

Taking the lower red *arbitrarily* as corresponding with the middle C, the octave is divided thus. (*See illustration.*)

This division was obtained in the following way.

The complete spectrum-band, greatly lengthened by sufficient distance, was thrown upon the screen by two bisulphide of carbon prisms—the source of white light being an unenclosed arc-lamp. An opaque diaphragm was then interposed close to the screen with an extremely narrow slit in it, and the fine slice of colour rays passing through it was made to correspond in position on the spectrum-band and approximately as to its rate of vibration to the notes of the musical scale in their relative intervals.

The narrow ribbon of colour, thus cut off from the spectrum-band, was then accurately matched and apparatus designed for producing it in larger quantity in the colour-organ and placing it under the control of the corresponding musical note upon its keyboard. The keys of the colour-organ were then connected with suitable mechanism for allowing these several colours to appear on the screen

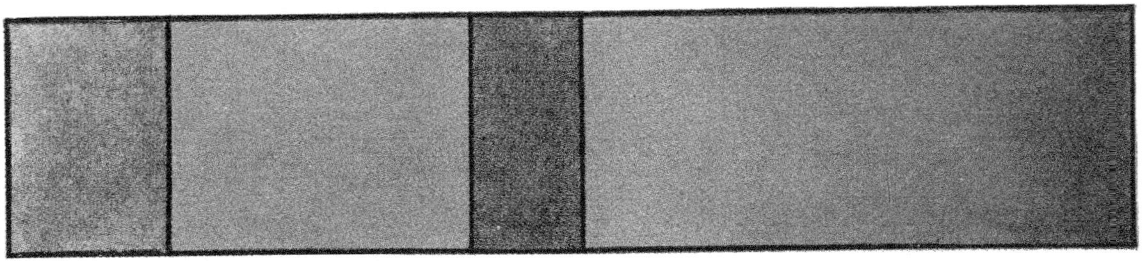

Illustrating a colour phrase, in which the fourth note is gradually increased in strength by the swell pedal of the colour organ.

as soon as the keys are depressed. The designing of this mechanism has been one of the great difficulties in the construction of the various instruments, as it was, of course, absolutely necessary that it should be responsive to the slightest touch upon the keys, and yet had to be far more elaborate than the action of a pianoforte.

A swell pedal was also provided, and if moved in one direction the brilliancy and intensity of the colour is increased throughout the whole of the length of the scale, if in the other, the colour effect is made more tender. Another stop enables either softened or "staccato" productions of the colour upon the screen to be given.

It is, of course, quite clear that, in order to use an instrument provided with a keyboard like that just described, it is necessary to devise some method of musical notation. Any absolutely new method would bring with it various difficulties, the foremost among them being the necessity for the executant to learn the new method, and for any composer in mobile colour also to be familiar with it. It would seem, therefore, that there is a good deal to be said for the adoption of a method which is already in use. This decided the author to employ the ordinary musical system—at any rate for all the preliminary experiments carried out by him—and it was soon found to be so convenient as not to make it worth while to abandon it in the later ones.

The keyboard of the colour-organ has therefore been arranged precisely in the same way as that of an organ or a piano ; and, as has already been stated, the spectrum-band has been divided up into similar intervals.

This division of the intervals, or notes, corresponding to those of the musical scale, is not quite as simple as it would first appear to be, because of the fact that the rate of dispersion at one end of the spectrum-band is considerably greater than at the other. At the red end, where the dispersion is greatest, the spaces between the points from which the colour is obtained have to be greater in order to provide for the slower increase in rate of vibration, and at the violet end they are consequently closer together. This, however, is

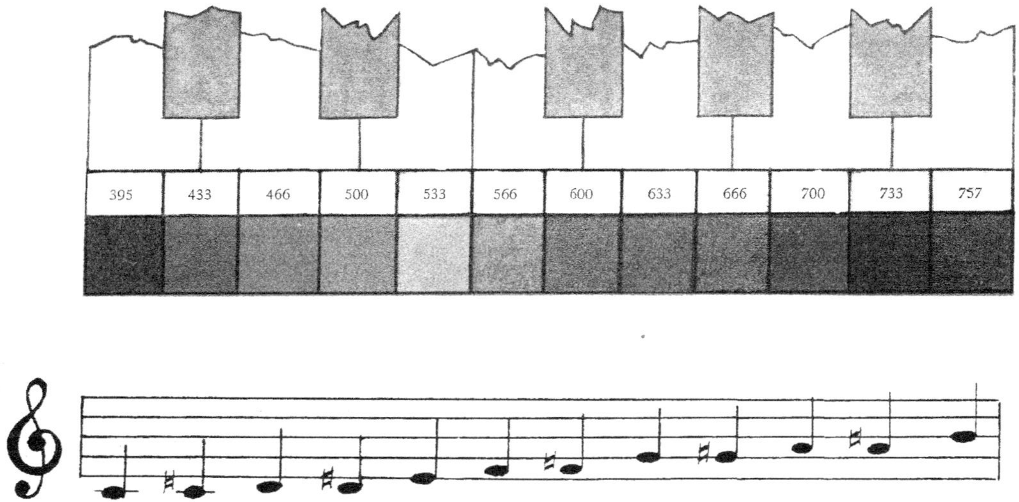

To shew normal division of colour scale upon keyboard of colour organ, colour musical methods of execution are employed. The figures in the spaces above the colours give the approximate frequencies of aether vibration in millions of millions per second. The colours cannot be accurately given in pigments, and of course do not correspond more than roughly to those produced by the instrument.

merely a matter of careful adjustment, as the increase progresses regularly upon a definite formula as in the case of a mathematical curve; and let it be again clearly understood that the division of the scale is merely a secondary matter and that other colour scales might perhaps be used with great advantage.

The method of musical notation being adopted as to the treble and bass clefs, time values of notes, etc., the ordinary musical directions such as *diminuendo*, *crescendo*, *allegro*, etc., can, of course, be used, and it becomes relatively easy for the executant to use the ordinary form of colour-organ.

Later on it was found convenient to have an alternative arrangement under which the spectrum-band can be spread over the whole of the five or six octaves of the keyboard. By the use of a pneumatic device, the simple withdrawal of a stop has the effect of doing this. A musical system of notation can still be employed, but when this stop is in use, of course, any direct translation of a musical composition is impossible, and a score written with the intention of using this arrangement of the keyboard would appear to the ordinary musician to be quite chaotic. Its chief advantage is to make extemporization in colour easier, and no more need be said for the present about its other uses.

Leaving the musical method of notation aside, we come to another mode of placing the colour effects under the control of the performer, to which some reference has already been made. It is that of using the three primary colours only, and combining them in various degrees of relative strength upon the screen. Under this arrangement each of the three colours can be projected in varying degrees of strength ranging from full power up to white light. Each colour is under the control of a lever, to which is attached an index showing the executant the strength of the colour he is using. The needle of this index passes along a curved scale, upon which figures or letters can be placed at intervals. Two of the levers are moved by the right and left hands of the executant, and the third by the foot. The whole arrangement places the performer more in the position of the violinist

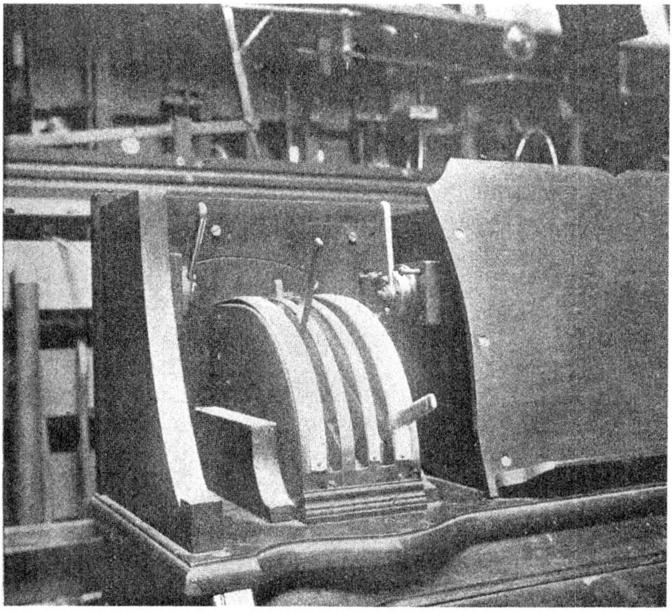

Levers of a three-colour instrument used conjointly with keyboard colour-organ.

who has to find his note upon the string, than in that of the pianist who has each note definitely settled for him by the keyboard. The great advantage of this three-colour system is that almost infinite gradation as to intensity, and some approach to infinity as to variety of tint, can be obtained by its means; but, except for extemporization, it is, strange to say, much more difficult to use than the colour-organ of the keyboard type. A composition in colour can be written for it, either upon the musical method or in various other ways.

In using any but the musical method, however, the difficulty of easily expressing the duration of a note has to be overcome, or showing whether it is long or short, or accentuated, and so forth. An example is given below of the method of notation employed.

Each space represents a given note as indicated by its number on the index scale, and the length of the space determines the relative length of the note in the bar. The letters R. Y. and B. are the initials of the primaries.

To make the matter clearer by recapitulation:

When using the keyboard colour-organ, whenever a note is depressed its corresponding colour appears upon the screen, and if a chord is struck, combined colours also make their appearance. It will easily be understood that although the intervals taken along the length of the spectrum-band—to give its division into the octave of tones and semitones—are small, as in the case of the pianoforte or organ, there are spaces of colour between these intervals. The keyboard form of instrument cannot therefore provide quite the whole range of colours which appear in nature, although the combinations which are placed at our command are almost limitless.

There is one point of interest which may be mentioned here. When we are using coloured light instead of pigment, although the effects produced are much more beautiful than those obtainable with pigments, it does not seem so easy to obtain some of the grey tints with which suitable pigments will provide us. Greyness is, however, a relative term. In

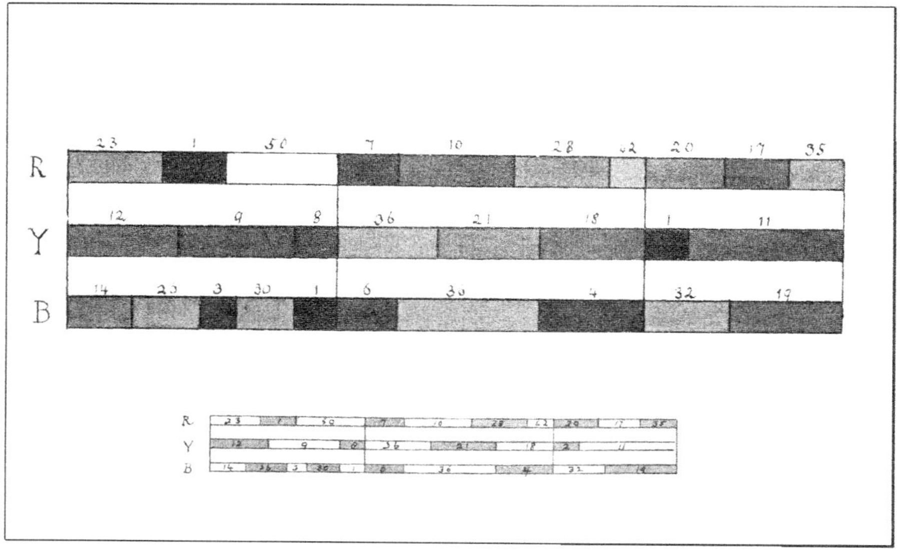

SYSTEM OF NOTATION FOR THREE-COLOUR INSTRUMENT.

The figures give the required position of the lever for each colour upon its scale, the tint within the space below it indicating approximately the strength of the colour. The length of the space gives duration of the note. Three bars of different time are given.

The lower illustration shows a smaller size of the musical staff in which the depth of the colour is not indicated.

the case of pigments a mixture of the three primaries in varying proportions tends to produce black or grey; but in the case of light, this mixture tends towards the production of whiteness. With paints or pigments, therefore, the mixture of many colours produces blackness or duskiness of the resultant tints; whereas, with the colour-organ, the more colours upon the screen the greater the approximation to white light. In using pigments, therefore, greyness is produced by a lowering of the luminosity; while with mobile colour instruments, on the other hand, it is due to increased luminosity. In both cases we have to compare grey or relative greyness with its surroundings, and with mobile colour the sensation of greyness is largely dependent upon the contrast between the colour upon the screen and the whiteness and strength of the two bands of light upon each side of it, which serve as standards for the eye to measure by, the other uses of which will be explained later on.

Although the present forms of colour-music instruments have cost me a large amount of time and thought and are the outcome of many modifications and experiments, there is still room for improvement in many respects, and I hope to carry out some of these improvements in the future or to be the means of suggesting them to those who may follow me in the pursuit of the subject.

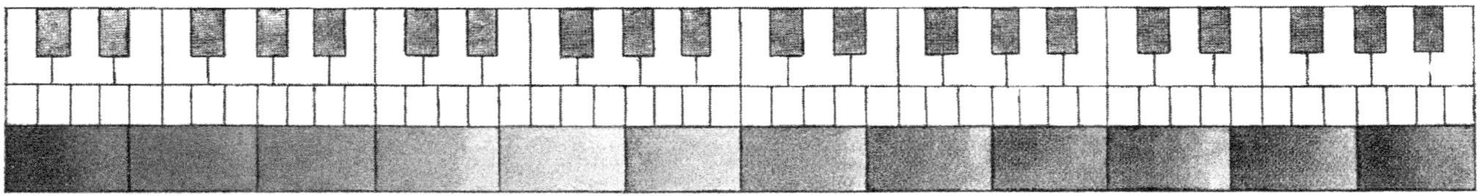

To shew division of colour scale when the spectrum is extended over the whole length of the key-board of the colour organ by spectrum stop.

CHAPTER VII

EFFECTS PRODUCED BY COLOUR-MUSIC

COLOUR and sound cannot, of course, be adequately described in words, nevertheless at this stage it may be as well to attempt to give some idea of the kind of effects produced by the colour-organ.

Imagine a darkened concert-room. At one end there is a large screen of white drapery in folds surrounded with black and framed by two bands of pure white light. Upon this we will suppose, as an example of a simple colour composition, that there appears the faintest possible flush of rose colour, which very gradually fades away while we are enjoying its purity and subtlety of tint, and we return to darkness. Then, with an interval, it is repeated in three successive phases, the last of which is stronger and more prolonged.

While it is still lingering upon the screen a rapid series of touches of pale lavender notes of colour begin to flit across it, gradually strengthening into deep violet. This, again becomes shot with amethyst, and afterwards, changing gradually into a broken tint of ruby, gives a return to the warmer tones of the opening passage.

A delicate primrose now appears, and with little runs and flushes of pulsation leads through several passages of indescribable cinnamon colour to deep topaz. Then suddenly interweavings of strange green and peacock-blue, with now and then a touch of pure white, make us seem to feel the tremulousness of the Mediterranean on a breezy day, and as the colour deepens there are harmonies of violet and blue-green which recall its waves under a Tramontana sky. More and more powerful they grow, and the eye revels in the depth and magnificence of the colour as the executant strikes chord after chord amongst the bass notes of the instrument.

Then suddenly the screen is again dark, and there is only a rhythmic and echoing beat of the dying colour from time to time upon it. At last this disappears also, and there is another silent pause, then one hesitating tint of faded rose as at the opening of the composition.

Upon this follows a stronger return of the colour, and as the screen once more begins to glow with note after note of red and scarlet, we are prepared for the rapid crescendo which finally leads up to a series of staccato and forte chords of pure crimson which almost startle us with the force of their colour before they die away into blackness.

This is an extremely simple example, but it may suffice to show the kind of effect produced by an unadorned form of mobile colour not accompanied by music.

Let us now try to obtain some idea of a colour-music composition associated with music. It was found after the first experiments that the beauty of colour compositions could be felt and appreciated without any musical accompaniment, but that, in some cases, it added greatly to their interest.

We will suppose for the moment an orchestral composition as being accompanied by colour. Let us assume that the composition opens with a Wagnerian trumpet-blast. The screen is at the same moment flooded by an intense orange which palpitates with the harmonic colours corresponding to a subordinate passage upon some of the other orchestral instruments. The blast ceases, there is a faint echo of it upon the violins while the screen pulsates with pale lemon and saffron, hardly discernible. Again comes the blare of the trumpets, and once more the screen flames with orange modulations.

This is the opening, let us say, of a passage of pathetic character in which accidentals often intervene and the key tends to become minor. The colour scheme, without being a direct translation, sympathizes with this—it is low in tone and shows slight discords, and then gradually in consonance with the sound-music develops a more joyous character. At last a modified form of the opening phrase is again reached both in sound and colour. This leads to fresh departures, and so the dual composition proceeds.

It might be tedious to describe it further, but this may suffice to give an idea of one kind of partnership which can be established between colour and sound.

So far, however, we have only considered the simple admixture of varying colour upon the screen by means of the first form of the colour-organ. This does not, however, by any means exhaust the resources of the instrument or the possibilities opened up by mobile colour. A few instances may be given of other ways in which the actual colour effects can be produced.

Let us imagine a low-toned tint upon the screen. Upon this is thrown a single spot of some other colour. That spot can be kept stationary or it can be made to move. It can be equal in intensity or can have a focussing point of brilliancy within it. If it moves it can be made to move rapidly or slowly, and if it moves very rapidly it will produce the effect upon the eye of a line or a pattern.[1]

[1] Professors Ayrton and Perry made some interesting experiments with a single spot of colour thrown upon the white ground of a screen and made to move rhythmically, some years ago in Japan. I was informed of this after some of my first colour-music experiments had been made public, and a further reference to the subject will be found in Chapter XIII.

Other spots may be added to it, also stationary, or in slow or rapid movement, and if in movement these movements may be in some sort of harmony or inter-relation.

Again reverting to our simple tint of colour upon the screen, we may imagine a second colour being thrown upon it and a net or reticulated diaphragm interposed in the path of the rays. The result will be that a portion of the second colour will be cut off by the solid parts of the net or diaphragm, and an interweaving of two colours, partly mingled and partly separated, will appear. If a third set of rays of different colours be projected upon it at the same time from another angle, there will, of course, be a mingling of three separate colours.

This on a large scale is very much what happens when the three primary colours are mingled in microscopically small dots by the three-colour printing process, but there is this important difference that each of two, three, or more interwoven colours can be instantaneously altered by the executant seated at the keyboard.

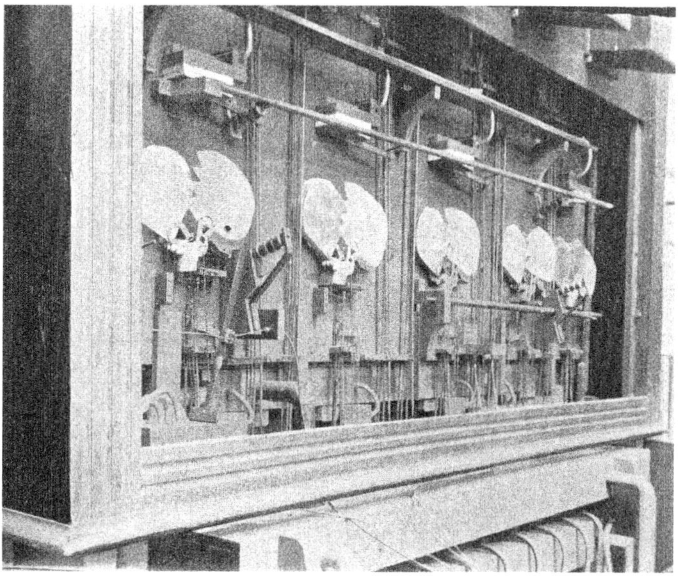

Part of the "action" of a keyboard colour-organ, with colour-producing diaphragms removed.

In this way results can be obtained of very great beauty, comparable to the interweavings of colour produced by a limpid sea reflecting a sunset.

In cold print all this sounds mere assertion, but I can only ask the reader to believe that the colour actually produced is far more beautiful than can be imagined or described.

The screen itself may also take various forms in order to resolve and break up the colours. I have experimented with various substances and materials, with opaque white drapery, combined with gauze veils at various distances, and other arrangements, in order to produce different effects. If it is wished still further to elaborate the complexity of the colour, the diaphragms can be made to move, and very remarkable results are produced by these movements. Some idea may be formed of them by imagining the delicate markings upon a shell to be seen in process of rapid formation and disappearance, by the movements of currents and eddies upon the surface of running water, and to some extent by the changing forms of a fleecy sky.

Advancing further in the direction of colour effects with a certain amount of form in them, it may be interesting to refer to another series of experiments which I have carried out.

It occurred to me that it might be interesting to substitute what are known as the "Watts-Hughes" sound-forms for the diaphragms above referred to, or to project the "Watts-Hughes" forms upon the screen in simple black and white at the same time as the colour tints. These sound forms are produced by causing musical notes to act upon films of liquid water-colour spread upon glass plates. When a musical note, or a series of musical notes, is played by a rather loud-sounding musical instrument, or sung by the human voice through a suitable trumpet placed close to one of these liquid films, the colour arranges itself in strange and decorative patterns upon the glass. The effects obtained upon the screen by interposing these plates are beautiful, but it would seem difficult to make use of them in writing a colour composition, though perhaps further experiment may show this to be possible.

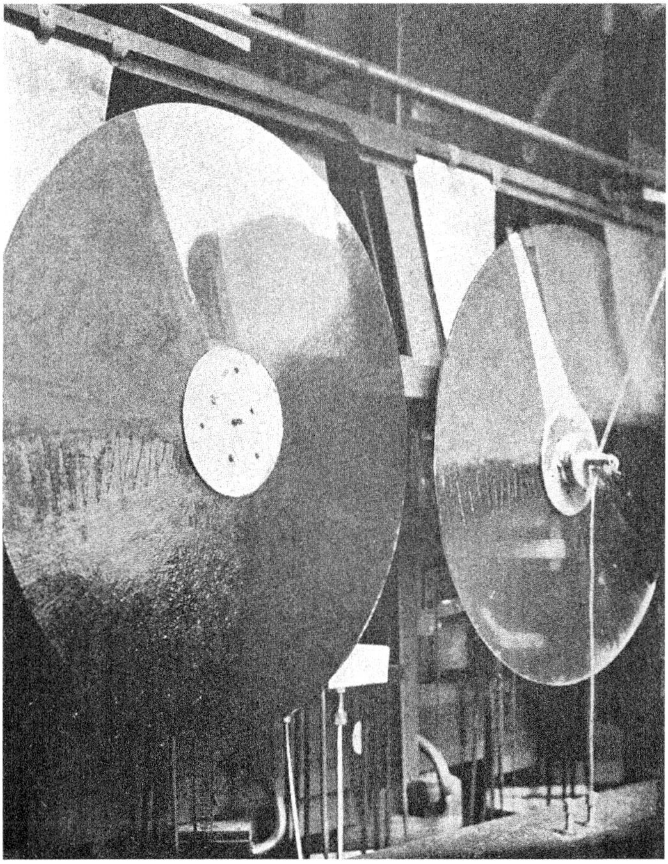

Portion of a three-colour instrument.

Any method of introducing form into the colour upon the screen should be under the control of the executant, and the forms above mentioned being produced separately, cannot of course be under his control. They are only referred to because the results obtained have been remarkable and suggestive. The best method which I have devised of using them experimentally is to throw them faintly on the screen with pure white light, the colour being super-imposed upon them while in movement. This movement is given by a specially designed apparatus.

There are various other ways of modifying the colour effects upon the screen, which may perhaps some day be employed in orchestral compositions, but for the present it would seem preferable to adhere to the simpler methods of direct projection and admixture of colour, with but occasional use of form.

Some reference has been made to modifications of the screen, i.e. the reflecting surface upon which the colour is received.

The simplest form of screen is a plain flat surface of white, like that used for a projection lantern—but many advantages are obtained by varying this.

If the white drapery is hung in folds instead of being tightly stretched, the effects of colour upon it are more interesting because they have more "quality" in them; and substances with a certain amount of texture, like white velvet, are better than absolutely smooth ones. The screen may also be modified by layers of white cords at a little distance from it, hung vertically, and this gives a very remarkable resolution of the compound tints. There are other modifications about which nothing further need now be said.

Thus far we have considered the production of colour-music by one, or at most two executants, but great variety and splendour of effects could be obtained by the use of several mobile colour-instruments used simultaneously.

This side of the subject the writer has not followed very far, but it is evident that the field for experiment is large. Electricity makes the production and control of colour far easier than it has ever been before, and other supplementary forms of colour-instru-

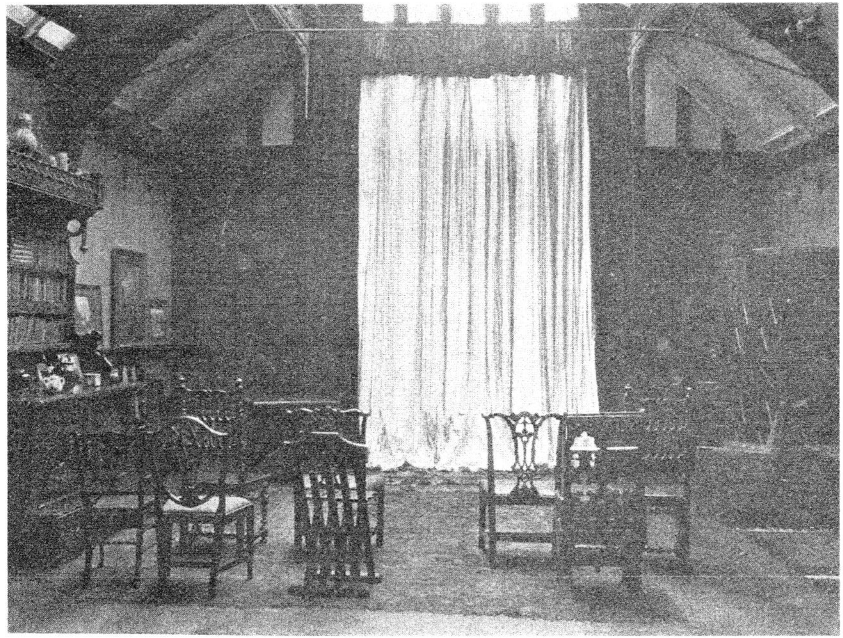

Simple form of screen as used in the author's studio.

ment in which the colour is also evolved and controlled by electricity might be devised.

As a partial explanation of the great beauty of the colour obtained upon the screen, it must be remembered that all the colours visible upon it are produced by the admixture of coloured light and not of pigments. In colour-music therefore, as already pointed out, the greater the number of colours combined upon the screen the greater the tendency, roughly speaking, towards increased luminosity. This partly accounts for the extreme purity and beauty of the colour when properly combined upon the screen. Successive contrast—that is, contrasts of colours following each other, but not presented to the eye at the same moment—probably also has much to do with this exceptional beauty. Simultaneous contrast also exists when a colour-chord is broken up into its constituents by the diaphragms, or by the surface of the screen. So that in colour-music we have two kinds of contrast acting upon us, whereas in painting there is but one.

Another fact that strikes most of those who

see mobile colour effects for the first time, is that they are introduced to a number of colours which they have never seen before and to which they can give no definite names. The colour-organ is, in fact, an easy means of producing those ranges of colour which it is difficult or impossible to obtain by means of paints, dyes, or other pigments, and which are rare in nature or in other forms of art.

As already mentioned, the chief difficulty in appreciating colour-music at the outset lies in being unable to appreciate rapid changes of colour upon the screen. Some persons do not feel this difficulty at all, whilst with others it only disappears after some weeks of training, but as it disappears the desire for increased rapidity of change steadily grows. At first the succession of chords can hardly be slow enough to give satisfaction, while later on and after more experience the contrasting effect of extremely rapid passages is eagerly demanded by the eye and by the mind. This is interesting as showing the educative effect of colour-music upon the powers of the eye.

It is not easy to account for this difficulty as

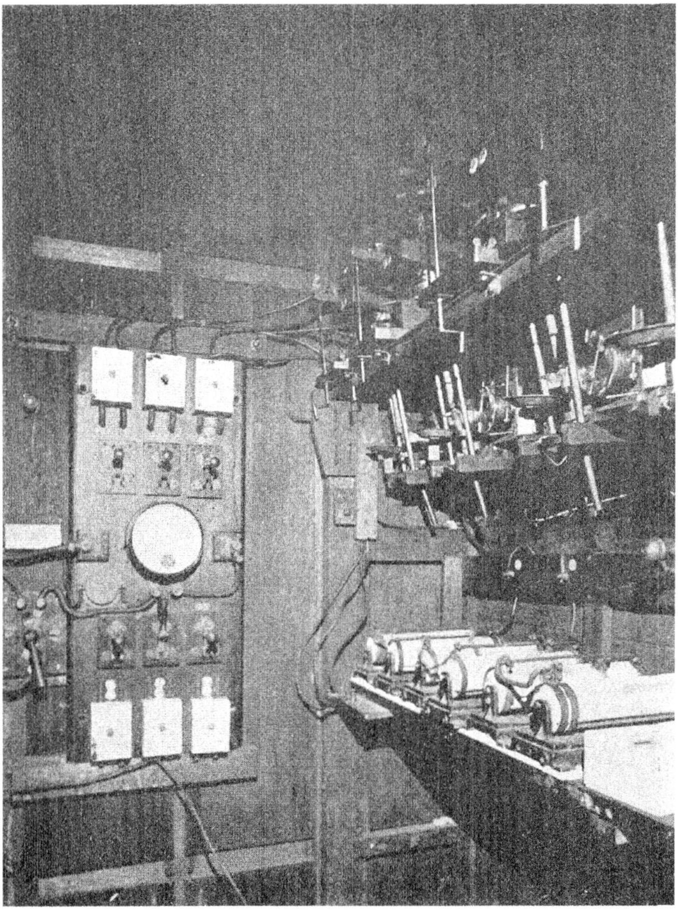

The sources of light in a colour-organ of 13,000 candle-power.

to rapidity at the outset, as it is quite clear that our eyes are accustomed to rapid changes of colour under ordinary circumstances. The rapidity of change in a tumbling sea under a brilliant sky is extreme, and yet we enjoy it thoroughly. So also is the rapidity of alteration of colour in moving objects and yet we can appreciate it; and in an express train the eye finds little difficulty in watching the rapid changes of colour presented to us by the landscape as it flies past us.

My early experiments led me to think that the difficulty was really due to alteration of intensity or luminosity of colour, rather than to that of tint or character of the colour, and it occurred to me that the effect of this alteration of intensity upon the eye might be greatly lessened if the colour-field upon the screen were surrounded by a background of pure white light. This acted successfully to a great extent, and in the newer forms of instrument two vertical bars or stripes of strong and pure white light are placed upon each side of the colour-field and opposed by black.

Experience has shown that in a very short

time displays of mobile colour awaken a rapidly increased desire to see more of it. There is no colour either in nature or elsewhere of quite the same kind either as to its variety, strength, or delicacy, and to those who love colour—or perhaps even still more, to those who have a latent sensitiveness to colour of which they are almost unconscious—the new art opens up an entirely new field of pleasure and interest.

The first impressions received being, as already noted, those of the beauty of the colour and of its variety, there usually follows after this the demand, as in music, for a kind of rhythm in the colour composition. The player, for instance, gives us a passage of warm tints, of orange and rose colour, succeeded by cooler contrasts. The eye and mind then seem to demand a return to, or echo of, warmer colours. Or, if we translate this into time, if a composition opens with several long-drawn chords of colour succeeded by rapid phrases, there is a tendency in most people to desire to return to the balancing of effect of further slow and single chords.

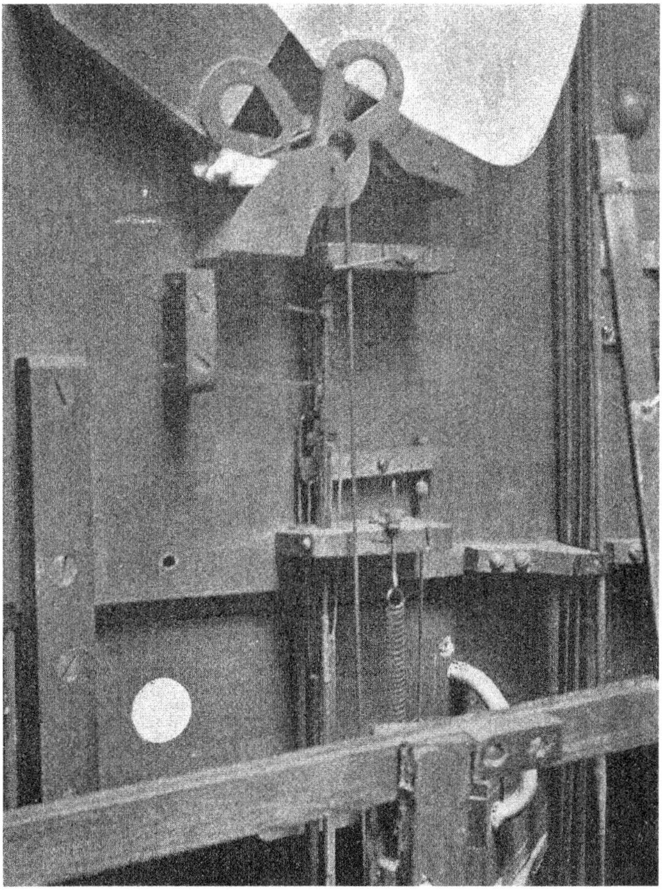

Part of the "action" of the inner diaphragms for giving intervals of relative strength in the colour for each octave.

The regular beat of a composition in well-marked time can easily be felt in colour, and time plays a far more important part than one would have supposed likely or possible in colour composition. To some extent it seems to take the place of form, that is, form in the sense in which the artist uses the word, though form as understood by the musician is certainly also felt in mobile colour.

The author has made many experiments with regard to the introduction of form, as the painter understands it, in the colour projected upon the screen, and has come to the conclusion that if used at all it should be indefinite or merely decorative and not in any sense realistic. The kind of form, for instance, which we see in cirrus clouds, while very beautiful in itself, has no definite meaning and is not calculated to distract the mind from the beauty of the cloud colour and yet is sufficiently interesting in itself. This kind of form introduced into the colour perhaps gives an added interest to it in slow compositions, but in rapid ones the eye and the mind have quite enough to do to appreciate and enjoy the colour itself without the addition of form, which would seem to be an unnecessary complication. The whole question of the introduction of decorative form is, however, a very interesting one and might well be explored farther. In music we are perfectly satisfied with compositions which do not express definite ideas, and in colour there seems to be no reason why this should not also be so if our colour sense is sufficiently developed. If stringed instruments had never been invented, could it have been for a moment supposed that a whole audience would sit spell-bound under the sounds produced by drawing a horse-hair bow over a tightened gut-string without definite words or ideas attached to such sounds? It is simply the insufficient training of the colour sense in many people that makes them demand form in addition to colour, or prevents them from enjoying colour for its own sake.

CHAPTER VIII

THE COLOUR SENSE AND ITS DECAY

THE decay of the colour sense has been referred to already, but it may be as well for us to consider the subject a little more fully, for if this decay is occurring it forms an important part of the plea for the further development of a pure colour art.

There is, I believe, some danger of the need for a better education of the colour sense being overlooked or under-rated, because many of us are unaware of the extent to which it has deteriorated and is deteriorating, and because we happen to be in contact with cultured or artistic people amongst whom there has been a slight revival of the feeling for colour.

It is perfectly true that a certain improvement in colour as used in house decoration and furniture has taken place, and that the scope of that improvement has somewhat widened.

But it still remains relatively small, and the great majority of the lower middle and working classes are not only absolutely inartistic in their tastes, but, as far as colour is concerned, incapable of appreciating good colour to an extent which it is difficult for some of us who have always lived in the art world to realize. Let us beware of concluding because we hear much talk in drawing-rooms or country houses about what is, or is not, artistic in colour, and much positive assertion upon the subject, that there is any widespread revival of the capacity for appreciating fine colour. Any such complaisant belief will be rudely shattered if almost any twenty people be taken at random and their feeling for colour be put to practical tests, or if we leave the average British workman to carry out the simplest piece of colour decoration upon his own initiative. This applies to most other European countries with nearly equal force, and we shall understand the position better, and see more clearly what we have lost and what are a few of the possibilities we are drifting away from, if we compare this state of feeling about colour,

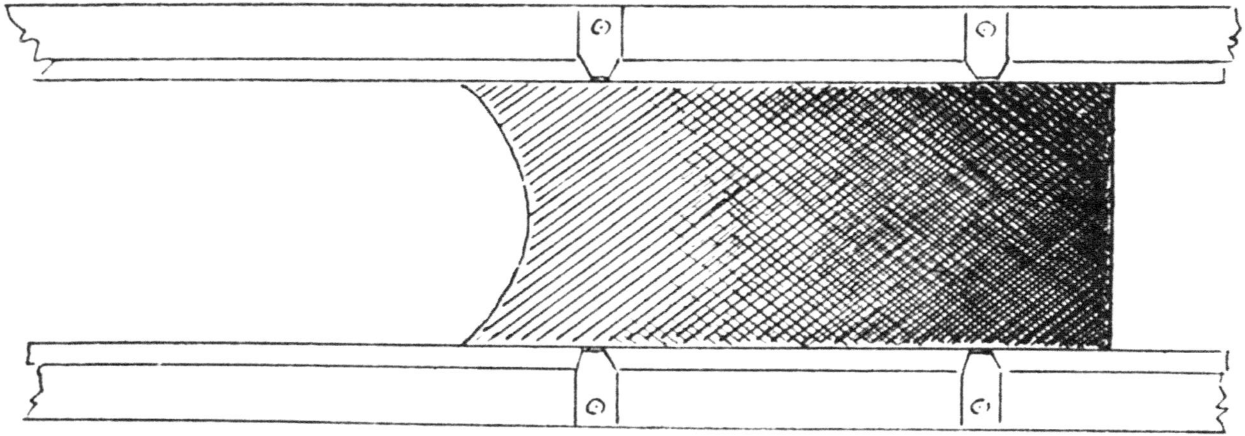

To show the construction of the diaphragms for giving *piano* and *forte* effects. The diaphragms consist of transparent mica crossed by innumerable lines which break up the light more at one end than the other.

firstly, with what it was in the Middle Ages; and secondly, with what it still is in many Eastern countries.

If we go back to mediæval times we find good colour everywhere in pictures, mosaics, and illuminated manuscripts, in the costumes of the people, in stained glass and decorative frescoes, in pottery and textiles; and in these and other things there is evidence of its having been present amongst all classes. Do we not continually return to the art works of these great colour periods and study them with care and reverence, while our best artists are almost hopeless of excelling them in refinement and strength? Does not the glass of Chartres, Le Mans or Fairford, or that of so many of the great German and Spanish cathedrals, not only excite our highest admiration, but our envy; and is it not rare for our most skilled colourists to reach the colour harmonies of the craftsmen who produced the enamels of Limoges, the mosaics of St. Mark's, Ravenna, Monreale or Cefalu? Can we compare, with any satisfaction, the average decorative coloured fabrics produced in Manchester, or other of our manufacturing towns, with the exquisite woven materials which were once common throughout Europe, and which still linger in a few out-of-the-way districts?

If we turn from European mediæval art to that of the East, we find the contrast with the present appreciation of colour in Europe—at any rate in the decorative arts—still more marked. Persia, India, Japan, and China have all had their decorative colour arts for centuries past, and they retain them to a great extent to this day. Eastern colour is not only strong and splendid, but is also subtle and delicate to an extent which we can hardly appreciate; and though here and there there may be a tendency for it, at the present day, to run into the stereotyped forms which descend from generation to generation without much change, this cannot be said to be so everywhere. The craftsmen of China and Japan are still able to design in colour, to obtain ideas from nature and transmute them into exquisite decorative colour schemes. If it be argued that the colour sense in Eastern nations has from very early times been stronger and better than in Western ones, surely the reply is that we should profit by their example, and endeavour to render our eyes as sensitive to colour and our minds as open to its influence as theirs; that we should, in fact, make special endeavours to bring our appreciation of colour up to their standards of the past as well as the present. The artistic colour sense must have been gradually developed in them as in us, and we should study the mode of its development even though our modern Western surroundings, apart from unspoilt nature, may be ugly and colourless as compared with those of the East, and our opportunities for seeing and enjoying colour fewer. This very ugliness and absence of colour is the outcome of our neglect, and due to the decay or non-development of the colour sense.

It can scarcely be disputed that at the present day large numbers of people are almost entirely insensible to colour, living in the world without being conscious that nature is full of beautiful colour harmonies, and never stopping to ask themselves how much of the beauty and interest of the surroundings of life are dependent on colour, or in the least realizing that there is urgent need for cultivation of the colour sense.

It is not, however, necessary to press the point. Even if the opinions expressed are considered pessimistic or over-stated, it is better to see clearly our weak points than to under-rate them, and we shall at least lose nothing by being on our guard against the decay of the colour sense, whether it is, or is not, as serious as some of us consider it to be.

Turning to another aspect of the question, I think it can be shown that the possession of a refined colour sense is of far more importance to a nation than its possession of a widespread musical one.

The defence of this bold assertion—which will, it may be feared, raise the ire of many musicians—may enable us better to see the position.

I have not the slightest wish to disparage music, which to me is one of the greatest of the arts, and one of the greatest pleasures in life, but it is at least conceivable that we might live (as man did once live in the early centuries) without other music than that of the birds or streams, and it is evident that there are at present thousands of people who hear hardly a note of music from one year's end to another, so that music is not essential to life.

But unless we are blind, or colour-blind, it is impossible for any of us to escape the influence of colour, be it good or bad. No object of any kind (unless it be black or white) is without colour. It is everywhere in nature, most of whose beauty is chiefly dependent upon it. In land and sea and sky it is omnipresent and in ever-changing variety—it is in every house and street, in every room and garden and field. We are constantly under its action—beautiful or ugly, healthful or morbid. We cannot escape from it if we would.

Is it not certain, then, that as it enters so much into our surroundings we cannot safely afford to know nothing about it, or to neglect to study it intelligently and cultivate our feeling for it?

Not only is it on all sides of us in nature pure and simple, but it is also practically everywhere in man's handiwork. All he produces (unless it be sooty black or absolutely white) has colour, and to a very large extent that colour is within his choice, and depends on his taste and the degree of the development of his colour sense. He selects the colours for most of the things he makes, modifies the natural colour of objects in a thousand ways, and has, in fact, the choice between good and bad colour constantly presented to him, and cannot escape from that choice. Moreover, upon his sensitiveness to colour depends to no small extent the effectiveness of his investigations in many sciences and his capacity for producing work of various kinds.

He stands, therefore, in a relation to colour very different from his relation to music, of which, if he is indifferent to it, he need have little or none; and colour must therefore be of more immediate importance to him in his daily life.

The doubt will, however, at once arise in some minds whether, after all, this question of colour and the colour sense is really of so much importance—whether it does matter

To illustrate inharmonious contrast of blue and rose-red, rendered less unpleasant by intermediate colour.

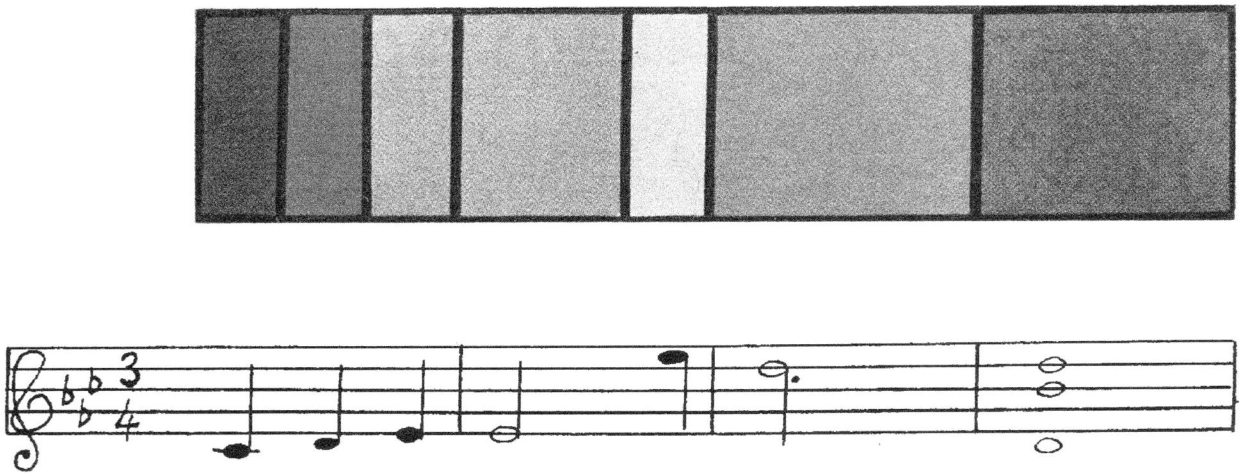

Example of a simple colour phrase in correspondence with musical notation.

NOTE.—It must be understood that the colours are merely diagramatic, and give little idea of their purity as actually seen upon the screen.

much if we are surrounded by bad colour or not, or whether we do or do not neglect to train and develop our feeling for colour.

To these questions the following points may be submitted in proof of its importance :

Firstly : Neglect tends to degrade and destroy the great colour sense with which we have been endowed, just as disuse of any member of the body usually brings about its atrophy or disease.

Secondly : Because much in civilization besides art is dependent upon a widespread and refined colour sense, without which many channels of observation are closed. For example, delicate questions of colour enter into biological, chemical, and spectroscopic research.

Thirdly : Our intellectual and even our literary capacity is injured if we do not possess a keen sense of colour. Without it our great poets could never have written many of the best passages in some of their most imaginative poems, for to give only one instance—the delicate colour harmonies of sea or sky would never have suggested many a subtle metaphor or stimulated many a delightful phantasy.

Fourthly: The absence of a refined colour sense, as already pointed out, affects us very prejudicially in every kind of art, handicraft or manufacture into which colour enters; and if, speaking from a national point of view, our capacity for colour falls below that of other nations, we shall not be able to compete with them in many of these.

Fifthly: It has been shown that colour has a direct influence upon health, mental and even physical, and this influence is probably greater than we have yet ascertained, and cannot be properly studied without the possession of the colour faculty.

Sixthly: Colour stands in a very similar relation to us to that which music occupies as a means of emotional expression, and the increase in the happiness and interest of life due to music will probably find a parallel in the pleasure and interest derivable from colour.

The importance of the retention and development of a refined colour sense being admitted, two further questions at once arise: firstly, whether it is possible to develop the colour faculty by education in the individual and in the race; and, secondly, whether colour-music has any such educative influence.

As to the first of these questions. It is sometimes asserted that it is impossible to develop the musical faculty in those who do not possess it, that without a natural talent for music a musical education is of very little use. When we come to examine this assertion, however, we find that it is but a half-truth. There are doubtless persons who, having no musical ear whatever, can by no possibility be taught to appreciate music, much less become musicians. But for the majority of people, starting with some slight appreciation of music, it is quite certain that much can be done by education to develop their pleasure and interest in it. We know that this is so, and were it not most of our study of music in schools and colleges would be useless. The recent improvements in the musical education of children upon new aural methods have also proved it.

Turning from music to colour, there are of course those who are colour-blind, and there are many intermediate stages between total colour-blindness and a full sensitiveness to all the colours upon the spectrum-band. But the majority of people unquestionably have a certain appreciation of colour, even though it be slight or latent, and experience has shown that it can be increased and refined by education. Almost every artist realizes this. He knows from experience that the pictures he has seen and admired in which colour plays an important part have had an educative influence upon him. He knows that his study of nature has had a similar influence, and it cannot for a moment be denied that as a rule those persons who are brought up in artistic surroundings become more sensitive to colour and are less satisfied with the crude combinations which are sufficient to please the uneducated.

In America the education of the colour sense in children has been much more systematized than it has here. There are several excellent handbooks upon the subject, and the

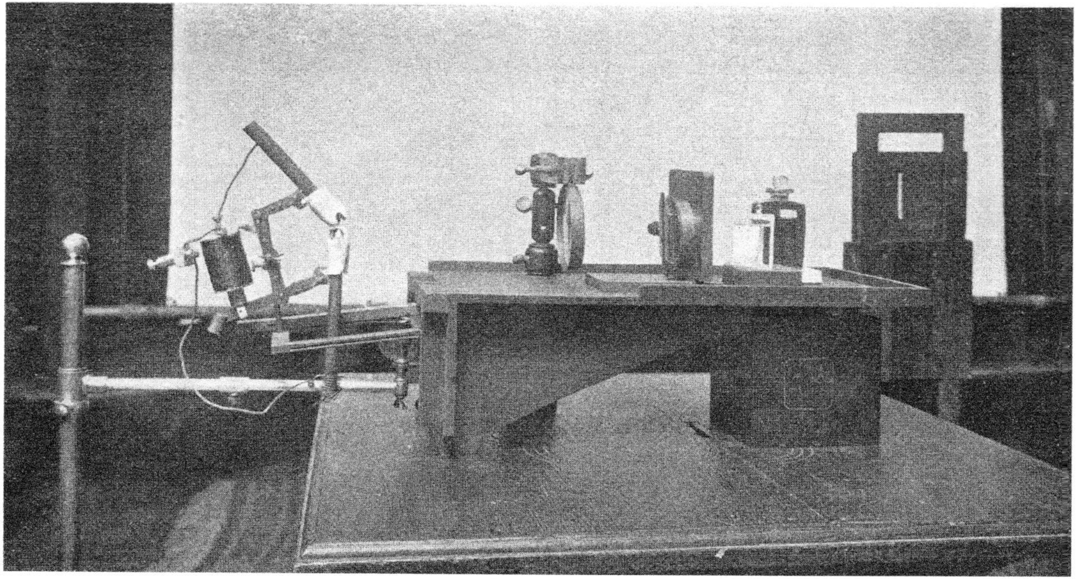

Apparatus used for producing spectrum and obtaining position ot colour intervals or "notes."
The box for enclosing the arc-lamp has been removed in order to show the latter.

results obtained in elementary and other schools have, I believe, been very satisfactory. In Germany, and here and there in England also, systematic training in the matching of colours and distinguishing between tints varying very slightly has also shown a movement in the right direction.

Passing from the general question of the possibility of this education—as to which there can be little difference of opinion—we now have to consider whether colour-music has any such educative influence. This is, of course, purely a matter of experience, and it can only be stated in general terms that experiment has shown that it has such an influence. The more the eye is trained to notice very slight differences of tint in colour, the more sensitive does it become to these differences. In colour-music not only is an immense variety of tints presented to the eye, but the changes in these tints are often very rapid. At first they are not fully appreciated, but in course of time the eye gradually learns to follow and to enjoy the rapidity of change, and it also becomes more sensitive to very slight differences of combination. On general grounds also it may be reasonably argued that the use of any faculty tends to strengthen and develop it; and it is therefore probable, if not certain, that an art devoting itself entirely to colour would, and must, develop the special faculty to which it appeals. There can, in fact, be very little doubt that the art of mobile colour does stimulate and strengthen the colour sense even in a comparatively short time, and, were it in more general use, its effects and influence would of course be wider, and therefore the contentions as to its importance in this respect on general grounds would seem to be well founded.

CHAPTER IX

THE EMOTIONAL INFLUENCES OF COLOUR

THE reference in the last chapter to the emotional influences of colour brings us back to the original contention that not only is a pure colour art possible in theory, but that in practice it has wider capabilities and power of education than can easily be realized.

It is difficult for many people, however, to understand that colour can be enjoyed and appreciated apart from form in at all the same kind of way that musical sound can be enjoyed in music. How, they say, can you isolate colour and produce it apart from form and make it interesting or beautiful? In reply, let us go to Nature for examples of how she does something of the same kind.

There are few people who cannot admire a sunset. Yet in many sunsets there is little form, and in some there is none. The lower expanse of a cloudless sky may, for instance, be suffused with primrose, orange or crimson, slowly changing either as to depth and intensity, or in respect of its actual colour. The latter may perhaps darken through tints of amber into blue and violet, or fade into pale peacock-green and ashy grey through endless subtle gradations, and yet cloud-forms may be entirely absent. But who shall say that such a series of colour harmonies is without beauty or interest?

To take another instance from nature. In a wide expanse of sea there may be little form—if we exclude a certain amount of structure to be seen in the nearer waves or ripples—and the beauty of its effect often depends almost entirely upon its colour, fluctuating in intensity and full of texture, but appealing to us mainly as colour alone. Yet how exquisite may be the varieties of tint in almost any given space of it, with gradations and interweavings of green and turquoise, deep blue and violet, with sparkle of pearly grey and depths of dark indigo and purple.

Many other examples from nature might be

given, but these two will suffice to show that colour can be appreciated in nature for its own sake apart from form ; and, upon reflection, most people will admit that even under these conditions it acts upon us emotionally.

Even when a sunset has beautiful form as well as beautiful colour, it is usually the colour that strikes most people and remains in their memory, and produces the chief emotional impression.

The writer recalls a sunset at Ruta, near Genoa, to which this would probably apply, and it may also serve as a further example of nature's compositions in mobile colour.

As the sun sank across the Bay of Genoa the sloping mountains of the Riviera, clad with olives, accentuated by rocky peaks, and with the pale white towers of towns and villages scattered along the coast-line, were all bathed in a warm golden glow of sunlight. The sea was a liquid peacock-blue shot with green and violet, and the long line of the more distant Maritime Alps, stretching out across the horizon, told against the sky in a tender shade of greenish blue.

The effect thus began with a harmony in subdued gold and blue. As the sun neared the horizon, cloudlets formed above the distant peaks of the mountains and arranged themselves into those subtle fan-like groups which are often so exquisite in form and colour. At first these were of a pale dove colour, deepening from minute to minute and accentuating by contrast the light behind them. High above them appeared a few fleecy strands of vapour which soon drifted into delicate rose-coloured filaments continually changing their shape and gradually overhanging the lower fields of colour with a lace-like canopy across the whole width of the sky. Meanwhile the glowing light upon the nearer mountains and woods had been shut off and they had sunk into a tender green-grey, warmed in places by feeble tones of umber and madder. The distant mountains remained of the same deep peacock-blue, but the sea began to assume that strange rare colour of wine which is sometimes described by the Greek poets.

The first chord of this evening symphony of colour had given place to a series of others in which grey and rose were contrasted with grey-green, and in which the purple of the sea seemed as if it were a somewhat disturbing accidental note.

Further changes then took place, and the sky behind the mountains and the dove-coloured clouds became of a lemon tint streaked with topaz which gradually turned into a cool cinnamon, while glowing lakelets of aqua-marine appeared in the lower sky. Meanwhile the topmost cloud filaments, far overhead, were deepening in colour, and from pale rose had become crimson, while the background of pure sky had changed almost to violet gradating downwards into paler tones.

Finally the splendour of the upper colouring faded away and the crimson filaments became a dusky grey touched here and there with a faint flush of pink. The sea darkened, and lines of current showed themselves upon its surface in cooler tones. The horizon on the other hand became suffused with ruby light, and the far-off mountains stood out sharply against it like the lead lines of a stained-glass window. Everything then deepened rapidly, and at last there was only one note of dull vermilion amongst the dying chords of grey and umber.

I think it may fairly be claimed that this, like many another sunset, was a piece of natural colour-music, and that it was well calculated to act on the emotions and to lead the mind from impressions of joyful beauty to the restful peace of night, though unlike the compositions of the colour musician it could never be seen again in all its fulness and variety. No doubt some of its impressiveness may have been due to the place and the poetic ideas associated with it, but how much less impressive would the whole scene have been under the glare of the midday sun or without the colour harmonies which have been described. It cannot, in fact, be denied that colour has an emotional influence in nature as it certainly has in pictorial art, and our own experiences, as well as the investigations of the psychologist, go to show that that influence is to a considerable extent independent of form.

If, then, colour in nature both with and

without form is interesting and beautiful, and if we are able by means of the colour-organ to obtain somewhat similar effects to those in nature, it may be argued as probable that we could arouse emotions of a similar kind. This is found from experiment to be the case ; and the next question is how far these emotional influences can be extended, and whether they can be made to assist in educating the colour sense.

It may be safely asserted that hardly any two persons are equally sensitive to the action of colour upon their eyes and minds ; and, in testing the effects of colour-music upon various people, this appears in a very marked way. We find, of course, exactly the same thing with regard to music. There are some to whom music is the keenest joy in life, others to whom it is a moderate pleasure, others who are indifferent to it, and, finally, those who will candidly tell you that it is a pain to them.

It might, therefore be expected that colour-music would be variously appreciated by different people, and this has proved to be the case. For some of those who see it for the first time there is a good deal about it which it is difficult for them to understand or appreciate, while there are others who find keen enjoyment and interest in it from the beginning. But it has been found that, within broad lines, the emotional effects produced by given passages upon different people are similar. That is to say, a colour-phrase of well-marked emotional tendencies will induce the same kind of mental attitude in various people. But, as in music, when we get away from these broad divisions of effect, the emotional results of less marked passages are much more uncertain.

There is one difficulty which has to be faced from the first, namely, that the full emotional effect of mobile colour upon the mind cannot be obtained without use of the contrast between slow and fast passages. But unfortunately, as has been said, in most cases, a spectator to whom mobile colour is a new, or nearly new, experience, cannot follow fast changes without considerable difficulty, and certainly cannot properly appreciate them. His eye is uneducated and puzzled. From this it will be easily understood that there are certain difficulties in showing effects of mobile colour except of an elementary description to untrained spectators. The appreciation of colour-music, however, rapidly develops after a few days' experience of it, but education and explanation are absolutely necessary at the outset.

Something has already been said about the expression of pathos and of joyfulness by means of colour, but it may be well here to give an example. Any sequence of colour which changes gradually from brightness and purity into depth of tone and greyness will, by general consent, be more or less pathetic. It is quite true that into this change enters the mere alteration of tone as distinct from tint, or, in other words, of light and darkness as opposed to colour. That is, however, also the case more or less in music, and it is difficult, if not impossible, to separate tone from tint in questions of emotional expression. But the very fact that the adjective "sad" is constantly applied to colour shows a general recognition of the fact of some colours being less suggestive of joy and brightness than others. Upon the instrument itself it is easy to show colour passages which have a pathetic tendency, and it is equally certain that phrases which are thoroughly suggestive of brightness and pleasure can be given, while between these two extremes lie rich fields of intermediate emotional possibilities.

To take an extreme example of emotional expression in colour, let us imagine a low-toned tint of dark purple which is slowly varied by successive chords of cooler and cooler colour until the purple has gradually changed into a deep blue with indefinite fluctuations towards absolute blackness. Now let us imagine a few short notes of half-developed red, then one blaze of deep crimson, and then a return to absolute darkness with faint suggestions of the previous purple and peacock-blue. I do not think that such a passage would have any other significance for the majority of people if its emotional effect were analysed than that of theatrical tragedy, though, as in music, this significance will always remain an indefinite and disputable one.

Speaking generally, the popular idea that low-toned colours are less exciting than bright ones, is borne out by mobile colour experiments.

As in nature, iridescence produces some of the most beautiful results in colour-music, and in rapid passages iridescent contrasts and harmonies affect the mind more than slow successions of plain colours or chords. These iridescent effects can be obtained in various ways—for example, by breaking up the component colours by diaphragms before they reach the screen, or by the surface of the screen itself, and very rapid successions of colour notes also produce the impression of iridescence.

If we examine a natural object which has iridescent colouring—for instance, the surface of some shells, or a piece of iridescent glass—we shall, I think, be led to the conclusion that great part of the beauty of the colour depends upon the minute contrasts contained within it. Red shades off into violet or green, in extremely small streaks and bars, and the violently contrasting colours are not large enough in quantity to be disagreeable—for quantity is an important element in questions of colour contrast—and yet they are sufficient to be exciting to the eye and the senses. Iridescence in nature always attracts us, and excites pleasurable emotions. We invariably admire it in the sunlit spray of the torrent, the plumage of the bird or the wing of the dragon-fly—and colour-music gives us the power of bringing it into being at our will and using it as an æsthetic influence.

CHAPTER X

THE EDUCATIONAL INFLUENCES OF COLOUR-MUSIC

SIDE by side with the advantages of the new art as a wholesome emotional stimulus like music are its educational effects upon the colour sense. It is very remarkable to note how rapidly it produces increased sensitiveness to slight divergencies of colour, and how, after a short time, the eye can appreciate these differences much more quickly.

At first in any rapid passages of mobile colour most of the slight changes are scarcely felt at all, and it is only after a week or two that those compositions in which they most appear begin to give the greater satisfaction. Primarily it is the strong contrasts and the vivid colour combinations which most appeal to people, while later the delicate and subtle passages produce the greater impression and are more keenly enjoyed. In music, of course, we find the same thing, though perhaps not in so marked a degree.

There is also another side to the matter. Hitherto colours have chiefly been produced by mixing them on the palette or in the dye-vat, or in some other more or less laborious way; their production has also been, to a considerable extent at any rate, dependent as to their range and variety upon the character and scope of the pigments used. With the colour-organ, however, an almost infinite variety of colour combinations can be obtained with no more trouble than in sitting down to the keyboard and running the fingers over the keys, and a vast variety of very exquisite tints are obtained with ease which it is extremely difficult and often impossible to produce by paints or dyes. Among these colours are thousands to which no name can be given, many of which one has never seen before, and the memory for colour is exercised in endeavouring to retain some recollection of them. Not only, therefore, is the colour sense rendered more sensitive, but the memory for colour is also trained, and in any art dealing with colour the memory plays a very important part. It is, in fact, to a large extent, due to the absence of a strong memory for colour that a great deal of modern decorative and imaginative art work leaves so much to be desired, as is now generally admitted amongst artists.

If the decorative painter has not got a well-developed colour memory, he will be unable to retain the impressions of beautiful colour harmonies which he sees in nature, and make use of them in his designs. Even in a direct transcript or study from nature the memory comes into play, for effects change from moment to moment, and the mere observation of a colour and the attempt to mix it on the palette is in itself an act of memory.

In watching the effects produced by the colour-organ upon the screen, slow and simple compositions should be studied at first; and as an exercise and training for the eye, it is a good plan for the observer to take the colours tint by tint and guess at the combinations which produce them, verifying them afterwards by reference to the keyboard.

The amount of pleasure and interest derived from colour compositions varies immensely with individuals. An interesting instance of this was the case of a well-known London doctor, who told the author, after first seeing a recital of colour-music, that he was absolutely unappreciative of any form of "sound-music," that it was, in fact, a pain to him, and that he had always detested it; "but," he said, "from the moment that I first saw a display of mobile colour, I realized what I had missed all my life through my inability to appreciate music. It opened up a new world of sensations to me and gave me the greatest mental pleasure I have ever experienced." This clearly shows that to some persons mobile colour would, or does, fill the place which music cannot occupy in their lives.

On the other hand, there can be little doubt that to some, though they would hardly own it, colour of any kind is more or less unpleasant, and they would prefer to live in a monotonic world. One must therefore be prepared for a great variety of opinions with regard to any such art as that of mobile colour.

The majority of people will probably derive a moderate but increasing pleasure from it. There are many to whom it at once provides a surpassingly interesting source of enjoyment and education, and some to whom, like my medical friend, it will open up an entirely new world of sensations; and there are others, again, to whom it will be supremely distasteful. It is well to recognize this to avoid disappointment, and be prepared for very divergent expressions of opinion about it.

Speaking broadly, it appeals most to those who have had an artistic training into which colour has entered, and it is less attractive to those whose interests centre in music. This is not what the author personally expected. He imagined that the connection with music being so close on some points, those who would take the greatest interest in mobile colour would be musicians; but, with some striking exceptions amongst distinguished musicians, the musical world, as far as it has yet come into contact with colour-music, has been at first inclined to see points of divergence rather than those of analogy and to look upon the art as a possible rival. A similar attitude is often adopted towards any new departure in science or art, and there is no reason for resenting it; it merely makes the co-operation of those amongst musicians who are able to take a sympathetic view and welcome the endeavour to open up new fields of investigation all the more valuable.

In some cases musicians, on the other hand, are very susceptible to the influences of colour. The German author Finck says, in reference to Wagner in the following curious passage, that "splendour, beauty, light, all the components of colour, were claimed by him as the rights of genius; from these in his life he gave in art the rich clangtones and tints which distinguish his music from all others. Wagner's love of colour in tones extended itself to his actual surroundings, and the influence of the glorious colouring with which he constantly surrounded himself is to be felt in every note of music he ever wrote. Catulle Mèndes describes him as having been attired in coat and trousers of golden satin embroidered with pearls and flowers; for he had a passionate love for luminous stuffs that spread themselves like sheets of flame. Velvets and silks abounded in his drawing-room in broad masses and flowing pleats, anywhere, without pretext of furniture, without other reason than their beauty of colour, to give him the enchantment of their glorious brilliancy. Wagner fully realized the influence of these colour surroundings on his genius and his music, for he wrote, in a letter to Frau Wille, 'Is it really such an outrageous demand if I claim a right to the little bit of luxury I like; I who am preparing enjoyment for the world, for thousands? I am differently organized from other men. I must have beauty, colour, light.'"

With this testimony to the influence of colour upon the mind of a great musical composer, it is surely not too much to hope, or even to expect, that colour-music with its endless variety and magnificence of colour effects may well be of use in the future as a stimulating influence to musicians. Wagner's operas, as we all know, when they were first performed were attacked with insensate fury in France, and abused by the musical critics in England. If, therefore, colour-music should have aroused some slight opposition in the musical world, as well as have received some tributes of warm appreciation, there is no cause for surprise or discouragement. Wagner did not disdain to call in the assistance of colour both in his operas and in his surroundings, and were he alive now the writer believes that he would have found in him a warm supporter of some of the claims put forward on behalf of a mobile colour art. The educational effects of such an art are probably not confined to its action upon those into whose work or interests colour largely enters, but may well exercise an indirect psychological influence upon other arts of quite a different kind.

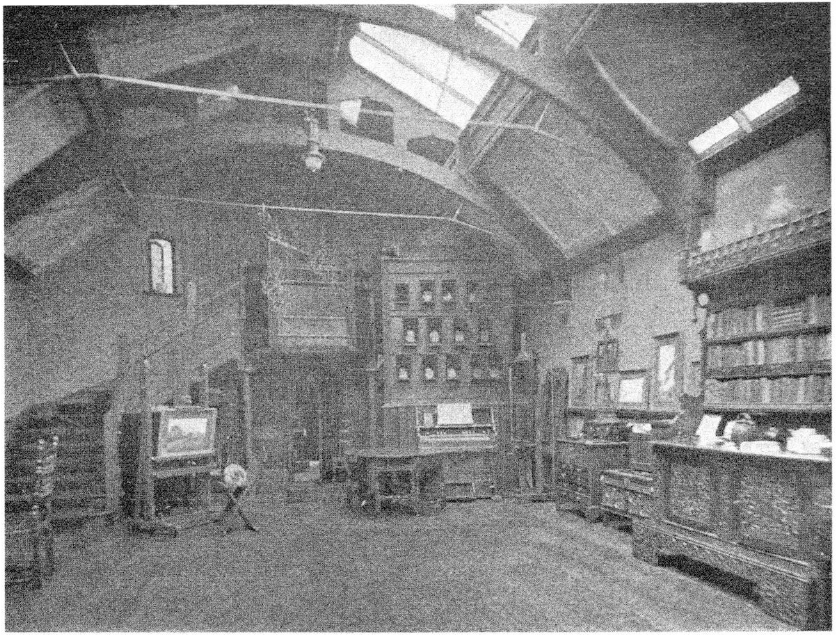

Keyboard colour-organ as used in the author's studio.

CHAPTER XI

MOBILE COLOUR AND THE ARTIST

TURNING from musicians to painters, colour-music, of course, makes a much more direct appeal to the latter. To them the two specially new qualities in regard to this presentment of colour are, its separation from form and the introduction of time and rhythm. At first the absence of form makes the full appreciation of the colour somewhat difficult to them, every artist being trained to regard colour as occupying more or less definite spaces and shapes. But, on the other hand, the extremely subtle changes and interweavings of colour, the new methods of producing texture and quality, the rapid contrasts, the interesting changes of harmony, and the joy of being able to produce and study colour with the ease afforded by the colour-organ, makes them at once appreciative of the new art and more open to see its present and future possibilities than the musicians. Sir Hubert von Herkomer's remarks as to mobile colour will have been read with interest as bearing upon this point—all the more so, perhaps, from the fact that he is an able musical composer as well as a great painter.

An artist thinks little of undertaking a long and tedious journey in order to be able to watch and study the magnificent colour harmonies of southern seas; the brilliant effects of sunlight upon the white buildings and costumes of Tunis or Tangier; or to give himself the opportunity of making a few rapid transcriptions of sunsets only to be seen in the sierras of Spain or the deserts of Egypt. When, therefore, he is provided with an instrument by means of which he can study and analyse somewhat similar effects of colour at a moment's notice, he feels that a new power is placed within his grasp and appreciates its acquisition. It is first the technical qualities of colour that will most appeal to him. He is principally interested in the impressions produced by the interweaving of opposing colours and the resultant effects of luminosity and other beautiful qualities, and also by the æsthetic emotions produced by contrasts into which the element of time enters. Just as in a picture a contrast is largely influenced by the relative size of contrasting colour patches, or, in other words, by the relative masses of colour, so in mobile colour contrast is greatly modified in its effects on the eye and mind by the length of time during which the contrasting colours remain upon the screen. If, for instance, it is flooded with a deep red for a second or two, and a short sharp note of sapphire-blue is then struck, the contrast will be greater than that produced by two brief notes of scarlet and blue of equal duration. A whole series of rapid notes of colour of equal length which are more or less in contrast to each other affect the colour-senses less strongly than the same colours in contrast with others when of longer duration upon the screen.

Of special interest also to artists is the introduction of the element of time into gradated effects of colour by means of mobile colour instruments. In a picture or in a decorative design, gradation—that is to say, the gradual increase of the strength of colour over a given area—often occurs. In the works of the great landscape painters—such, for instance, as Turner, where the problems of atmosphere and space have interested him so greatly—gradation of colour is present almost everywhere. But it is, as it were, fixed gradation ; it may begin slowly and may rapidly increase in depth and intensity over a given space until it culminates in a strong point or focus. Its rate of change may also be quite equal and steady with no rapid increase and no rapid decrease, but in both cases, once stated, it is fixed and definite, whereas when colour is produced by the colour-organ under conditions of gradation, whether it be towards intensification or of weakening of the colour, it grows, or wanes, under the eye of the spectator and can be quickened, or retarded, at the will of the executant. Gradation of colour under such conditions becomes much more interesting.

Mobile colour is also of practical aid to the

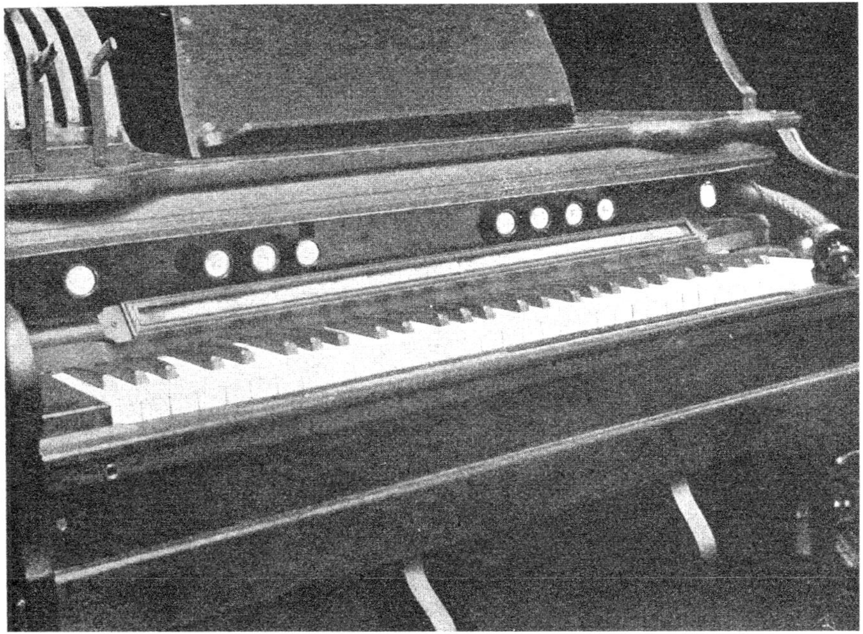

Keyboard of a colour-organ.

artist, because it enables him to try almost any scheme of colour he may have in his mind without the laborious process of transferring it to canvas or paper. He can sit down at the keyboard of the colour instrument, and starting from some chord of colour which pleases him can try various sequences of other colours and other combinations without the least difficulty. He can come back to his original chord and try fresh ones without having to clean his palette or provide a new canvas, and he can, at any moment, if he wishes to make a study of the effects he has decided upon, reproduce these colour schemes upon the screen and make notes of them before he begins his picture.

Many artists wisely keep objects of beautiful colour in their studios in order to be able to bring their minds into tune with the beauty of colour in nature or art. Some choose Oriental china, others Limoges enamel, others the plumage of birds or collections of gems and minerals, others, again, mediæval and oriental draperies or stained glass. But the artist who has access to a mobile colour instrument—which it is to be hoped will some day take such a simplified form that it will be within the reach of everyone—can at any time sit down and obtain thousands of suggestions, almost at haphazard.

This is one of the uses of the colour-organ for the artist. But what is of more importance to us for the moment is the emotional effect of mobile colour. Less sensitive as a rule than the musician to rhythm and all the complexities of time and counter-point, he is, by his training, much more open to receive emotional influences from the colour itself. It is, however, interesting to note that owing, as a rule, to this training, or perhaps to the very constitution of his mind and feeling, he will have an instinctive preference for certain schemes and combinations of colour rather than others. As the music of colour floods the screen, his preference for certain arrangements, or symphonies of colour, will be very marked, and it is curious to note the great divergencies of opinion amongst artists with regard to the preferability of some arrangements over others. The pleasure or pain produced by colour are much more pronounced, in most cases, with the artist than with the ordinary spectator, and it is therefore to the artist that the new art must look in the future, as it has up to the present time, for the greatest assistance in its development. Experience has shown that once having overcome the disconcerting realization of the fact that colour does not require form to make it beautiful or interesting, the eye of the artist becomes rapidly educated to appreciate the subtleties of colour-music.

A point that strikes most artists is that already alluded to, that however many colours are mixed upon the screen, there is no tendency towards deadness or impurity of colour as in the case of pigments. The greater the number of colours projected upon the screen, the greater the tendency towards white light; whereas in pigments, the greater the number of colours mixed upon the canvas, the greater the tendency towards blackness.

Vast numbers of combinations appear in colour-music which are seldom or never seen in art and very rarely in nature, and these are specially worthy of the painter's attention. One practical difficulty is that the colour appears in a darkened room, and can therefore only be compared with other tints produced in a similar way, and not with local colour of objects placed near the screen. But a special arrangement for comparison of the local colour of particular objects can be made by throwing detached beams of white light from an arc-lamp upon them. The two narrow bands or strips of pure white light usually projected upon the screen at each side of the colour-field also give a standard of comparison between the colours upon it and absolute white, and enable the depth and intensity of low tones to be better appreciated. If no such bands of light are used, low-toned colours, by reason of their being surrounded by darkness, are apt to appear too luminous, and their full strength cannot be realized. Somewhat the same conditions exist in stained glass windows in a dark church, and it was probably in order to enable the beauty of the sombre colours which the great stained glass designers of the Middle Ages often used that they frequently surrounded their pictorial designs by fields of white or grey glass. This is very marked in the windows at Fairford, and in much German glass, and the principle has been adopted by a whole school of modern English glass painters in imitation of them.

Another very important effect of the white bands is to prevent, as has already been said, the colour changes from becoming too dazzling to the eye and too violent in their effect. Their width is an important point and has to be found experimentally. If they are too wide, the brilliancy of the paler tints is injured; if, on the other hand, they are too narrow, the depth of the darker ones is not fully appreciated.

The use of the colour-organ in training the memory for colours may become important to young artists, many of whom neglect this training and regret it later in their careers. There are many people who have a keen musical faculty in other respects, but have no musical memory, and so there are many excellent artists who have a very feeble memory for colour, largely, perhaps, because they have not cultivated it systematically. Endless exercises in memory training for colour are possible with the colour-organ, and many interesting experiments in this direction have been made.

CHAPTER XII

SOME SCIENTIFIC OPINIONS

CONSIDERING the question of the analogy between colour and musical sounds purely from the scientific standpoint, there is, broadly speaking, a general agreement amongst scientific men that there are some remarkable points of resemblance between the respective modes of being of the spectrum-band and the musical octave. In both, the sensations produced upon the eye and the ear are due to variations of frequency of pulsation in the air and the luminiferous ether respectively. But, starting from this broad general statement of fact, there are divergencies of opinion as to how far further resemblances extend, and the question has perhaps been additionally complicated lately by the wide acceptance of the electron theory. As long as we confine it to physical science the path for the investigator to follow is, as far as it will take him, a fairly clear one. Physical facts as to the production of colour and of sound can, within certain limits, be definitely stated and compared. But when we come to the consideration of the effects of colour and of sound upon our eyes and ears, and through them upon our minds and emotions, upon memory and association, and upon those springs of suggestion and mental impulse which are so closely connected with art, we are in an altogether different domain and one within which there must necessarily be almost endlessly varied opinions.

Amongst scientific men we shall therefore not be surprised to find that some attach considerable weight to the analogy between the spectrum-band and the octave, and the action of colour and sound upon us mentally and emotionally; and that others attach very little and endeavour to confine themselves solely to the physical outlook. We may, perhaps, go as far as to say that valuable and helpful as is the opinion of men of science with regard to the latter, it is to those who have been trained to observe and study the emotional effects of colour and sound upon us, and whose lives have been spent in experimenting upon these influences through the medium of their work—namely, to the artist, to the musician, and also to the psychologist—that we should turn for further assistance in investigating the difficult and interesting questions connected with our subject, many of which press for solution.

But, at the same time, it is of great interest to compare the opinions of various scientific men of eminence, and in this chapter it is therefore proposed to give a brief summary of some of these opinions.

The general points of resemblance between colour and sound struck the earlier men of science very forcibly, and there are numerous references to them in their publications. There is not, however, much profit in going back to these opinions, as the scientific outlook, even with regard to physical science, changes so rapidly; but the following extracts from the works of the earlier authorities of our own time may be of interest:

Prof. Tyndall wrote :

"The pitch of sound is wholly determined by the rapidity of the vibration. *What pitch is to the ear in acoustics, colour is to the eye in the undulatory theory of light.* . . . Nevertheless, this great theory of undulation, like many another truth, had to establish by hot conflict its rights and existence. Illustrious names were arrayed against it."[1]

In Ganot's *Handbook of Physics* occurs the following :

"The analogy between the phenomena of light and sound is very close. . . . A red light is due to a comparatively long undulation and corresponds to a deep sound ; while a violet light is due to a short undulation and corresponds to an acuter sound."[2]

Prof. H. Schellen, in his well-known work upon *Spectrum Analysis*, states :

"Different colours are only produced by the different degrees of rapidity with which the ether vibrations recur, just as the various notes in music depend upon the rapidity of the suc-

[1] Prof. Tyndall, *On Light.*

[2] Ganot's *Physics*. Edited by E. Atkinson, PH.D., F.C.S.

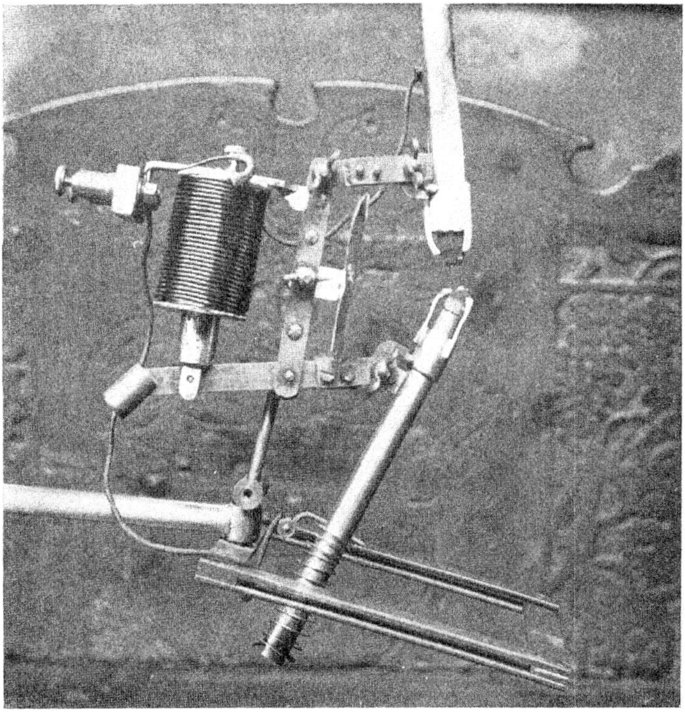

One of the patterns of arc-lamp, specially designed for mobile colour instruments.

cession of the vibrations of air. Colours are to the eye what musical tones are to the ear." [1]

Or again, in Preston's *Theory of Light* the author writes:

"As the pitch (or musical colour) of a note is determined by the frequency of its vibrations, so it is the frequency of the vibrations in the luminiferous ether that determines the colour."

In the last edition of the *Textbook of Physics* by A. W. Duff (1910) the matter is still referred to thus:

"It is a matter of common experience that the colour of a beam of light does not change when it enters water, hence frequency rather than wave-length determines colour. Colour is therefore analogous to pitch in sound."

Professor Heinrich Rubens, the great investigator of the infra-red rays, would also appear to group them in octaves as a con-

[1] Prof. H. Schellen, *Spectrum Analysis*. Edited by Sir W. de W. Abney, F.R.S.

venient method of nomenclature; but I am not aware how far he considers the musical analogy to extend.

Professor R. A. Gregory, who tells me that he considers that the analogies between musical sounds and colour are remarkably close, makes the following statement with regard to the musical octave, which is exceptionally clearly put and may be of interest in any comparison between the two scales of colour and sound.

"The major diatonic scale, such as is represented by the sequence of the white notes of a piano, commencing with the middle C, is built up in the following manner: a second major chord is obtained by starting from C^1, the octave of C, and descending in the ratio 6 : 5 : 4. This gives frequencies of 48, 40, and 32; and these correspond to the notes C^1, A, and F. This set of three notes is known as the 'sub-dominant chord.' Finally, a third major chord is obtained by starting from G, and ascending in the ratio 4 : 5 : 6. This gives frequencies of 36, 45, and 54; and these correspond to the notes G, B, and D^1. This is known as the 'dominant chord.' The note D^1 is above the octave of C, and its lower octave D, having a frequency 27, falls between C and E. Thus we obtain the following sequence of notes into which the octave may be divided :

Notes	C	D	E	F	G	A	B	C
Vibrations per second	256	288	320	341·3	384	426·6	480	512
Frequency	24	27	30	32	36	40	45	48
Interval (compared with C)	1	$\frac{9}{8}$	$\frac{5}{4}$	$\frac{4}{3}$	$\frac{3}{2}$	$\frac{5}{3}$	$\frac{15}{8}$	2 ”[1]

Leaving the strictly physical side of the matter for a moment, the following observations by Helmholtz are interesting as showing that he felt the limitations of the older arts into which colour enters, and that they therefore occupied a totally different position from music and had less to do with what he calls "pure sensation." They almost suggest regret at the absence of any art using colour for the purpose of influencing the emotions in a similar way to that in which music uses harmonic sounds:

"Music stands in a much closer connection with pure sensation than any other of the arts. The latter rather deal with what the senses apprehend, that is, with the images of outward

[1] *A Classbook of Physics*, by Prof. R. A. Gregory, p. 345.

objects, collected by physical processes from immediate sensation. Poetry aims most distinctly of all at merely exciting the formation of images, by addressing itself especially to imagination and memory, and it is only by subordinate auxiliaries of a more musical kind, such as rhythm and imitations of sounds, that it appeals to the immediate sensation of hearing. Hence its effects depend mainly on psychical action. The plastic arts, although they make use of the sensation of sight, address the eye almost in the same way as poetry addresses the ear. Their main purpose is to excite in us the image of an external object of determinate form and colour. The spectator is essentially intended to interest himself in this image and enjoy its beauty ; not to dwell upon the means by which it was created." [1]

Many modern painters would not entirely agree with this limitation of the scope of painting, and it has become the fashion to refer much to the means by which a pictorial effect is produced in present-day art criticism, but, nevertheless, Helmholtz' contention is in the main a true one, that music has hitherto stood

[1] Helmholtz, *Sensations of Tone*, *p.* 2.

alone as an art in its close connection with pure sensation, and that the other arts being more or less tied to the expression of form and definite ideas cannot use colour in the same kind of way as music uses sound.

Dr. G. D. Macdonald published an interesting book some years since upon "The agreement of the musical and colorific scales," and stated, *inter alia*, that "the inference is therefore legitimate that if the analogy of the musical scale were taken as a guide, the special points of the spectrum whose respective vibrations would compose a well-tempered diatonic scale of colour may readily be chosen."[1] This, of course, is matter of opinion, and I give the statement with all reservation.

Professor Grove was also struck by the closeness of the apparent relation between sound and colour, and, though the artistic possibilities of the use of colour in similar ways to sound did not strike him in reference to the subject, he said in his *Correlation of Physical Forces* that "the analogies in the

[1] *Sound and Colour*, by Dr. G. D. Macdonald, F.R.S.

progression of sound and light are very numerous."

To summarize briefly. The physicist rightly confines his attention to the physical facts to be observed with regard to the production of colour in the spectrum and in other ways, to theories concerning the nature of light and colour, and to deductions which may be drawn from their physical phenomena, and to what they can tell us with regard to the sources from which they emanate and their chemical, electrical, and other material effects. He experiments upon sound in a similar way and considers it from a like standpoint, and he notes points of physical analogy between the two sets of phenomena, but he leaves the intricate question of the effects of colour and sound upon our senses and our minds to the biologist and the psychologist, as also the deductions which they may draw from their observations. Harmony and discord, contrasts and blending in sound and in colour are, for instance, questions directly concerned with the impressions produced upon us, are complicated by various psychical considerations, and are therefore more or less outside the domain of physical science. The latter with its clear and unbiased vision gives us its invaluable assistance up to a certain point, but there it leaves us, as to this question of colour sensations and their mental influences, to pursue our own experiments and make our own deductions.

CHAPTER XIII

REMARKS UPON CRITICISMS AND APPRECIATIONS OF COLOUR-MUSIC

IN this chapter it is proposed to consider some of the points which have arisen during the long series of experiments made in mobile colour, and also to give a brief summary of some of the critical and other opinions from outside sources.

These two classes of opinions and criticisms are, of course, very diverse both in character and value. The small group of musicians, artists, and others who have followed or taken part in the experiments carried out personally by the author, and have watched the construction and reconstruction of the colour-organ and similar instruments, have been in a very much better position to discover weak points and appreciate strong ones than those who have merely been present at one or two public lectures where it has not been possible to enter into long explanations or discussion of the objects aimed at, the questions at issue, and the difficulties which have had to be overcome. With the former these could be talked over as they arose, and from time to time alterations could be made in the mechanical construction of the instruments, and the principles on which they have been designed could be revised, so as to take advantage of fresh experiences and criticisms.

With regard to articles upon the subject there has been much intelligent appreciation of the views put forward, and but little of the hostility which usually greets a new departure. It was quite inevitable that there should be some misconceptions, both as to the theories advanced and the results to be achieved; but by reprinting portions of some of the articles that have appeared the opportunity is afforded of clearing away some of these misunderstandings, and I therefore propose to adopt this course.

Before doing so, however, it may be as well once more to state the position claimed for colour-music.

The first and most important contention I have put forward has been, and still is, that there is a broad general resemblance between the effect produced upon the mind and the emotions by colour and by musical sounds. Going further, I, with many others, consider that with both colour and sound this general resemblance in emotional effect is largely dependent upon proportion and contrast coupled with harmony and dissonance, that this makes the general analogy still closer, and that there are other important points of resemblance. Whether, or how far, the physical analogy between the spectrum-band and the octave holds good or has its counterpart in sensation, is, it may once again be said, a secondary matter and one open to question, but on broad lines I submit that the deeper points of resemblance between the effects of colour and musical sounds upon us are so strong that they cannot be disputed by any unprejudiced person, though the support of this contention must depend to a great extent upon actual experiment and demonstration, and it is unavoidable that the question should be complicated by variations in individual capabilities of receiving emotional impressions, either from music or from colour.

Quite apart from any resemblance to or dependence upon music, a mobile colour art has a *raison d'être* and firm and solid foundations upon which it can be built up, as already contended elsewhere.

Returning now to the main subject of this chapter, the first impressions received from colour-music are as a rule those of the varying beauty of the colour itself, with which for the time being the eye is satisfied, without the mind attempting to analyse the sequences of colour or to inquire whether any method is behind the effects produced.

This would seem to correspond to the stage in the appreciation of music in which all that is demanded is something pleasant to the ear, and in which an untrained auditor is unable to take in the details or the deeper musical significance of a serious work.

The next step is usually that of the recognition of colour phrases, of the repetition of these in varied form, and of there being a general intention or structure in a colour-music composition.

Curiously enough, experiment has shown beyond possibility of doubt that for most people a colour composition which has been based or modelled upon an already existing musical one is more interesting and produces finer effects than most original compositions. I do not wish to attach any undue weight to this, as it is probably owing to the fact that mobile colour has yet to find its great composers, and that the experience required to write original colour compositions has yet to a large extent to be acquired, but it is a strong argument for using musical precedents as a temporary assistance.

When the colour phrase as shown upon the screen becomes easily grasped and recognized, the next demand made by the eye and the mind appears to be for some sort of predominant tendency in the colour—for something which, figuratively speaking, might correspond to "key" in music, but which would also partially include other general characteristics of a musical work. As in painting, a colour composition may be either warm or cool in tendency, or with strong or merely delicate transitions and variations. It may also, for instance, be written in a general key of some one particular colour which is predominant throughout, and in which contrast is very sparingly used, or it may be greatly broken up and with rapid alternations of contrast.

Contrast is more demanded at first and less later on, and there are many other points of this kind which are of interest, but into which it would be tedious to enter at any length in the absence of actual demonstration.

One of the difficulties with which mobile colour has had to deal is that of wide fluctuations of luminosity in the compound tints, and various mechanical devices have been designed and experimented with in the construction of the instrument in order to overcome this. To a large extent it has been now avoided, and it has been found that extreme and disagreeable alternations in luminosity are chiefly due to ineptitude in composition or extemporization.

Turning for the moment from the results of actual experiment to outside criticisms, it has been asserted that one difficulty with which colour-music has to deal is, that the eye is incapable of appreciating changes of colour as rapid as the changes of tone which occur in music. If this were so, it would merely be an argument against the direct translation of rapid sound-music compositions into colour-music. The art of mobile colour does not, however, make such translations or adaptations one of its chief objects, and it might, in fact, abandon them altogether and yet leave its main purposes untouched.

It is, moreover, demonstrable that, so far from the eye being unable to appreciate changes as rapid as those which the ear can follow, its capacity is much greater in this respect. In photography it is found impossible to design a shutter so rapid in its action as to enable the most sensitive photographic plate to seize the image of some very rapidly moving bodies. These are therefore sometimes exposed in the dark, and illuminated for an infinitesimal portion of a second by an electric spark of a duration far shorter than that of any musical note. If we take two such electric sparks of different colours and allow them to appear in a darkened space, the eye will, notwithstanding, be perfectly capable of distinguishing between their respective colours. No musical note at all approaches an electric spark as to its shortness of duration, and therefore the whole contention as to the inferiority of the eye in this respect falls to the ground. This, however, should be frankly admitted, namely, that rapid colour changes are at first fatiguing, and that to appreciate them in colour-music requires some training and experience. At first there is a sensation of dazzle, but, as previously stated, this gradually disappears, and is after a time, with most people, entirely lost. So much so is this the case that, as pointed out, the preference for slow compositions soon gives place to the desire for more and more rapid ones.

A difficulty that occurred to the mind of a musical critic was that in music the high notes, namely those of rapid vibrations, are cheerful and light; while to him the more pleasing and exhilarating colours, such as red, have the lowest vibrations. In reply it may be said that this is a purely personal impression and cannot be taken as a normal one. In the construction of the forms of colour-organ provided with a keyboard, the upper octaves are paler and lighter than the lower ones. If, therefore, there is anything in the contention that cheerfulness and light are intimately associated, that association is taken account of in the arrangement of the colour scale in these instruments. But, as a matter of fact, few people would agree with this critic in thinking that low-toned reds such as are found at the red end of the spectrum-band are the most cheerful colours. Nothing is much more cheerful and exhilarating than the strong or opalescent blue of the sky or of many flowers.

With regard to this point, in the careful researches which have been carried out in Germany as to the relatively pleasant effect of different colours upon the eye, satisfactory results could of course only be obtained by taking averages from a large number of people, and in the present stage of education, or rather of ignorance, with regard to colour it is quite impossible to found any arguments upon isolated instances of preference for individual colours, or, even taking a wider view, upon those attaching to one end of the colour scale or the other.

Another critic who evidently felt the initial difficulty of appreciating rapid colour changes wrote in an excellent article upon the subject: "For those—and they are many—who love colour for its own sake, the new art seems to offer endless possibilities of pleasure, and their only grief will be that each beautiful colour is only seen for a short moment before it is succeeded by another." He went on to say that, "though the training of the last few thousand years or so has enabled us to detect tune in sound, we are as yet unable to detect it in colour." We have already discussed rapidity of change and its advantages, and with regard to "tune" it may be said that a melody is nothing more than a pleasing succession of notes arranged in some rhythmical order, some shorter, some longer, some pleasant in sequence, some less so. In colour it is quite possible to have the same kind of arrangement, and many persons can, even at first sight, receive pleasure from such a colour phrase or melody, and can remember it perfectly. Both the power of recalling it and the pleasure of seeing it are, of course, rapidly increased by education of the eye, and it is quite true that it may need a long period of time for average audiences to gain an appreciation of colour-music at all equal to that they now have of sound. This is, however, not an argument against the art, but rather one in favour of giving increased opportunities for studying it. The writer went on to say that he fails to see how emotion can be awakened "unless a distinct faculty for appreciating tune is developed"; but in colour, just as in music, experiment shows that an emotional impression can be produced even by a sequence of two or three notes, and it is probable that colour is much more independent of definite melody or tune than is music.

Turning from tune to form, some of those whose impressions of mobile colour effects I have tested experimentally feel in the first instance a certain uneasiness when form—that is to say, a space of colour of a definite and distinctive shape—is entirely absent. Seeing colour they seem instinctively to demand form also, though in a short time the desire for it lessens and finally disappears. This is but what might be expected. We are accustomed to associate colour with the shapes of objects, and at first it surprises and somewhat puzzles us to see it separated from them and presented to us for its own sake. Then after a time, having our attention confined to colour alone, we begin to appreciate it more and more, and to realize how beautiful and impressive it may be apart from any form whatever.

But this initial difficulty has to be faced and will always recur at first, and we must not only be prepared for it with those who are new spectators, but also with the larger number of persons who only hear or read descriptions of colour-music. How, they ask, can colour be interesting without form? And all that can be said is that actual experience of it is the only satisfactory reply to the question.

It would seem that what really take the place of the additional interest which form gives to fixed or stationary colour are the elements of change and of rhythm which a mobile colour system introduces.

The increase in the desire for rapid changes contrasting with slower ones, already several times referred to, seems to point to this conclusion, and form, in the sense in which the musician uses the word in speaking of a musical composition, gradually enters into or attaches itself to the colour in the mind of the spectator.

There will always be a certain number of people who perhaps having little natural liking either for music or for colour—or who, caring much for music, have little feeling for other forms of art—will ask whether mobile colour has any "practical objects," or whether it can be turned to any "practical use." They ask this in all sincerity and with no desire to be hypercritical. The question has, to a certain extent, already been dealt with, but may be answered rather more fully here. The art of mobile colour stands in the same kind of relation to the practical side of life as music or painting occupy. It cannot actually produce a pattern for a fabric or a subject for a picture, but it can stimulate and develop the senses and faculties upon which the ability to design in colour depends; and better than this, it can bring a new source of interest and refreshment as well as a refining influence into life, just as music has done.

Any art that develops the faculties which enable mankind better to enjoy and appreciate the infinite beauty of nature is worth cultivating, and it is impossible to say to what its study may lead, or for what useful purposes it may not ultimately be turned to account.

One or two writers, in referring to my early lectures on the subject, whilst admiring the beauty of the colour effects produced, and admitting the plea for the development of a mobile colour art, were nevertheless of opinion that it should not be associated with music. Their grounds appeared to be, firstly, that they did not admit closeness of the musical analogy in some respects—a point I have fully dealt with elsewhere—and that they considered it unnecessary to associate colour with music in order to enhance and increase the emotional influence of the latter upon the hearers or spectators.

This view is based upon a misapprehension. I have never asserted or thought that all, or even most, forms of music would gain by being associated with or accompanied by mobile colour. My contention has been, and still is, that mobile colour, if not always used as a separate art, may with advantage be associated with music in compositions in which each gives and sacrifices something in order to produce a combined art, and occasionally also may be used as an addition to already existing musical works, which seem to allow of this. There is a very obvious precedent for this in opera, in which the musical score sacrifices something to the words and action, and, on the other hand, the latter concede a good deal to the music, so that a co-partnership is established of mutual benefit. I think upon reflection it will be admitted that there is a good deal to be said for a similar co-partnership between colour and musical sound.

Another of the writers referred to made a curious criticism. He said: "Music is absolutely an art of proportion, the charm of a chord consisting of the proportions to one another of vibration of its component notes. A quick ear always feels a note as a vibrating tone and can soon be trained to detect the different components of simple chords. Does any painter, even the most competent, recognize vibration as part of colour? Could he resolve a compound colour with certainty into its components, saying at once which of these components was quickest in vibration? Can our enjoyment of colour be shown in any way to be due to a sense of vibration?" To this it may be replied that in every picture, in every decorative design, in every colour pattern, the question of proportion of the colour tints and the colour masses enters, and also that any artist can determine almost at a glance what are the tints and what are the pigments, and the degrees of strength which build up any given space of colour in a picture.

As to vibration in colour, a whole school of painters endeavour to express their sense of the vibratory origin of colour by technical processes which emphasize it, so much so that some few have even called themselves Vibrationists.

A certain number of criticisms resolve themselves into various forms of expressed doubt as to whether the asserted analogy between colour and music holds good at all points. In the previous chapters of this book I have entered somewhat fully into this question ; but it may be here restated once more that I do not consider the analogy to be a close one in every respect, however certain and important it may be in others. If it were precisely similar at all points, there would, in fact, be less to be said for the development of this new form of art. If colour were completely analogous or identical in its effects upon our minds to those produced by music, there would be little advantage in using it for such an art. But it appeals to another sense capable of stimulating similar emotions upon which an art somewhat resembling music can be built up—but arousing other interests, developing other faculties, and opening up other possibilities.

The disinclination of some to allow that colour should be put into partnership with music has already been referred to; but there are others, again, who seem to feel that the chief emotional use for mobile colour will be in illustration and emphasis of musical compositions. It has nevertheless been asserted by one writer that, though this association of the two arts seems desirable, "the eye can grasp but an octave of colour, while the more delicate and complex ear possesses some ten thousand fibres, each vibrating in sympathy with the musical note. The pitch and intensity of a sound may be arbitrarily represented in colour, but what about the qualities of tone? This third attribute of a note or chord finds something wanting in the sister science."

In reply to this, it may be said again that, as a matter of fact, the number of tints appreciable by the eye exceeds by hundreds of thousands, perhaps millions, the number of tones appreciable by the ear. It is quite true that there is only one octave of colour, but the intercombination between the component colours of that octave in the vast ranges of tones they possess, gives us the almost endless variety of colours which we see in nature and in art, whereas it is scientifically demonstrated that the tones appreciable by the ear are not at all comparable in their number to these.[1]

The second objection as to quality of tone in music not being represented in colour opens up an interesting point. *Timbre* in music is produced by the admixture, greater or less, of harmonics with the ground-note which is being sounded ; or with each of the notes composing a chord. If the vibrations of air producing a given note are recorded by an optical curve by means of a suitable instrument, with a needle attached to a sensitive diaphragm which traces it upon a smoked glass, these harmonics clearly show themselves as small notches or wave crests upon the main line of the pulsations of the diaphragm, being

[1] See reference to this in the chapter upon the psychology of the subject.

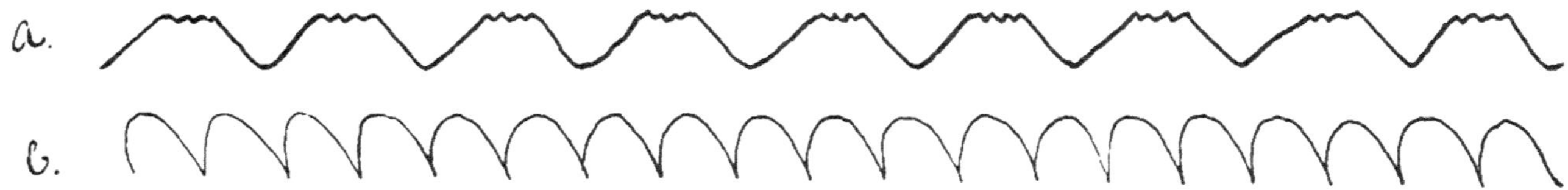

To Illustrate "Timbre."

The upper line (*a*) shows curves produced by a musical note with *timbre* harmonics, the lower line (*b*) those given by a tuning-fork nearly free from harmonics.

as it were the ripples upon the surface of a wave.

In colour we have, as a matter of fact, somewhat similar harmonic interruptions. If a particular colour is taken, say a general tone of rose colour, and its texture is broken up by slight tendencies to violet, to warmer red or to orange, an effect is produced upon the eye which may be said to be analogous to that of *timbre* in music. An absolutely pure colour thrown upon the screen, or made visible in some other way, may be taken from one point upon the spectrum-band, and will then correspond to an absolutely pure musical note without harmonics. But nearly the same colour sensation, though an enhanced one as to beauty and interest, may be produced by slightly altering the original ground tint and breaking into it with almost imperceptible streaks, dots, mottlings, or texture-producing marks of other divergent colours, in such a way as to give the same general impression as did the original colour yet with a different texture. This in pigments is a process well known to the artist, and he relies upon it for some of his most beautiful colour effects. *Timbre* in music corresponds, in fact, somewhat nearly to "quality" or texture produced by harmonious or divergent tints in the case of colour.

CHAPTER XIV

SOME FURTHER REMARKS AND SOME PAST PROPOSALS

IN various articles which have appeared upon colour-music reference has been made to cases of what are commonly called "colour-hearing"; that is to say, to instances of persons who, on hearing a given note or a particular phrase in music, always have a strong mental impression of a particular colour or set of colours. Cases of this kind are established facts, and have been referred to again and again by various well-known philosophic writers and psychologists, amongst others by Locke and Nussbaum. Little attempt has, however, been made to tabulate or systematize them, and no writer upon the subject, so far as I am aware, has yet shown that for the same notes similar colour-imaginings or sensations are aroused in various people. It would seem rather that the colours suggested are more or less arbitrary, or perhaps derived from some obscure associations, and therefore the subject has not much interest for the student of colour-music except in one important respect, namely, as a further piece of circumstantial evidence of there being some closeness of origin or common foundations in the senses and in the brain upon which, as it were, the emotional or psychological influences of colour and sound are based.

These associations of certain colours with certain sounds may perhaps have given the first impulse to some of the ideas as to a possible relationship between colour and music to which occasional reference may be found in early literature. Probably the earliest suggestion of an analogy (as distinguished from the possibility of a separate art) was made by Aristotle in the following passage :

> "Colours may mutually relate like musical concords for their pleasantest arrangement ; like those concords mutually proportionate."

The idea of an independent colour art somewhat analogous to that of music has also crossed a few minds at intervals during the past centuries. Since some of my earlier experiments I have made diligent search in the British Museum and elsewhere for any records of these ideas, but literary evidence of them is very sparse, and it is only within comparatively recent times that there have been more than very fragmentary or obscure allusions to the subject.

The first account I can discover of an attempt to give practical form to the conception of a colour art occurs in the following disjointed description, written from the somewhat amusingly hostile musical standpoint of the time:

"Lewis Bertrand Castel, a Jesuit of Montpellier, whose 'Physical System' ranks amongst the best philosophical works of the early part of the eighteenth century, studied vision and the nature of colours, as blended or contrasted with each other, till his imagination getting the better of his understanding he confounded the eye with the ear and associated the harmony of tints with that of sounds.

Infatuated with this idea, he invented what he called an Ocular Harpsichord, which was strung with coloured tapes instead of wires, and being placed in a dark room, when the keys were touched the transparent tapes, which respectively corresponded with them, became visible; and the various successions and combinations of colours, consequent to this operation, produced effects on the sight, which his fancy assimilated to the impressions made on the ear by melody and harmony."[1]

After this curious attempt to show a correlation the subject seems to have again dropped into obscurity.

Coming to more recent speculations, an interesting book upon *Sound and Colour* was published by Dr. G. D. Macdonald, F.R.S., and there exists a pamphlet by the late Lady Archibald Campbell entitled *Rainbow Music, or the Philosophy of Harmony in Colour Grouping.* She employed what she considered to be the analogy between the octave and the rainbow for suggestions for the decoration of a room

[1] *Assimilation of Colours to Musical Sounds*, by Dr. Bushby. Published 1825.

for which, amongst other materials, to obtain her colour combinations, she used coloured shells.

Professor J. Perry's experiments in Japan have also already been referred to. He and Prof. Ayrton designed an apparatus for determining the effects produced by a spot or spots of coloured light made to move in lines or curves upon a screen.[1]

The following remarkable forecast in reference to a possible mobile colour art, which appeared in the Rev. H. R. Haweis's *Music and Morals*, was brought to my attention when completing my first experiments :

"Colour now stands in the same kind of relation to the painter's art as sound amongst the Greeks did to the art of the gymnast. But just as we speak of the classic age as a time long before the era of real music, so by and by posterity may allude to the present age as an age before the colour-art was known —an age in which colour had not yet developed into a language of pure emotion, but was

[1] If any further experiments by others should have taken place, particulars of these would be welcomed by me.

simply used as an accessory to drawing, as music was once to bodily exercise and rhythmic recitation. And here I will express my conviction that a colour-art exactly analogous to the sound-art of music is possible, and is amongst the arts which have to be traversed in the future, as sculpture, architecture, painting, and music have been in the past. Nor do I see why it should not equal any of these in the splendour of its results and variety of its applications. Had we but a system of colour-notation which would as intensely and instantaneously connect itself with every possible tint, and possess the power of combining colours before the mind's eye, as a page of its music combines sounds through the eye to the mind's ear—had we but instruments, or some appropriate art mechanism, for rendering such colour-notation into real waves of colour before the bodily eye, we should then have actually realized a new art, the extent and grandeur of whose developments it is simply impossible to estimate. . . . But what a majestic symphony might not be played with such orchestral blazes of incomparable hues! What delicate melodies composed of single floating lights, changing and melting from one slow intensity to another through the dark, until some tender dawn of opal from below might perchance receive the last fluttering pulse of ruby flame, and prepare the eye for some new passage of exquisite colour! Why should we not go down to the palace of the people and assist at a real colour prelude or symphony, as we now go down to hear a work by Mozart or Mendelssohn?"[1]

The colour organ and allied mobile colour instruments have, to some extent at least, realized the hopes expressed. It should be added that Mr. Haweis afterwards took a keen interest in the results obtained, and his death deprived the new art of a strong supporter and eloquent champion of its claims.

Shortly after one of my first demonstrations of colour-music, an article of considerable interest, by Mr. William Schooling, appeared in *The Nineteenth Century*, to which the editor added a footnote stating that it had been in his hands for a year or two. Mr. Schooling's views, therefore, were formed quite independently of my own, and are consequently

[1] *Music and Morals*, p. 32.

the more valuable in support of the general theory of a mobile colour art, though, as I had been carrying out experimental work for some years previously, and had discussed various points involved with many friends, it is not impossible that some of these may have reached the writer through indirect channels. Mr. Schooling asked the following questions:

[1] "Is it possible to create an art that shall appeal to us in a kindred way to music, and to educate our perceptions so that we may appreciate the melody and harmony of sound? The analogy of colour to sound is one consideration that may lead us to think that we can perhaps answer 'Yes.' Objectively, and as a matter of physical science, the two are so far alike that both are wave-motions, though of different kinds; the pitch of a sound and the colour of a light are both dependent on the number of vibrations; violet light and high notes result from frequent vibrations; red light and low notes from comparatively few vibrations, and probably, though not of necessity, they would arouse similar sensations.

[1] Reprinted by kind permission of the proprietor of the *Nineteenth Century and After.*

The thunder of a storm might conceivably be represented by low notes and red colour, the lightning by high notes and violet light.

"The range of audible sound comprises about eleven octaves, the range of musical sound about seven ; the range of visible light is less than one octave ; the range of artistic colour may perhaps be less, as in the case of sound ; but the seemingly narrow limits of colour to less than one octave is more verbal than real, for if we consider that the limits of musical sound lie between 40 and 4000 vibrations in a second, while the limits of visible light lie between 460 millions of millions and 680 millions of millions in the same time, it would seem probable that a larger number of colours and tints could be appreciated by the eye than notes by the ear, and that, therefore, the variation producible by combination of colours is greater than the variations possible by musical combination into chords, while the change from tint to tint could be incomparably more gradual and delicate than the change from note to note. But how far it would be possible or desirable to have scales of colour starting from different points and with intervals between the tints or colours, dependent on certain proportions between their respective vibrations, I am not prepared to guess."

Mr. Schooling went on to describe a possible colour-music instrument in the following terms:

"The first to suggest itself is naturally a series of vacuum tubes or vacuous chambers that could be had in any desired variety, that could be illuminated in succession or combination by the use of a keyboard, on playing the notes on which the electric current would pass through different tubes. Contacts would be made so easily that the most elaborate chords or combinations of colours could be played with the utmost simplicity, and the intensity of the light, corresponding to the loudness of sound, could be varied, as in a piano, by using a pedal to alter the intensity of the current, so causing the tubes to shine with a brilliant light or to glow in the softest of hues."

I think some interesting results might be obtained with an instrument of the kind suggested, though so far as I know none has been constructed ; but by its means separate colours only, or at most groups of separate colours, could be produced and not compound tints, which would greatly limit its range. Any fresh proposals, however, as to new principles for the construction of colour-music instruments are to be welcomed. The points raised by Mr. Schooling as to the wider scope of a mobile colour art as compared with music are of special interest, and the notes (see p. 173) as to the immensely greater sensitiveness of the visual nerves as compared with the aural give much support to these contentions.

CHAPTER XV

COLOUR-MUSIC AND PSYCHOLOGY

SO far as men of science are concerned it is quite clear that it is to the psychologist that colour-music, or any form of mobile colour art, will be especially interesting; and it is chiefly to the psychologist that we must look for assistance in analysing the impressions which are produced by colour-music. To Dr. William Brown, of King's College, London, I am much indebted for assistance in exploring the psychological outlook, up to the present time, upon colour and its sensory and emotional influences; and in view of his valuable contributions to psychological science the note in this book to which his name is attached will, I am sure, be read with interest.

The physicist can tell us much that is valuable as to the constitution of light, the production of colour, the rate of vibration in the luminiferous ether which corresponds to a given colour, the points of resemblance and dissimilitude between colour and sound, and various other matters of the highest importance.

The biologist can take us a step further and help us to understand the action of light upon the nerve terminations of the retina behind the lenses of the eye, and he can follow the tremulous air waves of music for us up to the point of their impingement upon the basilar membrane of the ear, and perhaps even a little further. But the object of colour-music is to make an appeal to the mind and the emotions, to the mental sense of colour, and to its intellectual or emotional effects upon us; and when we come to these questions we have to part company with the physicist and the biologist and enter the domain of psychology.

As a matter of fact, up to within the last few years psychology has unfortunately investigated the subject but little. One may almost say that the emotional effects of colour are only just beginning to be studied, and it is one of my hopes that colour-music will give a new impulse to further investigations, and to obtaining additional records of experimental facts upon which we may be able to build in the future.

There are many questions which careful psychological experiment might be able to answer for us, such, for instance, as—

(1) How far similar colours affect the majority of people in a similar way? This investigation has been commenced in Germany by Professor Exner, but only with regard to single colours. As I have already mentioned, he experimented upon a large number of people, chiefly as to their choice of what they considered the most beautiful colours, and upon some points he obtained great unanimity of opinion. But he discovered, and quite frankly admits, that contrasts of adjacent colour at once upset most of his conclusions.

This brings us to another important question for psychologists, and one which I would venture to suggest for their further consideration, namely—

(2) What are the influences of contrast in

colour, what are the normal or average limits of agreeableness in contrasts, what are those of discordancy, and what, on the other hand, are those of harmony?

On these points individual opinions are of little value. Experiments must be spread over a large number of persons of varying education, and perhaps also of race, and the hasty conclusions which have been arrived at by many writers upon colour theories should from the outset be re-examined and the whole question considered anew.

Some past theories with regard to colour, such, for instance, as Goethe's, and even those of great experimentalists like Young and Helmholtz, have had a cramping influence upon psychological investigation, valuable as have been many of their contentions or suggestions in other respects.

An entirely new set of questions for the psychologist are, in addition, opened up by the introduction of the elements of time and rhythm into colour, which it is now possible to study by means of colour-music instruments. Such questions, for instance, as—

(3) What counterpart does rhythm in music find in colour?

(4) Does education of the colour sense by means of the rhythm introduced by colour-music tend to evolve an increased demand for colour rhythm in the majority of persons?

(5) Can rhythm in colour be with advantage more complex than in music?

Other interesting points for consideration are:

(6) Upon what conditions do tragic, pathetic, and joyful emotions evoked by colour depend, and do they upon broad lines coincide in different people with similar colour effects?

Dr. W. Brown is of opinion that music creates a set of emotions different from and apart from our ordinary emotional experiences, and evolved, as it were, in a higher plane of our consciousness. He agrees with me in thinking that these, though different in character from what may be called normal emotions, nevertheless assist in stimulating the latter, and it seems probable to me that the same view holds good with regard to colour-music effects, and that indefinable emotions are produced as well as those to which we can put some sort of name. It is probable that if this is true, part of the stimulating, helpful, or restful effect of music is dependent upon these super-emotions as we might call them, and this opens up a most interesting field of inquiry.

There are many other points which might be suggested as suitable for psychological study and investigation, with the help of a mobile colour art. Meanwhile, it may be interesting to give a few short extracts from psychological writers who have dealt with colour.

In *Music—its Laws and Evolution*, by the eminent French scientific author, Monsieur Combarieu, the following passage occurs: "We will point this out by taking for a brief comparison two given realms—music and light. The two senses to which they correspond, the eye and the ear, alone receive impressions which systematize themselves into a work of art. Smell, taste, and feeling, though susceptible to the highest education, and in no way limited to a utilitarian part, have not given rise to creations of a truly æsthetic character. To show the analogy between sound and light, music and colours, will be to realize, on an essential point, the problem of harmony we have traced out."

This is a portion of an argument in favour of the unity or similarity of action of colour and sound upon us, and the writer goes on to say: "Are the two senses of hearing and of sight formed by the same evolution and by a similar process? This is what the facts of history would seem to affirm."

So far as physiological investigations have been made upon points of analogy between the action of colour and sound upon us, they would seem to support very strongly the general contention of the analogy being a close one.

With regard to the question of the effect of rhythm in colour, some very valuable experiments have been made by Dr. B. Berliner, which he records in his work *Der Ansteig der reinen Farbenerregung in Sehorgan.* He there states that "a rhythmic movement or repetition of colours in varying intensities produces the maximum effect of sensation upon the optic nerve, and hence upon the mind." This I have found to be corroborated by experiments in colour-music.

The same writer considers that he has proved that various colours have similar degrees of power in exciting particular sensations even under varying conditions of lightness or darkness of the colours.

Other experiments upon this question have also been carried out by the psychologist Arthur Mitzscherling.[1]

Before accepting these conclusions as to the effect of degrees of lightness or darkness, we should have to understand exactly what the experimenter means by sensations. Results obtained from colour-music would seem to show that lightness or darkness has a great deal to do with the impressions obtained from given colours.

Elsewhere reference has been made to one great difficulty which at once presents itself in

[1] *Die Farben-Kurven bei Reduktion auf gleichen Helligkeit.*

comparing a musical note with its corresponding colour upon the spectrum-band when similarly divided, in that the whole construction of the diatonic scale is very arbitrary, and that it is inevitable that any colour scale must also be so to some extent.

In reference to the diatonic scale and the use of musical precedents for mobile colour purposes, the following remarks by Dr. Max Meyer in a paper on *Elements of a Psychological Theory of Melody* are of interest as showing the dissatisfaction which many feel as to the non-scientific and unrepresentative character of the diatonic scale in music. After remarking that there are plenty of books on musical theories written by professional musicians, physicists, physiologists, and others—but that in his opinion the psychological laws upon which music is founded have not yet been determined—he goes on to say: "The wrong path, much frequented, which inevitably leads back to the starting-point, is the adoption of the theory that the basis of all music is the so-called diatonic scale, represented by the numbers 24, 27, 30, 32, 36, 40, 45, 48. . . . This so-called diatonic scale which is the basis of all discussions in Helmholtz's *Tonempfindungen* was introduced into the modern theory of music by Zarlino in 1558. It was accepted by Rameau in his *Traité de l'Harmonie*, 1721. According to Rameau (and Helmholtz) no numbers play any part in music except 1, 2, 3, 4, 5, and 6. This is certainly not a law derived inductively from observed facts, but a dogma, because one may, as Poole rightly states, very easily observe that the 7 acts psychologically in a way corresponding to the action of 2, 3, and 5; whereas, indeed, with other prime numbers, as 11, 13, etc., this is not the case. . . . There can be no doubt that the tempered scale cannot be made the basis of a theory of music, that theoretic conclusions drawn from considerations regarding the interval of the tempered scale have no scientific foundation. A scientific theory of music can only be a theory describing the laws of music performed in just intonation, but in just intonation that *really* is to be called 'just,' not in that *seemingly* just intonation of Helmholtz, which—as can be proved by experiment—does not deserve this name." This dissatisfaction with the diatonic scale and its inconclusive construction, as already said, complicates the whole question of similarity between the two scales.

Schopenhauer in *Die Welt als Wille und Vorstellung* fully recognizes the immensely important position which colour occupies, or ought to occupy, in relation to human life and civilization, and develops his views in many eloquent passages ; but he naturally regards the whole question from the philosophic and not from the practical point of view.

Some interesting observations have been made by E. Bullough in *The Perception Problem in the Æsthetic Appreciation of Single Colours,* but they are mostly too abstruse to be of much assistance in attacking the questions to which a mobile colour art gives rise. As a matter of fact, many of these break entirely new ground, and special investigations are required to explore them.

To sum up. Psychology has only just begun to explore the emotional effects of colour, but in the main its conclusions, so far as they go, are highly favourable to the general theory of colour-music and tend to support the contentions that a mobile colour art has serious and important claims upon our attention.

APPENDIX

THE following comparative table of visual and auditory sensations will be of interest as showing some of the points of resemblance and difference between these. It also opens up further questions for future investigation.

COMPARATIVE TABLE OF VISUAL AND AUDITORY SENSATIONS

SOME POINTS OF RESEMBLANCE AND DIFFERENCE

VISUAL SENSATIONS	AUDITORY SENSATIONS
1. *Physical stimulus*, produced by transverse waves in the ether between the limits of 440 billion vibrations per second and 770, approximately. Change set up in the sense-organs a chemical one.	1. *Physical stimulus*, produced by longitudinal waves in the air between limits of 20 and 22,000 per second (varies in individuals). Change set up in the sense-organ—the basilar membrane—is probably physical.
The vibration-frequency of extreme violet approaches twice that of extreme red at the opposite end of the spectrum.	Any audible wave-frequency being doubled comprises between these extremes the musical sensations contained within the octave.

Visual Sensations	Auditory Sensations
2. Hue, saturation, and intensity are dependent in the main upon wave-length, wave-complexity, and wave-amplitude respectively.	2. Pitch, timbre, and loudness are dependent in the main upon wave-length, wave-complexity, and wave-amplitude respectively.
3. A series of greys extending from white to black are due to a mixture of rays of all wave-lengths. Non-neutral greys are due to predominance of some rays of particular wave-lengths.	3. Noise, as distinguished from musical tones, probably due to a mixture of all tones. Noises may differ in pitch. This is due to predominance of certain tones.
4. From a physiological point of view well-marked turning-points in the spectrum are at yellow, green, blue, and red.	4. Salient points in the musical scale—in order of closeness of physiological relation to the fundamental tone—are octave, fifth, fourth, major third, minor third and sixth.
5. Colour mixtures or fusion of colours.	5. Combination tones, interruption tones, beats, etc.
6. Simultaneous colour contrast. This occurs usually when two or more colours occupy visibly separate spaces in proximity to each other.	6. Tonal fusion, or the sensation produced by a number of notes in a united chord or noise. Ebbingham follows Stumpf in considering that it is a characteristic

Visual Sensations	Auditory Sensations
But it may also occur when these spaces are so small as to be separately indistinguishable, as in the case of many colours in flowers or insects, or in three-colour photographic processes, and this would seem to correspond to some extent to tonal fusion, i.e. a number of notes combined in a chord.	peculiarity of hearing that it is possible to distinguish individual tones in a combination—"die allgemeine Fähigkeit eine objectiv zugleich vorhandene Mehrzahl von Tönen auch subjecktiv als eine solche zŭ erkennen." But this distinction seems somewhat artificial, the real difference being that whereas the constituent tones do not occupy separate spaces, in the case of contrasting colours they must do so.
7. Successive colour contrast—including "after images." (Successive contrast is an important feature of colour-music).	7. Less marked than in colour, but as to "after-images" a similar effect probably occurs in the realm of sound, but of very short duration. The question has yet to be explored.

If the spectrum and the octave be divided into similar intervals in accordance with the diatonic scale, the following table shows the approximate frequencies of relative vibration and the relative colours corresponding to each note or interval. The verbal description of these colours is, however, of course an inadequate and inaccurate one. Colours, like musical tones, cannot be properly described in words. Greenish blue, for instance, may mean any one of many thousand shades of the colour with varying tendencies towards green and blue.

It is also nearly, if not quite, impossible to represent pure spectrum colours by means of pigments. Any diagrams in this book into which colour enters must therefore, like the following table, be taken merely as approximate statements.

TO SHOW DIVISION OF COLOUR SCALE UPON KEYBOARD COLOUR-ORGAN WITH MIDDLE C CORRESPONDING TO LOWEST RED OF SPECTRUM

Approximate ether vibrations Mil. mil. per sec.	Approximate colour	Musical note	Vibrations per sec.
395·0	Deep red	(Middle) C	256·0
433·0	Crimson	C#	277·0
466·0	Orange-crimson	D	298·0
500·0	Orange	D#	319·0
533·0	Yellow	E	341·0
566·0	Yellow-green	F	362·0
600·0	Green	F#	383·0
633·0	Bluish green	G	405·0
666·0	Blue-green	G#	426·0
700·0	Indigo	A	447·0
733·0	Deep blue	A#	469·0
757·0	Violet	B	490·0
Invisible		C_1	512·0

The subjoined quotations from articles upon colour-music are inserted here for the following reasons:

1. Because in the absence of ocular demonstration for the majority of readers of this book, it seems well to include some few descriptions of the effects produced upon entirely unprejudiced eyes and minds.

2. Because it affords an opportunity of making one or two further replies to criticisms which it seems fairer to quote verbatim.

In an article upon the subject, its author stated that "the keynote of the new art" was "mobility introduced into colour, enabling time, tone, and rhythm to be expressed in modulations." The keyboard of the colour-organ was described as being "like a palette on which all the subtle gradations of hue and tone are evolved but not fixed. Fleeting and momentary as sounds, the whole gamut of colour was thrown on to the screen in slow or rapid successions in infinite combinations . . . and in waves of intense and most lovely colour, the tints blending and neutralizing each other, and presenting subtle tones, taxing the eye to seize and follow them; now deepening into sombre hues, now passing into infinitely delicate gradations, and now bursting into full pure hues of surpassing beauty, the magic evanescent colour flitting across the vision in indefinable harmonies."

This is interesting as a description of the impressions made upon an unprejudiced person unknown to the author, who evidently belonged to those who, witnessing a demonstration of colour-music for the first time without any special training for it or experience of its possibilities, are yet able at once to appreciate and enjoy it.

In an article in *The Times* written after a demonstration of colour-music, after describing the effects produced and remarking that the tints with which the screen was filled were often very beautiful, the writer went on to say that "there is perhaps force in the suggestion that our eyes are not yet sufficiently practised to make us competent judges of colour as expressive of emotion; but it may be remarked that even were the physical analogy between sound and colour complete—which it is far from being—it does not follow that the emotional effects are analogous."

This is, of course, perfectly true, and the analogy has to be demonstrated. But to return to a question already somewhat fully discussed, the physical analogy in view of very similar physiological action through the nerves makes it probable that there would be similar emotional effects, and following upon this probability experiment shows this to a considerable extent, at any rate, to be so.

The following are extracts from another article:

"As concords and discords in proper relation and succession build up a musical structure to the ear, so they do to the eye. The trained ear anticipates certain successions of harmonies, and is held in suspense until the succession is completed. Likewise does the eye, artistically vexed for the moment by certain discordant combinations of colour, await in suspense the concord which must artistically follow."

The writer concludes with the following remarks: "Wherein the art differs from painting is, firstly, that the colours in their concord or discord are not necessarily associated with definite form. And, secondly, that whilst any picture, once painted, remains fixed in its single harmony of combination, the notes or colours of the colour-music flow successively one into the other, as if we could conceive a picture or a colour design in which the group or multitude of hues were constantly being replaced by others, under government of the same intellectual laws which regulate the musical successions."[1]

Many interesting articles have appeared on the Continent showing an intelligent appreciation of the subject, and the following curious extract from *Le Temps*, written in a vivacious and somewhat figurative style, may perhaps be read with interest:

"Dans l'exécution d'un morceau de musique, la succession des couleurs répond à l'agilité du doigté et au mouvement de la page écrite; l'instrument donnant en tons la mesure, le rythme et l'harmonie du son.

"A la première rencontre c'est la surprise, un peu l'éblouissement qui dominent; mais on s'habitue bientôt à discerner le coloris des maîtres, à reconnaître la pourpre de Richard Wagner, le bleu céleste de Mozart, les ors profonds et les rubis étincelants que charrie l'œuvre de Saint-Saëns; et l'on conçoit

[1] *Yorkshire Post.*

peut-être de la page entendue une impression plus vive, plus facile et plus sincère.

"Il en resulte que, grâce au 'colour-music,' on ne doit pas désespérer d'arriver à donner une sensation musicale à un sourd de naissance. L'inventeur ne pense nullement que cette sensation soit jamais parfaite et complète, mais il n'est pas douteux que la vue de ces lumières rythmées, furtives, vivantes, fasse naître dans les esprits mûres aux sons des idées de cadence, de mesure et un sentiment d'harmonie générale dont il est facile de pénétrer le sujet.

"Le prélude de *Lohengrin* n'a point la même 'couleur' qu'un refrain populaire. Longtemps avant l'instrument dont nous nous occupons, la critique musicale se servait volontiers de ce mot 'couleur' pour rendre des effets que sa technique ne lui permettait pas d'exprimer avec une netteté satisfaisante; mais Herold—qui usait volontiers de cette formule—ne soupçonnait pas sans doute que quelque jour un instrument mathématique traduirait cette couleur des maîtres pour nous montrer tous les soleils de la Crau dans 'l'Arlésienne' de Bizet, les horizons du Sahara dans le 'Désert' de Félicien David, des blancheurs de lis dans Gounod, des pâleurs d'aurore dans Léo Delibes, et des tempêtes, des gloires, des pourpres allumées, des embrasements de batailles dans une phrase de la Marseillaise qui passe.

"Quel peut devenir l'utilité du 'colour-music'? . . . C'est aux savants d'examiner, de mediter et de conclure. Un premier pas a été franchi dans une voie inexplorée, vers un but mystérieux."

COLOUR-MUSIC

This article, written some time since, of course lays far too much stress upon some of the experimental "direct translations" of musical writers which were then given, but as I have frequently explained, such translations, founded as they must be upon musical and colour scales, both of which are arbitrary although they show strong points of resemblance and produce very beautiful colour effects, are not the objective of colour-music.

Music and Colour

Recent Works on the Psychology of Music

The following conclusions, quoted from a summary, by W. B. Pillsbury, of papers read at the Fourth Congress of Experimental Psychology at Innsbruck, in April, 1910,[1] are of interest in regard to some of the points already discussed in the body of this book:

"W. Kohler presents a suggestive note on the possibly discontinuous character of the tone qualities. His experiments grew out of the tendency to refer a vowel quality to certain pitches. In two subjects he found that a note of about 265 V.D. was similar to *u*, 528 to *o*, 1054 to *a*. The suggestion is that these sounds have the same relation to the musical scale that the primary colours have to the spectrum. In answer to questions he asserted that there was a quality lower than *u* that corresponds to the *m* sound, and probably others still lower that give critical points for sensational qualities as the vowel sounds do for the upper notes."

[1] From the *Physiological Bulletin*, Vol. VIII, pp. 210–11.

APPENDIX

Primitive Musical Scales

"Messrs. Stumpf and Hornbostle reported on the results obtained from a study of the phonographic records of primitive music that the psychological institute at Berlin has been collecting. Prof. Stumpf discusses two conclusions that have already been reached. First the tendency to equal-interval scales of five and seven tones, second the widespread use of fifth and fourth relations in part songs. In the Javanese five-tone scale the notes are related $\frac{5}{2}$, the tones of the seven-note Siamese scale as $\frac{7}{2}$. These prove that the occidental scale is not the only relation that may be used in music. Stumpf rejects Wundt's suggestion that the scale has arisen from making the differences in the blocks of the zylophone or metallophone (the musical instruments used in Java) proportionately equal, for observation of the blocks show that they have been hollowed out in the course of tuning. It is evident that the tuning is by the ear rather than by the eye, and that the scales represent a maximum of beauty to the natives. On the problem of the harmonious relations of simultaneous tones, the author reaches the result, that the intervals of the octave, fourth, and fifth at first appeared by chance among a large number of other relations, and were selected and retained because they were the more pleasant on account of the close approach to the unison effect that makes the words more easily appreciated. These are only preliminary to the many results that may be expected from a careful study of phonographic records of primitive and other music."

The origin of and differences between musical scales are of importance in any consideration of the analogies between colour and music.

Origins of Polyphonic Music

V. Hornbostle suggests other ways in which polyphonic music might originate. The antiphonic parts might easily overlap, first by chance, then be repeated intentionally when the effect was found to be pleasant; or the use of falsetto that is found in primitive music might, in singing with others, give a consonant effect with the voices of others and be repeated through its agreeableness. Possibly the interval of the major second that is found among the Admiralty Islanders might have been developed through the failure of some voices to sing in unison. He also remarks on the complexity of the rhythm and of the melodic structure of primitive music.

The bearing of this upon Colour-Music

The history of the development of opinion amongst certain races as to what colours can be harmoniously combined would be of equal interest in connection with colour-music problems.

If this variety of scale, founded upon varieties of feeling, exists in music there is no cause for surprise at some divergency of feeling with regard to harmonious and discordant combinations in colour. A mobile colour art may well assist in bringing about more unanimity of opinion as to fundamental principles of harmony, and by its means experimental tests can be applied with great ease to large numbers of persons and the results tabulated and analysed. Such results may, and probably will, lead in the end to the construction of new colour scales to which the present forms of instrument could easily be adapted. They would also serve as the basis for new forms of mobile colour composition, and I have this object in view in present experimental work.

Musical scales and compositions must be founded more or less upon some general unanimity of opinion and feeling, amongst those to whom music appeals, as to what is beautiful in tone combinations and sequences and what is unpleasant, and the knowledge of that unanimity—which lies at the root of the art of the musician—has only been gradually acquired. Thus it must also be with colour. But it is only now—for the first time in the history of the uses of colour—that mobile colour instruments give a ready means of obtaining similar points of unanimity.

PRINTED BY
WILLIAM BRENDON AND SON, LTD.
PLYMOUTH

Printed in Great Britain
by Amazon

21849820R00145